Lenka Krátká

A HISTORY OF THE CZECHOSLOVAK OCEAN SHIPPING COMPANY, 1948–1989

How a Small, Landlocked Country Ran Maritime Business During the Cold War

ibidem-Verlag
Stuttgart

Bibliografische Information der Deutschen Nationalbibliothek
Die Deutsche Nationalbibliothek verzeichnet diese Publikation in der Deutschen Nationalbibliografie; detaillierte bibliografische Daten sind im Internet über http://dnb.d-nb.de abrufbar.

Bibliographic information published by the Deutsche Nationalbibliothek
Die Deutsche Nationalbibliothek lists this publication in the Deutsche Nationalbibliografie; detailed bibliographic data are available in the Internet at http://dnb.d-nb.de.

Grant Agency of the Czech Republic, the research grant Reg. No 315130.

∞

Gedruckt auf alterungsbeständigem, säurefreien Papier
Printed on acid-free paper

ISSN: 1614-3515

ISBN-13: 978-3-8382-0666-0

© *ibidem*-Verlag
Stuttgart 2015

Alle Rechte vorbehalten

Das Werk einschließlich aller seiner Teile ist urheberrechtlich geschützt. Jede Verwertung außerhalb der engen Grenzen des Urheberrechtsgesetzes ist ohne Zustimmung des Verlages unzulässig und strafbar. Dies gilt insbesondere für Vervielfältigungen, Übersetzungen, Mikroverfilmungen und elektronische Speicherformen sowie die Einspeicherung und Verarbeitung in elektronischen Systemen.

All rights reserved. No part of this publication may be reproduced, stored in or introduced into a retrieval system, or transmitted, in any form, or by any means (electronic, mechanical, photocopying, recording or otherwise) without the prior written permission of the publisher. Any person who does any unauthorized act in relation to this publication may be liable to criminal prosecution and civil claims for damages.

Printed in Germany

Soviet and Post-Soviet Politics and Society (SPPS) Vol. 146
ISSN 1614-3515

General Editor: Andreas Umland,
Institute for Euro-Atlantic Cooperation, Kyiv, umland@stanfordalumni.org

Commissioning Editor: Max Jakob Horstmann,
London, mjh@ibidem.eu

EDITORIAL COMMITTEE*

DOMESTIC & COMPARATIVE POLITICS
Prof. **Ellen Bos**, *Andrássy University of Budapest*
Dr. **Ingmar Bredies**, *FH Bund, Brühl*
Dr. **Andrey Kazantsev**, *MGIMO (U) MID RF, Moscow*
Prof. **Heiko Pleines**, *University of Bremen*
Prof. **Richard Sakwa**, *University of Kent at Canterbury*
Dr. **Sarah Whitmore**, *Oxford Brookes University*
Dr. **Harald Wydra**, *University of Cambridge*

SOCIETY, CLASS & ETHNICITY
Col. **David Glantz**, *"Journal of Slavic Military Studies"*
Dr. **Marlène Laruelle**, *George Washington University*
Dr. **Stephen Shulman**, *Southern Illinois University*
Prof. **Stefan Troebst**, *University of Leipzig*

POLITICAL ECONOMY & PUBLIC POLICY
Prof. em. **Marshall Goldman**, *Wellesley College, Mass.*
Dr. **Andreas Goldthau**, *Central European University*
Dr. **Robert Kravchuk**, *University of North Carolina*
Dr. **David Lane**, *University of Cambridge*
Dr. **Carol Leonard**, *University of Oxford*
Dr. **Maria Popova**, *McGill University, Montreal*

FOREIGN POLICY & INTERNATIONAL AFFAIRS
Dr. **Peter Duncan**, *University College London*
Dr. **Taras Kuzio**, *Johns Hopkins University*
Prof. **Gerhard Mangott**, *University of Innsbruck*
Dr. **Diana Schmidt-Pfister**, *University of Konstanz*
Dr. **Lisbeth Tarlow**, *Harvard University, Cambridge*
Dr. **Christian Wipperfürth**, *N-Ost Network, Berlin*
Dr. **William Zimmerman**, *University of Michigan*

HISTORY, CULTURE & THOUGHT
Dr. **Catherine Andreyev**, *University of Oxford*
Prof. **Mark Bassin**, *Södertörn University*
Prof. **Karsten Brüggemann**, *Tallinn University*
Dr. **Alexander Etkind**, *University of Cambridge*
Dr. **Gasan Gusejnov**, *Moscow State University*
Prof. em. **Walter Laqueur**, *Georgetown University*
Prof. **Leonid Luks**, *Catholic University of Eichstaett*
Dr. **Olga Malinova**, *Russian Academy of Sciences*
Prof. **Andrei Rogatchevski**, *University of Tromsø*
Dr. **Mark Tauger**, *West Virginia University*
Dr. **Stefan Wiederkehr**, *BBAW, Berlin*

ADVISORY BOARD*

Prof. **Dominique Arel**, *University of Ottawa*
Prof. **Jörg Baberowski**, *Humboldt University of Berlin*
Prof. **Margarita Balmaceda**, *Seton Hall University*
Dr. **John Barber**, *University of Cambridge*
Prof. **Timm Beichelt**, *European University Viadrina*
Dr. **Katrin Boeckh**, *University of Munich*
Prof. em. **Archie Brown**, *University of Oxford*
Dr. **Vyacheslav Bryukhovetsky**, *Kyiv-Mohyla Academy*
Prof. **Timothy Colton**, *Harvard University, Cambridge*
Prof. **Paul D'Anieri**, *University of Florida*
Dr. **Heike Dörrenbächer**, *DGO, Berlin*
Dr. **John Dunlop**, *Hoover Institution, Stanford, California*
Dr. **Sabine Fischer**, *SWP, Berlin*
Dr. **Geir Flikke**, *NUPI, Oslo*
Prof. **David Galbreath**, *University of Aberdeen*
Prof. **Alexander Galkin**, *Russian Academy of Sciences*
Prof. **Frank Golczewski**, *University of Hamburg*
Dr. **Nikolas Gvosdev**, *Naval War College, Newport, RI*
Prof. **Mark von Hagen**, *Arizona State University*
Dr. **Guido Hausmann**, *University of Freiburg i.Br.*
Prof. **Dale Herspring**, *Kansas State University*
Dr. **Stefani Hoffman**, *Hebrew University of Jerusalem*
Prof. **Mikhail Ilyin**, *MGIMO (U) MID RF, Moscow*
Prof. **Vladimir Kantor**, *Higher School of Economics*
Dr. **Ivan Katchanovski**, *University of Ottawa*
Prof. em. **Andrzej Korbonski**, *University of California*
Dr. **Iris Kempe**, *"Caucasus Analytical Digest"*
Prof. **Herbert Küpper**, *Institut für Ostrecht Regensburg*
Dr. **Rainer Lindner**, *CEEER, Berlin*
Dr. **Vladimir Malakhov**, *Russian Academy of Sciences*

Dr. **Luke March**, *University of Edinburgh*
Prof. **Michael McFaul**, *US Embassy at Moscow*
Prof. **Birgit Menzel**, *University of Mainz-Germersheim*
Prof. **Valery Mikhailenko**, *The Urals State University*
Prof. **Emil Pain**, *Higher School of Economics, Moscow*
Dr. **Oleg Podvintsev**, *Russian Academy of Sciences*
Prof. **Olga Popova**, *St. Petersburg State University*
Dr. **Alex Pravda**, *University of Oxford*
Dr. **Erik van Ree**, *University of Amsterdam*
Dr. **Joachim Rogall**, *Robert Bosch Foundation Stuttgart*
Prof. **Peter Rutland**, *Wesleyan University, Middletown*
Prof. **Marat Salikov**, *The Urals State Law Academy*
Dr. **Gwendolyn Sasse**, *University of Oxford*
Prof. **Jutta Scherrer**, *EHESS, Paris*
Prof. **Robert Service**, *University of Oxford*
Mr. **James Sherr**, *RIIA Chatham House London*
Dr. **Oxana Shevel**, *Tufts University, Medford*
Prof. **Eberhard Schneider**, *University of Siegen*
Prof. **Olexander Shnyrkov**, *Shevchenko University, Kyiv*
Prof. **Hans-Henning Schröder**, *SWP, Berlin*
Prof. **Yuri Shapoval**, *Ukrainian Academy of Sciences*
Prof. **Viktor Shnirelman**, *Russian Academy of Sciences*
Dr. **Lisa Sundstrom**, *University of British Columbia*
Dr. **Philip Walters**, *"Religion, State and Society", Oxford*
Prof. **Zenon Wasyliw**, *Ithaca College, New York State*
Dr. **Lucan Way**, *University of Toronto*
Dr. **Markus Wehner**, *"Frankfurter Allgemeine Zeitung"*
Dr. **Andrew Wilson**, *University College London*
Prof. **Jan Zielonka**, *University of Oxford*
Prof. **Andrei Zorin**, *University of Oxford*

* While the Editorial Committee and Advisory Board support the General Editor in the choice and improvement of manuscripts for publication, responsibility for remaining errors and misinterpretations in the series' volumes lies with the books' authors.

Soviet and Post-Soviet Politics and Society (SPPS)
ISSN 1614-3515

Founded in 2004 and refereed since 2007, SPPS makes available affordable English-, German-, and Russian-language studies on the history of the countries of the former Soviet bloc from the late Tsarist period to today. It publishes between 5 and 20 volumes per year and focuses on issues in transitions to and from democracy such as economic crisis, identity formation, civil society development, and constitutional reform in CEE and the NIS. SPPS also aims to highlight so far understudied themes in East European studies such as right-wing radicalism, religious life, higher education, or human rights protection. The authors and titles of all previously published volumes are listed at the end of this book. For a full description of the series and reviews of its books, see

www.ibidem-verlag.de/red/spps.

Editorial correspondence & manuscripts should be sent to: Dr. Andreas Umland, DAAD, German Embassy, vul. Bohdana Khmelnitskoho 25, UA-01901 Kyiv, Ukraine.
e-mail: umland@stanfordalumni.org

Business correspondence & review copy requests should be sent to: *ibidem* Press, Leuschnerstr. 40, 30457 Hannover, Germany; tel.: +49 511 2622200; fax: +49 511 2622201; spps@ibidem.eu.

Authors, reviewers, referees, and editors for (as well as all other persons sympathetic to) SPPS are invited to join its networks at
www.facebook.com/group.php?gid=52638198614
www.linkedin.com/groups?about=&gid=103012
www.xing.com/net/spps-ibidem-verlag/

Recent Volumes

138 David R. Marples, Frederick V. Mills (Eds.)
Ukraine's Euromaidan
Analyses of a Civil Revolution
ISBN 978-3-8382-0660-8

139 Bernd Kappenberg
Setting Signs for Europe
Why Diacritics Matter for
European Integration
With a foreword by Peter Schlobinski
ISBN 978-3-8382-0663-9

140 René Lenz
Internationalisierung, Kooperation
und Transfer
Externe bildungspolitische Akteure in der Russischen Föderation
Mit einem Vorwort von Frank Ettrich
ISBN 978-3-8382-0751-3

141 Juri Plusnin, Yana Zausaeva, Natalia Zhidkevich, Artemy Pozanenko
Wandering Workers
Mores, Behavior, Way of Life, and Political Status of Domestic Russian Labor Migrants
Translated by Julia Kazantseva
ISBN 978-3-8382-0653-0

142 Matthew Kott, David J. Smith (eds.)
Latvia – A Work in Progress?
100 Years of State- and Nation-building
ISBN 978-3-8382-0648-6

143 Инна Чувычкина (ред.)
Экспортные нефте- и газопроводы на постсоветском пространстве
Анализ трубопроводной политики в свете теории международных отношений
ISBN 978-3-8382-0822-0

144 Johann Zajaczkowski
Russland – eine pragmatische Großmacht?
Eine rollentheoretische Untersuchung russischer Außenpolitik am Beispiel der Zusammenarbeit mit den USA nach 9/11 und des Georgienkrieges von 2008
Mit einem Vorwort von Siegfried Schieder
ISBN 978-3-8382-0837-4

145 Boris Popivanov
Changing Images of the Left in Bulgaria
The Challenge of Post-Communism in the Early 21st Century
ISBN 978-3-8382-0667-7

Contents

Acknowledgements		**IX**
1	**Introduction: Maritime business in landlocked Czechoslovakia as a research topic**	**1**
	1.1 This book's dockyard: a brief account of the information sources	5
2	**Prologue: First attempts to run the maritime business after World War I**	**11**
3	**1950s: From the foundation of the People's Republic of China to the foundation of the Czechoslovak Ocean Shipping company**	**19**
	3.1 The economic Cold War and its impacts on Czechoslovakia	19
	3.2 The People's Republic of China comes into play	22
	3.3 The first "independent" attempts to establish a Czechoslovak merchant fleet	25
	3.4 The Republika—the first ship owned by the Czechoslovak state	28
	3.5 The top secret protocol on cooperation in shipping with the People's Republic of China	37
	3.6 Communist China's ship with a Czechoslovak communist hero's name	41
	3.7 Flourishing cooperation with communist China	46
	3.8 Czechoslovak Ocean Shipping Ltd.	54
	3.9 Financial results in the 1950s	57

4	**1960s: From the Caribbean Crisis to the mutiny on the ship Kladno**	**61**
	4.1 Czechoslovaks need more ships	64
	4.2 The People's Republic of China does not need more ships	66
	4.3 "Why do you yield to US imperialism?" (end of cooperation with the PRC)	71
	4.4 The last third of the 1960s—the development of an exclusively Czechoslovak shipping	77
	4.5 Financial results in the 1960s	80
	4.6 1968: "We dreaded that they would requisition our ships"	83
5	**1970s: The transition from ideological tasks to business tasks**	**91**
	5.1 Détente in abroad, "normalization" at home	91
	5.2 The company's performance after the suppression of the Prague Spring	101
	5.3 Financial results in the 1970s	111
6	**1980s: From a drop in earnings to fleet renewal**	**115**
	6.1 The company as an object of counterintelligence interests	115
	6.2 Problems in the Soviet bloc, problems in the COS	123
	6.3 Perestroika and the first (un)successful business attempts in shipping	129
	6.4 Financial results in the 1980s	137
7	**Epilogue: Czechoslovak and Czech maritime business after the Velvet Revolution**	**141**

8	Seafarers' lives and memories		**151**
	8.1	"Work on the sea is simply different" (an overview of seafarers' professions)	153
	8.2	"One had to decide" (the impacts of the communist regime on ocean shipping)	164
	8.3	"Is the sea salty? I really wanted to know!" (travelling and emigration)	171
	8.4	"To make some extra money" (salaries and black marketeering)	175
	8.5	"His wife sailed around the world with him" (family travelling)	183
	8.6	"She went never nuts, she always toughed it out" (the family life of the seafarer)	187
	8.7	"She was my sweetheart in Canada" (women, men and lovers)	189
	8.8	"Surrounded by creature comforts on the ship" (life on the ship)	191
9	Ship memoirs		**197**
10	Conclusion: Four decades of Czechoslovak shipping in a nutshell		**243**
	List of archival resources and interviews		**251**
	Summary in Czech and German		**269**

Acknowledgements

In February 2015 when I completed this book, five years had passed since the day I recorded the first oral history interview with a former seafarer. Sixteen other interviews followed. Two of the men I talked to in 2010 are no longer alive. I am grateful to all the men who shared their stories about their seafarer's life and about Czechoslovak naval ships with me. These interviews would not have been possible without research support for exploring the theme of shipping in Czechoslovakia using the oral history method. For this support I am particularly grateful to Professor Miroslav Vaněk, head of the Centre of Oral History at the Institute of Contemporary History of the Czech Academy of Sciences.

In order to give an as most complete picture as possible of shipping in Czechoslovakia, however, I needed to conduct deep archival research. Archivist, who are sometimes seen merely as "no name" people, in all the relevant archives (Security Services Archive; Archive of the Czech National Bank; Archive of the Ministry of Foreign Affairs) gave me important support in my research effort, and I am thankful to all of them. I am most grateful to the National Archive where the majority of the documents on shipping are stored, namely the archivist Bohumír Brom, who was very helpful in searching for materials about shipping and making them available for my work. I should not forget Miloslava Buriánková at the National Archive who prepared excellent tea for me whenever my throat was burning from the dust of the documents.

I am very much obliged to Max Jakob Horstmann, whom I met as a representative of the publisher and who believed that I could write a publishable book in English. I am also thankful for the invaluable support in language editing of the text provided by Šárka Císařová and Jan Kletvík from the Language Department of the Czech Academy of Sciences. Further reading, focusing on language, content, and formal shortcomings of the final text was carried out by Veronika Pehe from University College London, to whom I also owe my immense thanks.

I am particularly grateful to Pavel Mücke from the Centre of Oral History at the Institute of Contemporary History of the Czech Academy of Sciences, for proofreading the text and providing me with comments and useful suggestions before submitting this book to the publisher. Not only did he support me during the work, he also encouraged me at critical moments when I thought I could not complete the project successfully. My work would not have been possible without the institutional support of the Grant Agency of the Czech Republic, contributed within the research grant Reg. No. 315130, "Micro-histories" and "Macro-history" of Czech/Czechoslovak Travelling and Tourism (1945–1989).

Last but not least, I want to thank my dearest family, my husband Jiří Krátký and my daughter Tereza Krátká, for their understanding when I felt tired because of writing this book about Czechoslovak shipping and for their encouragement when I was losing energy.

1 Introduction: Maritime business in landlocked Czechoslovakia as a research topic

This book seeks to address the topic of ocean shipping, seafarers, and ocean ships in socialist Czechoslovakia (1948–1989), while also examining the processes that allowed Czechoslovak ships to cruise the oceans and for seafarers to live and work on them. Although this topic may seem rather specific and marginal in a landlocked country, seafaring in those times was a matter of pride for Czechoslovaks, especially for those men sailing the seas. Their families shared this pride but they often experienced loneliness when men set off for their work on a ship for long months. As hardly anybody was allowed to travel in socialist Czechoslovakia, many people envied seafarers their work and their opportunities to travel freely around the world, obtain foreign (Western) currency and buy goods perceived as luxurious and inaccessible. But envy was aroused not only because of travelling and money. It was also the exceptional nature of the seafarers' job, the sense of something distant, adventurous, and exotic. Looking closely at seafarers' lives, their destinies and memories, we get a completely different picture of the motivation behind their sea cruises—a profound love of the sea.

Initially, this book was supposed to portray the personal and professional life of Czechoslovak seafarers so that they would not sink into oblivion. This was mainly because the former Czechoslovak fleet no longer exists—approximately a decade after the Velvet Revolution, seafarers lost their ships and along the way, many of them lost their purpose in life. However, centring this book on seafarers only would involve two dangers. First, it is impossible to write about seafarers without reflecting on the company they worked for and the role of the state during the socialist period, when private enterprises were excluded from the economy. Second, building up the book (only) around the seafarers' memories could overwhelm the reader with the sadness and nostalgia that these men often indulge in when speaking or writing about their past spent on the sea. Thus, approaching this topic only through memoirs could lead to biased and oversimplified conclusions similar to those that are today presented by seafarers themselves or by the media. The most frequent comments include, for instance, that they worked for a prosperous company, worked hard and thus could be proud of their work and ships, of that Viktor Kožený,[1] with the help of government officials, stole their ships and were it not for him, they would be sailing the ships successfully to this day.

As we will see throughout the book, these voices are generally right; nevertheless, the issue becomes more complicated when covering the topic of maritime business in Czechoslovakia before 1989 in its entirety and colourfulness. The following essential questions arise: Why did a landlocked country establish this kind of maritime business? Whom did this business serve? Who profited from it? For what purposes was the business operated? Was it really prosperous throughout its existence? And how did "ordinary" people live within this business? Did they profit from it? Did they like it? Answering these questions will fill gap in knowledge about the Czechoslovak fleet and maritime business.

The book is framed by two main milestones—1948 and 1989. The year 1948 is perceived as the year when the changes initiated after WWII were completed, with the February communist coup d'état on the top. It was the moment of reversal in Czechoslovakia when ownership relations changed completely, together with business conditions and institutional structure. Consequently, the transport sector changed too. The "real" history of the post-WWII seafaring trade began shortly after the New Year in 1950. The other milestone was the year 1989 when Czechoslovakia became a democracy and market economy. The political, economic, and social changes in the post-November period affected the further development (and subsequent termination) of the maritime business in Czechoslovakia (the Czech Republic respectively) so fundamentally that they would require an independent research project.

The book takes into account three interrelated factors: 1) the development of maritime business in Czechoslovakia and of the Czechoslovak Ocean Shipping company; 2) the circumstances of the Cold War; and 3) the internal political and economic situation in Czechoslovakia influenced by the wider political context due to its affiliation to one side of the bilateral conflict. These factors represent the "macro" perspective of

---

1   For more on Viktor Kožený's activities, see the "Epilogue".

the book and reflect the shipping company's activities in the political and economic sphere of the socialist state and its planned economy. Along with the macro perspective, this book also offers a "micro" perspective aimed at everyday life on ships, and at the pros and cons of the seafarers' jobs. Last but not least, the picture of shipping would not be complete without "memories" of the 44 ships run by the Czechoslovak/Czech[2] Ocean Shipping company.

The book strives to give the most comprehensive picture of the history of maritime business in Czechoslovakia as well as of the shipping company that had been dealing with the whole business. It starts with a short prologue reflecting on the main issues of the maritime business in the interwar period. What follows is a chapter about the 1950s. In its first part, it describes the wider Cold War context and the economic circumstances of the conflict, since the Cold War was to a great extent an economic war.[3] Then the chapter covering the 1950s attempts to capture the very beginning of maritime business in Czechoslovakia in the 1950s by describing the fate of the first Czechoslovak ship Republika and the cooperation with the People's Republic of China (PRC) within this sector.

The following chapter moves to the 1960s, a decade marked by a gradual increase in the number of ships cruising under the Czechoslovak flag. In addition, by the mid-1960s Czechoslovakia finished its cooperation with the PRC and consequently consolidated an exclusively Czechoslovak company in maritime business. Yet another dramatic moment arrived in 1968, a year that holds a crucial place in the history of post-WWII Czechoslovakia. The main events (democratization attempts followed by the invasion of Warsaw Pact armies into Czechoslovakia) are therefore reflected in the context of the treatise on maritime business. The chapter will disclose how seafarers lived through these "big" events

---

2   After the split of the Czechoslovak federation on 1 January 1993, the company was renamed to Czech Ocean Shipping.

3   Charles S. Maier, "The World Economy and the Cold War in the Middle of the Twentieth Century," in Melvyn P. Leffler and Arne Westad Odd, eds., *The Cambridge History of the Cold War, Volume I* (Cambridge: Cambridge University Press, 2010), 44–46.

on selected ships as well as the wider consequences of the affairs for the further development of the enterprise.

The events of 1968 had an important impact on the company. After the invasion, the authorities (conservative, anti-reformist leaders in the Communist Party) took measures of so-called normalization in order to suppress all the democratizing tendencies and "return" the state back to the times before 1968. This "normalization" in its broader definition receives special attention in the chapter about the 1970s, as it dominated the entire period of the 1970s as well as the next decade. The main focus of this chapter is placed on the process of "normalization" within Czechoslovak Ocean Shipping, its consequences for both the company's operation and seafarers' lives.

The subsequent chapter about the 1980s concentrates on the further development of the enterprise and its main problems. Then it moves to the main impacts of *perestroika* in the company and their plans for the future. This chapter also introduces the topic of the State Security and its activities within the company and among the seafarers. Similarly as in the "Prologue", where I introduce the maritime business development in the interwar period, the "Epilogue", the chapter following the 1980s, briefly summarizes all the important processes in shipping after the Velvet Revolution until 1998, when the business ended.

While "Epilogue" is the last chapter dedicated to the "macro" perspective of the topic, the following chapter "Seafarers' lives and memoirs" focuses on the "micro" level—the lives and work of Czechoslovak seafarers (and their families to some extent). It covers the themes of working conditions including salaries and other benefits, life on ships, emigration, and the influence of the communist regime on ships. In brief, it gives an insight into everyday life reflected through seafarers' eyes. And because seafarers cannot be without ships, before the "Conclusion", I have also added a chapter about ship memoirs, which presents all the ships operated by the Czechoslovak/Czech Ocean Shipping company (or by the Czechoslovak state), their basic parameters, and moments of interest from the history of their running. The book closes with a comprehensive summary of possible answers to the questions of why, for what purpose and in whose favour this business was operated in

Czechoslovakia with the main conclusion that political and economic reasons were interrelated. The topic is covered through a complex combination of valuable primary sources together with other available information resources described below.

1.1 This book's dockyard: a brief account of the information sources

The marginality of the shipping sector in the history of landlocked Czechoslovakia corresponds with the marginality of the topic in historiography. Up to know, neither Czech nor Czechoslovak historiographers have paid attention to the topic, nor have other social scientists. Thus Czech historiography cannot offer any comprehensive book summarizing the history of the shipping sector and the Czechoslovak Ocean Shipping company during the existence of the socialist Czechoslovakia.

Let us go back to the metaphor of the subtitle. I consider archival resources the basic plates for the hull of the book—they create a substantial part of my knowledge basis; the vast majority of them are discussed here for the first time. Although the Czech law on archives belongs to the most liberal ones, gathering and collecting the archive sources was demanding and sometimes detective work. It is symptomatic that water presented the biggest problem here, though not seawater but the devastating flood in 2002, which destroyed part of the archival materials related to the topic. Still, based on the "surviving" fonds, it is possible to reconstruct the history of the Czechoslovak Ocean Shipping company and the Czechoslovak maritime business as a whole. The resources that proved to be most useful for my research were those stored in the following National Archive fonds: Office of the Prime Minister, Office of the Central Committee of the Communist Party of Czechoslovakia, Office of the Communist Party Central Committee's First Secretary Antonín Novotný; and the special fond dedicated to the Czechoslovak Ocean Shipping company, the substantial part of which was not damaged by the flood.

Other archive resources used in the book come mainly from the Archives of the Ministry of Foreign Affairs and the Security Services Archive. Documents stored in the Ministry's archives supplement the above mentioned fonds of the stated institutions, since they include information on some international issues (mainly bilateral ones) concerning the topic of maritime business. The Security Services Archive have a special importance because the company as well as seafarers were, for various reasons, objects of the State Security's interests. Today, documentation of these interests provides us with rather comprehensive information on the "object" of surveillance (contemporary terminology). However, before 1989 the State Security cancelled or destroyed several volumes: No. 1014 (the ship Lidice), No. 10149 (the ship Republika), No. 10150 (the ship Julius Fučík), No. 2344 (the ship Blaník), No. 1118, 8706, 22164 (Czechoslovak Ocean Shipping).[4] It means that almost all relevant documents are no longer accessible, with the exception of volume No. 4147 (Czechoslovak Ocean Shipping). Still, this volume, despite its time and content fragmentation (it includes various reports from 1959–1989 on various subjects) gives some important information mainly on the topics of black marketeering, customs offenses, seafarers' contact with foreigners and immigrants, and also some economic information about the company's trade and running of ships.

Other basic sources for this book are memories of former seafarers which—when I return to the shipbuilding metaphor—serve as material for the construction of the superstructure, i.e. the ship's cabins and deck where seafarers live. The memories presented in this book are the outputs of 17 oral history interviews (13 of them directly quoted throughout the book) that I recorded in the period between February and November 2010 with former Czechoslovak seafarers (16 from the Czech Republic and one from Slovakia). The set of interviews includes men of all levels of maritime hierarchy and all types of professions (deck, machine, kitchen, doctor; the only missing profession is a radio officer). Because of the rather wide age range of the narrators (the youngest narrator was born in 1964, the oldest in 1929) this collection encompasses almost the whole history of the Czechoslovak Ocean Shipping company. Interviews were taken in accordance with methodological, procedural, ethical, and legal aspects of the discipline of oral history. Still, narrators' statements cited in some parts of the book are named only with their initials. Alt-

---

4   Security Services Archive's letter from 20 August 2010.

hough I have at my disposal full consent to use the interviews in scientific and non-fictional texts, I decided for this arrangement to protect the privacy of those men who had been so kind as to share their life stories with me.[5]

Just as no ship is completely alone at sea, so this book is not alone in the "literary sea". Probably the first (and fairly representative) book on the Czechoslovak maritime business was published in 1958,[6] shortly before the foundation of Czechoslovak Ocean Shipping (COS); interestingly, it was then that independent maritime business in Czechoslovakia started to flourish. The seafaring theme in Czechoslovakia was dealt with in educational publications,[7] fictional works including both memoirs and factual elements;[8] and non-fiction texts[9] focusing on technical and factual data as well as on some aspects of ships operation. Towards the end of the communist regime, in 1989, a picture publication[10] was printed on the occasion of the 30th anniversary of the founding of the COS. All these books (apart from those for professional education purposes) were used primarily for the presentation of the Czechoslovak fleet, whereas older fictions served also for propaganda purposes and

---

5   During my oral history project I also identified some personal conflicts, persistent feelings of injustice, sometimes mutual finger pointing, accusations of infidelity, etc. That is the main reason why I do not quote the narrators' full names—to avoid damage to their present personal lives.

6   Václav Švarc, *Přes moře a oceány* [Across the Seas and Oceans] (Praha: Naše vojsko, 1958).

7   Jakub Frey, *Loď, moře, námořníci* [Ship, Sea, Seafarers] (Praha: Státní nakladatelství technické literatury, 1961), subsequent editions in 1967, 1976.

8   Bedřich Stožický, *Námořníkem na Atlantiku* [Sailing the Atlantic] (Praha: Státní nakladatelství dětské knihy, 1956); Bedřich Stožický, *Putující horizont* [Wandering Horizon] (Praha: Mladá fronta, 1958); Bohumil Černý, *Na daleké plavbě* [Long Voyage] (Praha: Lidová demokracie, 1963); Bedřich Stožický, *S palubou pod nohama* [On Board] (Praha: Blok, 1973); Jan Kozmík, *Plavby a návraty* [Voyages and Returns] (Praha: Albatros, 1979); Antonín Jakeš, *Poutník oceány* [The Pilgrim of the Ocean] (České Budějovice: Jihočeské nakladatelství, 1980).

9   Jaroslav Pacovský, *Mořští vlci na Blaníku* [The Seadogs on the Blaník] (Praha: Albatros, 1976); Jaroslav Pacovský and Vladimír Podlena, *Atlas lodí. Českoslo-venské námořní loďstvo* [The Atlas of Ships. Czechoslovak Shipping] (Praha: Nakladatelství dopravy a spojů, 1984).

10 Jiří Machota, *Československo na mořích a oceánech* [Czechoslovakia on Seas and Oceans] (Praha: Tisková agentura Orbis, 1989).

showed ship cruising and seafarers' work just as a broader framework for presentation of other topics.[11] Although these books include a substantial amount of factual information and technical data on individual ships, they cannot be considered a full-fledged source base since they do not state standard references and bibliography, ignoring the methodological principles of historical research.

The same methodological problem applies to the only post-communist "factual" book, *Fifty Years of Czechoslovak Ocean Shipping*.[12] Although the author, former economic assistant director in the COS, worked with some archival resources (as I learnt from the archive staff), the text omits any references, bibliography, and source base identification. Beside this, the abolition of censorship and new publishing opportunities after 1989 led to a "boom" in memoirs writing.[13]

Even though memoirs show some imperfections, e.g. when "amateur" writers forget or conceal some information or when they present themselves as "novelists" and mislead the reader, they still provide a certain picture of seafarers' lives and work and prove useful where no other resources are available. Significantly, the vast majority of the memoirs were not written at the outset of the democratic regime but only with the advent of the new millennium. This time lag can be explained by the fact that the former seafarers had grown older and want to give their testimony. What is more, the recent "flood" of publications dedicated to ocean shipping relates to a romantic view of the Czechoslovak maritime past. Though this book is not the first to address ocean shipping in the

---

11 For example: "the past thousands years recede into the background and this country opens up to a more joyful present. Thanks to the Aswan dam and to the new Saad el Aali and thanks to the decree of the nationalization of the Suez together with the new land reform, this ancient country receives fresh new blood". /Černý, *Na daleké plavbě*, 36./

12 Zdeněk Bastl, *Padesát let Československé námořní plavby* [Fifty Years of the Czechoslovak Ocean Shipping] (Praha: Mare-Czech, 2009).

13 Fifteen books published by Mare-Czech (www.mare-czech.cz): two by captain Antonín Fojtů (2006); one by chief engineer Michal Svoreň (2013); three by 2nd mate František Ptáček (two in 2009, one in 2014); six by ship doctor Otakar Mlejnek (2007, 2008, 2010, 2011, 2012, 2013); three by ship cook Pavel Braňka (2012, 2013, 2014); one by seafarer Vlastislav Ringel (2014). Other publishing houses released another three books: one by cook Jan Hájek (2000); one by cook Jiří Frank (2007); one by 2nd mate František Ptáček (1998).

decades of socialist Czechoslovakia, it is the first attempt to make sense of a large portion of archive resources, secondary literature providing the wider context,[14] some pop-cu tural images, and memories of contemporary witnesses. Using primary archival resources and other relevant materials and documents, this work becomes the first systematic attempt to process the history of maritime business in Czechoslovakia and the Czechoslovak Ocean Shipping company after WWII.

---

14   In addition to English historical and other specialized texts, I also used books by Czech authors which I considered useful (in some aspects irreplaceable), mainly with respect to specific topics (for example, the purges in the Communist Party, the "normalization" period, etc.) or the texts of authors who are leading experts in the field with a profound knowledge of the topic and context and history of former Czechoslovakia. Above all, these include economist Václav Průcha and historian Karel Kaplan, a prominent expert on post-WWII history in Czechoslovakia.

2 Prologue: First attempts to run the maritime business after World War I

After the dissolution of the Austro-Hungarian Empire, the newly formed Czechoslovak state paid for its independence by losing direct access to the sea, thus losing seaborne trade on international markets.[15] Consequently, in order to balance this disadvantageous position, the international community had "recognized, and in part addressed some of the constraints [the landlocked countries] faced through a number of international legal instruments".[16] One of the first instruments was the Treaty of Versailles, part XII on Ports, Waterways and Railways (articles 363 and 364), according to which Czechoslovakia acquired free access to the German ports Hamburg and Szczecin (part of Germany until the post-WWII rearrangement of the German/Poland borders).[17]

---

15 For Czechoslovakia it was vital to maintain its export-oriented economy as the market of the new state inherited no more than a third of the industrial capacities from the former monarchy and was short of raw materials, which had to be imported.

16 Kishor Uprety, *Transit Regime for Landlocked States* (Washington, DC: The World Bank, 2006), xi.

17 The Avalon Project. Documents in Law, History and Diplomacy, Yale Law School, "The Versailles Treaty June 28, 1919," http://avalon.law.yale.edu/subject_menus/versailles_menu.asp (as of 4 July 2014). After WWII Czechoslovakia built in Szczecin certain facilities; in the 1950s Czechoslovakia surrounded the territory in favour of Poland in exchange for a small border area of about 4 km². As for Hamburg, Czechoslovakia bought areas in the Peutehafen locality (13,600 m²) in 1929 and signed a lease agreement for 99 years with the City of Hamburg for areas in the localities of Saalehafen and Modauhafen (28,500 m²). The lease contract was adjusted by four additional protocols (1931, 1955, 1987, 1996). Protocol II from 1929 on special arrangements between Czechoslovakia and Germany (based on the decisions under the Versailles Treaty's Articles 363 and 364) set out the terms for the transition of property in the port of Hamburg to the Czechoslovak Republic. In the same year Czechoslovakia and the City of Hamburg concluded a purchase contract for lands between the Peuter area and the Peuter channel (13,574.2 m²) Today this land, including built-up and adjacent water areas, is recorded in the Hamburg registry as assets of the Czech Republic. /Ministry of Transport of the Czech Republic, "Form of Lease Contract. Article I," http://www.mdcr.cz/NR/rdonlyres/64EBE63F-49B5-40C6-B3B9-BBCC8FDED4B0/0/HamburkP%C5%99%C3%ADloha%C4%8D9.doc (as of 17 October 2014)./

Regarding the freedom of transport, article 338 of the Versailles Treaty included an arrangement establishing "an eventual general regime of transit freedom on navigable waterways".[18] The subsequent Covenant of the League of Nations (1919) in article 23e embedded "provision to secure freedom of communications and of transit and equitable treatment for the commerce of all Members of the League".[19] The final arrangement in this process was brought out by the League of Nations conference in Barcelona (1921) to impose equitable treatment in trade. At this conference,

> a new technical organ—the Organization of Communication and Transit (OCT)—was [formed and] charged with proposing measures to ensure freedom of communication and transit. [Several days later, as] a result of the OCT's work, the First General Conference on Communication and Transit (the Barcelona Conference) adopted a series of conventions concerning navigable waterways.[20]

For the topic discussed here, the Convention and Statute on Freedom of Transit signed on 20 April 1921 is particularly important; it stated that the contracting states take measures for regulating traffic across territory under their sovereignty in order to "facilitate free transit by rail or waterway on routes in use convenient for international transit".[21] In conformity with these steps in the international area, Czechoslovakia adopted relevant maritime legal acts. The first one was authorized on 15 April 1920,[22] defining Prague as the "home port" of Czechoslovak ships. Despite these favourable constitutional steps, the maritime business in the interwar period did not thrive.[23] The unfortunate fate of the very first

---

18 Uprety, *The Transit Regime for Landlocked States*, 48.
19 The Avalon Project. Documents in Law, History and Diplomacy, Yale Law School, "The Covenant of the League of Nations," http://avalon.law.yale.edu/20th_century/leagcov.asp#art23 (as of July 4 2014).
20 Uprety, *The Transit Regime for Landlocked States*, 48–49.
21 World Intellectual Property Organization, "Convention and Statute on Freedom of Transit (Authentic text)," http://www.wipo.int/wipolex/en/treaties/text.jsp?file_id=201915 (as of 4 August 2014).
22 "316/1920 Sb., Zákon o vlajce a rejstříku lodí námořních" [Law on the flag and naval vessel register], http://ftp.aspi.cz/opispdf/1920/058-1920.pdf, (as of July 7 2014). The Czechoslovak shipping register was set up in May 1920 by the Government's Regulation 345/1920 Coll.
23 As the historical records of the Czechoslovak Ship Register are hard to ac-

PROLOGUE 13

ship Kehrwieder [Come back] proves that ocean shipping in a landlocked country was to face a number of pitfalls (including various scheming activities). After its flag-raising in March 1920, the Kehrwieder cruised the Baltic and the North Sea for three years. By the end of 1923, the ship was supposed to be registered in Prague under the new name Rusalka. However, on her last voyage before the christening, the Kehrwieder was battered by the raging sea, and no one from the crew survived.[24] This information has been constartly recalled and forms part of Czechoslovak maritime history. Nevertheless, I found one more note in the archives: apparently the ship had been smuggling alcohol into Finland, and the Finnish customs officers probably sank it.

Smuggling alcohol became a profitable business after Finland declared the prohibition law known as *kieltolaki*[25] in 1919 (valid until 1932). Thus, almost all ships sailing in the interwar period under the Czechoslovak flag were probably engaged in this activity. Having no direct connection with the seashore and being a recently developed area of trade, the responsible authorities could not control all the business purposes of the Czechoslovak flag, and smugglers took advantage of it. This unstable situation also enabled some ships to sail for some time under the Czechoslovak flag without any registration.

The available sources offer very little information about ships sailings as Czechoslovak without being entered in the Prague Ship Register. Apart from the first ship Kehrwieder, I found the following twelve vessels: 2) the Praga (in 1928 she completed a voyage with a delivery of 40,000 rifles to the northern Chinese army; the cargo was leaked, which caused negative reactions especially amongst the Czechoslovak public; then she was renamed to the Hedwig Fischer),[26] 3) the Bohemia, 4) the Stella and 5) the Leda (smuggling spirits). Yet another three ships were op-

---

cess, I reconstructed the section on the first ships with the help of the records stored in the National Archive, fund ČNP [COS], part VII-A-16-5-1-6 and the picture publication about the ship Republika from 1958 /Švarc, *Přes moře a oceány.*/

24 Pacovský, *Mořští vlci na Blaníku*, 17.
25 "Alcohol Prohibition History," http://noliquor.us/liquor/alcohol_prohibition_history.html (as of 1 November 2014).
26 Otakar Franěk, *Zbraně pro celý svět* [Weapons for the Whole World] (Brno: Blok, 1970), 73.

erated by the Hamburg businessman Leo Glass, but they had a fictitious owner—the Czechoslovak citizen Anna Hablerová. Leo Glass's ships had the following names: 6) the Únor [February] and 7) the Srpen [August], neither of them received the right to a flag; only the Duben [April] was registered. Furthermore, Anna Hablerová gained a half-year flag right for the ships 8) the Magdalena, 9) the Smíchov and 10) the Tábor. The ship 11) Mělník owned by Gerhard Weiss was fined 20,000 crowns for unauthorized use of the flag; she also smuggled spirits. As for the last unregistered ship, 12) the Olomouc, the request for registration was withdrawn. In addition, in the interwar period the Czechoslovak citizen Pavlíček raised the Czechoslovak flag on the ship Leming without authorization in order to smuggle spirits to Finland.

But even ships that had been recorded in the Prague Ship Register smuggled spirits, mainly those owned by Erwin Spitzer, the co-owner of Swedish Shipping Co. Ltd. He was a "coat" owner, misusing the Czechoslovak flag for Latvians, Estonians, Lithuanians, and other ship owners smuggling spirits to Finland. To this purpose he registered the ships Dalibor, Neptun, Míla, Jiřina, Marie and (most probably also) Merkur. All these ships registered by Erwin Spitzer were deleted from the Prague Ship Register in 1934. Another "coat" person was the Berlin businessman Gerhard Weiss (while the real owner was the German citizen Jebens); Weiss managed to register the ships Plzeň and Litoměřice. All the above mentioned ships had a smaller tonnage, from 25 GRT[27] to 641 GRT (with the Litoměřice being the ship most involved in spirit smuggling). A much larger ship (3,049 GRT) was the Arna owned by Erich Veselý,[28] which sank in February 1928 at the Spanish coast. The ship master did not attempt to rescue the ship nor the documents, although he had enough time. Because of these strange circumstances there is suspicion of insurance fraud.[29]

---

27 In the text the following units and abbreviations are used: DWT—dead weight tonnage, the weight of total load (cargo, fuel, stores, passengers, crew); GRT—gross registered tonnage, the entire cubit content capacity.
28 The son of the Prague Credit Bank's director who ran the ship Erna before WWI; in December 1919 the Arna was confiscated by the Russian army.
29 NA_42: Basic information about the ships operated in the inter-war period.

In 1932 the Baťa concern purchased two ships—the Morava (3,463 GRT), which was supposed to transport caoutchouc from Malaysia, while the second ship, the Little Evy (461 GRT), was to transport leather within European ports. But when the Little Evy collided on 22 March 1934 in the Kiel Canal, she was sold at the beginning of 1935. The Morava did not live up to the company's expectations either. She made only one voyage from Gdynia to India with a footwear cargo and back with raw materials (caoutchouc and leather). Then she served for the transport of grain in the European area but already at the beginning of 1934 (after approximately fifteen months of running), she was sold.

The operation of both ships was negatively affected primarily by the 1930s Great Depression. The depression had a devastating impact on the operation of the most famous Czechoslovak ship in the interwar period—the Legie, the first Czechoslovak ship that entered into the ship register. Before I unfold the compelling story of the Legie, let me summarize the list of the ships registered under the Czechoslovak flag in the interwar period in chronological order from 1920 to 1932:

Record No.	Name	Ship owner	GRT
1	Legie	Bank of Czechoslovak Legionnaires	5,735.08
2	Arna	Erich Veselý, Praha	3,049.19
3	Dalibor	Erwin Spitzer, Gdansk	173.11
4	Neptun	Erwin Spitzer, Gdansk	243.10
5	Míla	Erwin Spitzer, Gdansk	149.71
6	Duben	Leo Glass, Hamburg	548.52
7	Plzeň	Gerhard Weiss, Berlin	79.02
8	Jiřina	Erwin Spitzer, Gdansk	339.01
9	Marie	Erwin Spitzer, Gdansk	127.61
10	Litoměřice	Gerhard Weiss, Berlin	640.66
11	Morava	Baťa, Zlín	3,462.68
12	Little Evy	Baťa, Zlín	461.12

Table 1: Chronological list of ships registered in the inter-war period

The ship Legie was purchased in Japan by Legiobanka shortly after the bank's foundation in 1920.[30] The bank management found this decision compliant with the bank officials' wishes "to get their own great ship" mainly because Czechoslovak legionnaires owned approximately 16,700 tonnes of the cargo in Vladivostok that needed to be transported.[31] The purchase was also justified by a favourable price, and thus Legiobanka bought the Japanese ship Taikai Maru, which sailed off from Vladivostok to Terst on 24 August 1920.

Gradually, however, the Legie's operation ceased to be effective, as the company's accounting records from the years 1927 and 1928 clearly illustrate. At that time the ship made round trips from Hamburg to Argentina or Brazil. But three collisions and subsequent repairs in 1927 meant financial losses. Another problem was the unused capacity of the vessel. In 1927 almost 30 per cent of the total capacity remained unused and the estimation for 1928 was similar.[32]

The following year the bank's management clearly concluded that this type of business was no longer profitable (despite the fact that the ship was in steady operation); as bank officials complained, they had essentially been providing a rather inexpensive means of promotion to the Czechoslovak state, since Legie was "the only oceanic ship operating regular business [...] not like other so-called Czechoslovak ships transporting contraband, be it weapons or spirits".[33] Finally, in October 1933, the management decided on the sale because of the catastrophic situa-

---

30 The foundation of Legiobanka, short name for the Czechoslovak Legions Bank [Banka československých legií], is closely related to the liberation movement of Czechoslovak legionnaires in Siberia (troops formed from the beginning of 1914 from Czechoslovak volunteers fighting for the Tsarist army in Russia). In November 1919 in Irkutsk, several leaders of the Czechoslovak Army in Russia decided to establish a financial and economic centre for the legionnaires. Its predecessor was Military Savings Bank [Vojenská spořitelna] established as a self-help initiative of the Czechoslovak Army in Russia. Together with the foundation of the bank, the Centrokomise started its business activities as a joint stock company in Vladivostok (running until 1921). /Daniela Brádlerová, *Banka československých legií v letech 1919–1938* [Czechoslovak Legions Bank in 1919–1938] (Praha: Filozofická fakulta Univerzity Karlovy, 2006, PhD. Thesis), 24–25./
31 CNB_1: Czechoslovak Legions Bank, ship purchase, 12 July 1920.
32 CNB_2: Czechoslovak Legions Bank, shipping department, 14 March 1928.
33 CNB_3: Czechoslovak Legions Bank, shipping department, 6 February 1929.

tion in maritime transport. The ship was sold to a Greek ship owner for a very reasonable price at that time, £6,250.[34] Reportedly, the ship was destroyed by Germans during WWII.

The case of Baťa ships and mainly that of the Legie indicate that maritime business in Czechoslovak conditions could be successfully run only by strong businesses (e.g. a bank or large business group). Even though their failure can be largely attributed to the Great Depression in the 1930s, these interwar "experiments" showed more disadvantages than advantages in running a private maritime business in Czechoslovakia. Still, the issue was to continue after WWII.

The Czechoslovak state established its maritime business after the 1948 communist coup d'état, and in many ways Czechoslovakia at the time can be considered a similarly strong "business entity" as the previously mentioned companies. As all efforts were aimed at post-war reconstruction, ocean shipping did not receive much attention in the first years after WWII and goods were transported by sea via contracting foreign tonnages. However, less than two years after the communist revolution, business affairs took an unexpected twist—not for economic reasons but for political ones, linked closely to the escalation of the Cold War. Surprisingly, the crucial variable here was the foundation of the People's Republic of China in 1949. The next chapter will explore this strange connection in greater detail, starting with the wider context of international political events and their impact on the political and economic situation in Czechoslovakia in the early 1950s.

---

34 CNB_4: Czechoslovak Legions Bank, ship purchase, ship sale, 11 October 1933.

3 1950s: From the foundation of the People's Republic of China to the foundation of the Czechoslovak Ocean Shipping company

As the chapter's title implies, the Czechoslovak maritime business owes its origins to the foundation of the communist Chinese state and the entire context of the Cold War. To understand better how s landlocked country could launch an ocean shipping operation, I will start by pointing out the essential milestones of the Cold War, focusing on the economic impacts of the Western embargo against the Soviet bloc countries. After presenting the basic conditions for the development of maritime business in Czechoslovakia, I will then lay out in detail the purchase and operation of the first Czechoslovak ship Republika and the cooperation with the People's Republic of China on purchasing and operating other ships. The chapter culminates with the main result of this cooperation—the foundation of the Czechoslovak Ocean Shipping company as an international joint stock company.

3.1 The economic Cold War and its impacts on Czechoslovakia

One of the most essential milestones of the Cold War was the famous "Long Telegram" written by the US diplomat George F. Kennan in February 1946, which "simplified Soviet post-war politics to a version of two camps" with the final aim of the Soviet side being the defeat of the capitalist system. Kennan's contemplations later contributed to creating a new conception of American foreign policy—the Truman Doctrine of retaining Communism (declared on 12 March 1947). Kennan's telegram was followed by Winston Churchill's speech on 5 March 1946 at Westminster College in Fulton, where he used the term Iron Curtain "for the dividing line between the two worlds".[35] Czechoslovakia fell under the Soviet sphere of influence of that Iron Curtain.

---

35 David C. Engerman, "Ideology and the Origins of the Cold War, 1917–1962," in Melvyn P. Leffler and Arne Westad Odd, eds., *The Cambridge History of the Cold War, Volume I* (Cambridge: Cambridge University Press, 2010), 35.

The competition between the two rival powers, the United States and the Soviet Union, was not limited to the field of military-political disputes or conflicts but also took the form of economic warfare with the main aim of depriving the enemy and weaken its (fighting) capacities. An indispensable element in escalating the Cold War was the economic embargo managed by the informal multilateral organization, the Coordinating Committee for Multilateral Export Controls (COCOM), which was used by the United States and associated countries in their effort to oversee the key materials and technology exported to communist countries.[36] It arose as a private and informal initiative whose development was triggered by 1) the intensification of the Cold War in the years 1948–1949, when the People's Democracies (socialist dictatorial regimes) had been established in Central and Eastern Europe, and by 2) important Cold War milestones, specifically "the proclamation of the People's Republic of China, the Berlin crisis, the Tito-Stalin split, and the explosion of the Soviet atomic bomb".[37]

Starting with the new economies in Central and Eastern Europe, the first years of the Cold War were characterized by strong pressure on national autarky.[38] The new policy within the Soviet bloc was interdependence, which was significantly strengthened by the activities of the Council for Mutual Economic Assistance (CMEA). This council was established in 1949 as a partial countermeasure to the Marshall Plan rejected by the Soviet bloc countries (although some of them, mainly Czechoslovakia and Poland, wanted to join the Marshall Plan). From the outset, CMEA activities evinced strong features of political expediency represented mainly by the international political plans of Moscow. Thus, they often acted rather as a brake on Czechoslovak economic development.

---

36 Congress of the United States, Office of Technology Assessment, Washington, D. C., *"Technology and East-West Trade,"* http://ota-cdn.fas.org/reports/7918.pdf (as of 10 December 2014), 153.
37 Ibid.
38 For example, in Czechoslovakia the foreign trade exchange between the years 1948–1953 increased from 39.7 to 78.4 per cent with socialist countries and decreased from 45.5 to 14.8 per cent with capitalist countries. /Václav Průcha, *Hospodářské a sociální dějiny Československa II, 1945–1992* [Economic and Social History of Czechoslovakia 1945–1992] (Praha: Doplněk, 2009), 571./

Furthermore, the Czechoslovak economy was severely affected by the communist revolution in 1948.[39] Yet another negative factor were the increased requirements on heavy armament industries caused primarily by the Korean War at the turn of the 1940s/1950s. When the conflict intensified and led to the establishment of NATO armed forces, the Soviet Union (and subsequently the whole bloc) had to "respond" to this process of armament. Thus from the end of 1950, army demands gradually came to dominate the economy, and all industries became subordinated to the requirements of arms production.

Consequently, Czechoslovakia, whose industry was one of the most developed in the Soviet bloc, was forced to implement a structural transformation of its economy—from a country focused on the production of consumer goods to an economy oriented towards heavy industries and arms production, in spite of the lack of domestic raw materials. However, when implementing these structural changes the government overestimated the real potential of the economy and set out impossible tasks given the conditions of the Czechoslovak economy.

During the first Five Year Plan (1949–1953) economic disproportions became larger, creating substantial barriers for economic growth; the production of food and consumer goods was lagging behind the preferred heavy industry. As a result, Czechoslovakia was hit by an economic crisis,[40] even though the crisis had different features due to the socialist state's economy being dominated by centralization, directive management methods and market exclusion.[41]

---

39 In consequence, the state-controlled directed economy was fully established, market mechanisms were removed from the economy, and private property and enterprises were completely nationalized. The most substantial changes transforming the market (multi-sector) economy into a single (state) sector economy occurred no later than in 1953.

40 The economists of socialist Czechoslovakia labelled the economic crisis as "economic imbalances".

41 There was no increase in unemployment, no decrease of the demand for certain products, but on the contrary there was unrealized purchase power, etc.

3.2 The People's Republic of China comes into play

Nobody would expect that the Czechoslovak Republic had sufficient financial resources and capacities to launch a shipping business under such economic conditions. But the leading authorities decided not only to develop ocean shipping, but also to cooperate with communist China[42] (the cooperation began no later than in 1950[43]). To understand why such a "strange" cooperation could start, we need to briefly sketch the context of the Cold War as well as the relationships between the United States, the Soviet Union (Eastern bloc) and the People's Republic of China.

The People's Republic of China (PRC) was formed under the leadership of the supreme official Mao Zedong on 1 October 1949, as a result of the civil war between the Communists and the Kuomintang. The political representation of the Kuomintang and the rest of its army found refuge on Taiwan Island, where they declared the Republic of China. This republic remained the official sovereign representative of China up until 1970, when the PRC was recognized by the United Nations.

For the United States, this course of events meant a great disappointment as well as a loss of power and prestige. As the United States had gradually expanded their interests in China since the mid-nineteenth century and intensified these efforts after WWII, the foundation of the PRC thwarted their plans. The Sino–Soviet alliance indicated that China had become Moscow's full-fledged partner[44] and this was further confirmed after the outbreak of the Korean War on 25 June 1950, especially when the People's Republic of China became involved in the conflict on

---

42 Hereafter the word China is used for the People's Republic of China (PRC) or communist China—unless otherwise stated.
43 The archival file is incomplete; I estimate the cooperation started in 1950 based on an available document from 11 September 1951, which stipulated details about the negotiation of time charters of Chinese ships and future ship purchases. /NA_1: Secret report from the Czechoslovak Embassy in Beijing for the Ministry of Foreign Affairs, 11 September 1951./
44 Shu Guang Zhang, *Economic Cold War: America's Embargo against China and the Sino–Soviet Alliance, 1949–1963* (Woodrow Wilson Center Press; Stanford: Stanford University Press, 2001), 17, 29.

North Korea's part.[45] The Truman administration responded by imposing "a total economic embargo against the Beijing regime",[46] which meant that the PRC's involvement in the Korean conflict not only deepened its international isolation, but also produced a greater dependence on the Soviet Union.

As for the maritime business, according to the US intelligence units, the PRC's "weak point" was its significant dependence on "foreign sources of petroleum, military equipment and supplies and certain semi processed raw materials" as well as the export of goods. Therefore, it was desirable for the United States to provide the widest possible naval blockade to weaken the regime. But controversies between the United States and the allies arose, and even after the United Nations embargo was proclaimed, "a large number of noncommunist countries' vessels continued carrying goods to China".[47] Still, the majority of the UN members acted in compliance with the embargo.[48]

Despite the difficulties in enforcing the embargo, "the Truman administration was able to persuade its chief allies, the U.K., France, Canada and Japan, to accept the establishment of China Committee (CHIN-

---

45 The PRC was declared a co-aggressor in this war. The United Nations Security Council adopted a resolution designating the Korean conflict as North Korea's attack on the Republic of Korea. The Soviet Union lost the opportunity to veto this resolution because it refused to attend the Security Council meeting as long as "the Kuomintang delegate is sitting there". Thus, the war in Korea decided about China's representation in the United Nations for the next twenty years (that of the Republic of China on Taiwan). /Ivana Bakešová, Čína ve XX. století, díl 2 [China in XX. Century] (Olomouc: Univerzita Palackého v Olomouci, 2003), 44–45./

46 Zhang, *Economic Cold War*, 31.

47 Ibid., 40.
    A significant event in this regard took place in August 1951, when a British ship carried strategic materials to a PRC destination. In mid-September, then, Washington disappointedly stated that the embargo was considerably impaired. /Ibid., 41–42./

48 For example, Danish ship owners refused to charter vessels for the PRC trade; Greece enacted a law prohibiting the chartering of vessels for the transport of embargoed goods for the PRC; Italy prohibited its public vessels (from 85 to 90 per cent of its total shipping) from transporting strategic materials for the PRC; Norway took similar measures. Thus, in 1951 the National Security Council reported that although "a substantial volume of goods continued to be shipped" to communist China, only little of this trade dealt with direct war materials. /Ibid., 43./

COM) of the Consultative group in Paris [COCOM] late in July 1952"[49] to coordinate international economic sanctions against the PRC. Beside this, all the COCOM countries prohibited

> sales of ships to communist China and had agreed to impose restrictions on sales of ships to the rest of the Soviet bloc. These restrictions, however, had not prevented the circumvention of controls and transfer of at least 27 vessels to Soviet bloc flags since October 1950.[50]

The combination of the naval blockade and the embargo brought a serious problem for the PRC regime, since the restrictions affected a great portion of the PRC's transport and purchase of naval vessels (including transactions required by all other Eastern bloc countries). Communist China had to now rely on cooperation with the Soviet Union and Eastern bloc countries. In practice, this cooperation entailed that the PRC used ship capacity of other (Soviet bloc) countries, i.e. purchased and operated ships under foreign flags, formally in foreign ownership.[51] However unusual it may seem, landlocked Czechoslovakia served this purpose as well.

Considering the wider geopolitical context, it is more than likely that this decision was to a great extent influenced by the fact that Czechoslovakia was under the Soviet sphere of influence. Czechoslovak officials made important decisions about Czechoslovak economic policy in accordance with the Soviet Union's (or CMEA) needs and on the instructions of a network of Soviet advisors.[52] This procedure was a result of the Soviet Union's approach to its satellites: Moscow, constantly worried about the coherence of the Eastern bloc and its interests in its sphere of influence, gave individual Communist Parties no choice but to implement the Soviet model of governance. Still there was room "for East Eu-

---

49   Ibid., 43.
50   Ibid., 46 (SE-27, Probable Effect of Various Possible Courses of Action with Respect to Communist China, 5 June 1952, FRUS, 14: 59–62).
51   One of the most important enterprises in this area was the Chinese-Polish Joint Stock Shipping Company Chipolbrok, which started cooperation in July 1950, officially established in June 1951. /"Chipolbrok History," http://www.chipolbrok.com.pl/strona.php?id=25 (as of 8 September 2014)./
52   Karel Kaplan, *Československo v RVHP 1949–1956* [Czechoslovakia in the Council for Mutual Economic Assistance 1949–1956] (Praha: Ústav pro soudobé dějiny AV ČR, 1995), 171–172.

ropean leaders to set their own priorities and initiate their own policies, but only within the contours dictated by Stalin and the Soviets".[53]

In practice, the "satellites" largely adopted a foreign policy that satisfied the superpower's interests while looking for their "own" approaches to foreign partners. Thus, for example, regarding the relationships with the PRC, Czechoslovakia was among the first countries that recognized communist China. In mid-June 1950 Czechoslovakia established diplomatic relations with the government in Beijing and signed an agreement on economic and cultural cooperation.[54] In this context, the PRC's international isolation, the COCOM/CHINCOM embargo, together with the increasing volume of trade between Czechoslovakia and the PRC,[55] were major precursors to establishing cooperation in shipping. Before outlining the planning process of maritime cooperation with the PRC, its scope and results, I will describe yet another, seemingly unrelated, process in the field—the independent[56] development of the Czechoslovak shipping.

3.3 The first "independent" attempts to establish a Czechoslovak merchant fleet

Regardless of the secret negotiations with the Chinese side, there had been voices in Czechoslovakia calling for maritime transport, or better, a single voice can be traced in archival materials. In May 1950, while the international negotiations on the Czechoslovak–Chinese cooperation were in progress, Jaroslav Tomandl, a planner in the national enterprise

---

53 Norman Naimark, "The Sovietization of Eastern Europe, 1944–1953," in Melvyn P. Leffler and Arne Westad Odd, eds., *The Cambridge History of the Cold War, Volume I* (Cambridge: Cambridge University Press, 2010), 195–196.
54 Bakešová, *Čína ve XX. století*, 15.
55 The need for ship transport capacity can be illustrated by the following document from 1959: "in Gdynia goods worth of approximately 200 million crowns had no ship space; if the ship space cannot be provided, we will ask the Chinese partner to decide about transport via land". /NA_2: Report No. 26 from negotiations between Mr. Böhnel from the Czechoslovak Embassy in Beijing and Chinese partner, 25 November 1951./
56 In fact, it is very unlikely that the below described events were conducted independently of the negotiation with the Chinese side. Especially, if we consider that after 1948, these activities had to be realized solely as a state business, which was part of the centrally planned economy.

Československá plavba labsko-oderská [Czechoslovak Elbe–Oder Shipping] asked the Prime Minister Antonín Zápotocký to investigate why the proposal for establishing maritime transport and designing of the Oder–Danube canal had not been realized yet. According to Jaroslav Tomandl, a national shipping enterprise would enable Czechoslovakia to 1) transport certain Czechoslovak goods with lower costs; 2) have a stronger position in negotiating maritime transport fees; 3) maintain total confidentiality while transporting the goods; 4) promote Czechoslovakia through the Czechoslovak flag and thereby demonstrate the socialist state's achievements.[57]

Prime Minister Zápotocký's Office actually started to examine the matter. I offer a hypothesis that—with respect to the ongoing negotiations with the PRC on the same issue (which were at least in a preparatory phase at this point)—Tomandl's letters could have served as a pretext for screening the opinions of relevant ministries.

In a response to this initiative, the Ministry of Transport stressed that maritime business had to be primarily dealt with in cooperation with the Council for Mutual Economic Assistance. At that time, the Ministry was in need of one or two ships mainly for necessary regular transports (e.g. imports of ore from Scandinavia, an essential material for the Czechoslovak economy in post-war years).[58]

The Ministry of Foreign Affairs was also asked to respond to Tomandl's initiative. The Ministry disclosed information about renting two coastal vessels for shipping Czechoslovak cargo from Hamburg to the ports of Benelux, Poland, and back. Yet another ship was rented from Norway to transport ore from Swedish ports. These charters were to show if the operation of ships was economically advantageous. Interestingly, the Ministry of Foreign Affairs made a wry comment that "the main support-

---

57 NA_3: Letter from the planner Jaroslav Tomandl, 15 May 1950.
    Reference to "the confidentiality of transport" indicates that the discussions of maritime transport development were from the very beginning accompanied by considerations about transporting so-called special cargos (i. e. mainly weapons, explosives, strategic chemicals, etc.).

58 "Since the Austro-Hungarian monarchy Czech industry had relied on high-quality Swedish iron ore and had built up its production lines accordingly". /Gertrude Enderle-Burcel et al., eds., *Gaps in the Iron Curtain* (Kraków: Jagiellonian University Press, 2014), 5./

ers of national maritime transport are a few old captains who just see themselves on ships ignoring the problems and risks of such business".[59] This statement is certainly paradoxical in the light of the Ministry's international negotiations in shipping that were going on at the same time.

3.3.1 Organizational background for shipping development in Czechoslovakia

After WWII, Czechoslovakia had to deal with several institutional arrangements to control the existing maritime business. After the February 1948 coup d'état and subsequent nationalization and centralization of the economy, the company Metrans was established (at the end of 1948) as a Czechoslovak joint stock company with a monopoly over international transport, international freight forwarding, and shipping.[60] Given the relatively small range of maritime transport services organized by Metrans, there was no need for other special organizational changes.

Very soon (approximately two years later), however, the government devised a new plan to establish an independent company for maritime transport. The scope of activities included the representation of foreign shipping companies, shipping space booking for shipments greater than 10 tonnes, all kinds of charters and finally, the purchase and operation of the first Czechoslovak seagoing ship.[61] This process culminated in

---

59 NA_4: Letter from the Foreign Trade Ministry for the Prime Minister's Cabinet, 4 January 1951.
60 It was a "direct response" to a new foreign trade conception reflecting the newly constructed economic system based on the Soviet model, where the sphere of external relations formed part of the centrally planned economy. On the basis of Act 119/1948 Coll., a state monopoly on foreign trade was established under the Foreign Trade Ministry and organizations created or authorized by the Ministry. Exclusive rights to the foreign trade business were also confirmed by the Constitution of 9 May 1948. /Aleš Skřivan and Petr Chalupecký, "K charakteru, problémům a roli zahraničního obchodu komunistického Československa," [Characteristics, Problems, and the Role of Foreign Trade of Communist Czechoslovakia] in Radek Soběhart, ed., Hospodářské dějiny Československa 1918–1992 [Economic History of Czechoslovakia 1918–1992] (Praha: SETOUTBOOKS.CZ, 2013), 137./
61 NA_5: Establishment of Čechofracht; proposal for the Deputy of the Prime Minister, 17 November 1951.

creating the company Čechofracht[62] by the arrangement of the Foreign Trade Minister in March 1952 (retrospectively valid from 1 January 1952). The relevant part of Metrans' administrative work, including the staff, was moved to Čechofracht. The new company had 50 employees—quite a significant number, taking into account that the shipping of Czechoslovak goods was then of minor importance and that the Czechoslovak state possessed only one ship. It was the Republika, purchased in 1951.

3.4 The Republika—the first ship owned by the Czechoslovak state

The contract for the first Czechoslovak ship Republika, a thirty-year old steamship (built in England in 1920 and originally named Evanthia), was signed on 26 September 1951. It was a Greek ship owned by Atchides, but it sailed under the Costa Rican flag.[63] While today this regime of ship operation under a foreign flag[64] is mainly used to decrease recurrent costs, in the 1950s this kind of operation also served political or security reasons (such as the Czechoslovak cooperation with the PRC), or

---

62   The name followed foreign examples, as similar specialized enterprises had already been established in the Soviet Union, Poland, and Hungary to remove capitalist ship owners from the market. The proposed name for the new company was Čechofracht as an analogy to similar Soviet and Polish companies (Sovfracht, Polfracht), thus demonstrating that the Czechoslovak company belonged to the camp of People's Democracies. /NA_5: Establishment of Čechofracht, Proposal for the Deputy of the Prime Minister, 17 November 1951./

63   NA_6: Document for the Political Secretary, Report about ship purchase, November 1951.

64   Flag of Convenience (FOC) is a practice allowing a ship's registration in a different country. This practice can reduce recurrent costs (fees for registration, taxes, employing cheap labour, etc.) and circumvent regulations of the country in which the owner is located (on working conditions, environmental regulations, etc.). Today ships are frequently registered in countries where the government has no oversight and no real connection with a ship or her owner (typically Liberia, Pana-ma). Compared to four per cent of FOC ships sailing in the 1950s, today these "open registrations" are used by more than 60 per cent of maritime shippers. /George Rose, "Flying the Flag, Fleeing the State," *The New York Times*, 24 April 2011, http://www.nytimes.com/2011/04/25/opinion/25george.html?_r=2&ref= opinion> (as of 9 November 2014)./

was intended for sale for a higher price to the "second part" of the bilateral world, where it was a scarce good (as was the case of Republika's purchase).

The purchase price of £375,000 (recalculated to 52,500,000 Czechoslovak crowns[65]) complied with contemporary market prices with respect to the quality, prompt delivery, and easy transfer (there were no problems with obtaining an export license from Costa Rica). Although the ship was in poor condition, it was able to transport goods to the embargoed market.

To ensure safe cruising, the Foreign Trade Ministry intended to carry out an overhaul repair of the Republika at the beginning of 1952, before she undertook her first voyage.[66] But the intention was dismissed (probably by higher Party bodies), and the ship was sent from Gdynia (after the ceremonial raising of the Czechoslovak flag) to the Norwegian port of Stavanger to undergo only basic repairs.

"The Norwegian dock was chosen because despite all the efforts, the people's democratic ports could not perform all the necessary repairs."[67] This practice shows (albeit merely episodically) that the Iron Curtain was not impermeable, even in the case of "enemy" countries such as Norway, a founding member of NATO. National business interests oriented towards earning prevailed over political/ideological frictions, and Czechoslovakia strove to benefit from the new opportunities as much as it could. In the same spirit, a report sent from the Czechoslovak Embassy in Beijing to the Ministry of Foreign Trade said: "I beg you to no longer allow repairs of the ship in Stavanger. The crew calls attention to £22,000, where some parts of the ship were removed and installed back without any repair; then the ship embarked on a voyage."[68] Although the available documents do not provide sufficient details about the state of

---

65 After the currency reform in 1953, the price was recalculated to approximately 10.2 million Czechoslovak crowns.
66 NA_7: Report on the classification repairs of the ship Republika, 7 July 1953.
67 NA_8: Draft letter about the Republika's christening for the Minister of Foreign Affairs, 1951.
68 NA_9: Letter from the Embassy in Beijing for the Foreign Trade Ministry, 27 September 1952.

repairs in Stavanger, it was certainly a mistake that the ship had set out to the Far East without having undergone overhaul repairs.

On 17 May 1952, the ship sailed out with a cargo of various Czechoslovak goods for the PRC (particularly machinery and iron materials). During this voyage other repairs had to be made, e.g. a few meters of boiler tubes had to be exchanged. Finally, on 16 June, the ship anchored in Takubar (Northern China) to unload the cargo and load approximately a tonne of general cargo (skins and bristles). About three weeks later, the Republika set out for Tsingtao to load approximately eight tonnes of ore. In the meantime, the representatives of the Czechoslovak Embassy reported on the situation on the ship. They pointed out that the crew's mood and the atmosphere on the ship was "unhealthy". The crew could be divided into three groups: 1) comrades who fully understand their political task and want to undertake further voyages to China; 2) comrades who no longer want to sail for health or personal reasons or for terrible conditions on the ship; and finally, 3) comrades who would be willing to work further on the ship but only under certain conditions (salary increase, cabin arrangements, etc.).[69] All these problems were attributed to poor political leadership.[70]

Yet on a closer look, not everything can be blamed on "weak political leadership." Most importantly, it was the "unpardonable situation in the ship's administration, thrown into such a disarray that it is virtually impossible to find out quantities of stock, the quantity of the distributed and purchased food, wages, vouchers for travelling to Czechoslovakia, etc." The ship's purser completely failed in his function, so most of the ship's administration was made by the captain himself and he did it to the detriment of his captain's duties, which naturally deteriorated the overall situation on the ship.[71] In fact, the incompetence of the ship purser shows that the problems on the Republika had more prosaic reasons— a substantial shortage of people who would be qualified in maritime transports and at the same time reliable for the communist regime.

---

69 NA_10: First voyage to China, 22 July 1952.
70 Until 1968, Czechoslovak ships were also occupied with the ship master's deputy for political affairs; a similar function was to be found in the army.
71 NA_10: First voyage to China, 22 July 1952.

The first voyage of the first ship Republika brought together important personages of the Czechoslovak fleet. The crew was supervised by the 57-year-old ship master, Bohumil Klos, a graduate from the Naval Academy in Yugoslav Bakar, and officer in the newly established Yugoslav navy after the dissolution of Austria-Hungary. The 46-year-old chief mate, Jakub Frey, had the same naval education, while the 45-year-old 2nd mate, Oleg Harna, graduated from the Naval Academy in Yugoslav Dubrovnik during WWII. The 22-year-old 3rd mate, Antonín Fojtů, graduated from the Academy in Polish Szczecin after WWII, and the cadets Milan Rusňák (22 years old) and Antonín Kantner (23 years old) both graduated from the Szczecin Academy.

All these men later became captains working for the Czechoslovak Ocean Shipping company for decades. On the first voyage of the Republika, they all had appropriate education and most of them even several years of experience (before entering the Czechoslovak fleet they had worked mainly on Polish ships). Most of the "ordinary" seamen and some machinics were recruited from the Československá plavba labsko-oderská [Czechoslovak Elbe-Oder Shipping]. Some mechanics came from the Škoda factory, while other crew members, such as stokers, the purser, the doctor, stewards, or cooks, had no experience with a ship's operation. Furthermore, 15 Polish seamen were hired for this voyage (to complement the other 36 Czechoslovaks on board).[72]

It needs to be said that because the early 1950s were the most severe period of the communist regime, and dominated by violence and injustice, people did not express their dissatisfaction unless they had good reasons (e.g. there were riots after the currency reform in 1953[73]). In this light, the work and life conditions on the ship must have been really critical. And moreover, due to the ship's poor technical condition, the crew may have experienced fear for their lives and safety. The life-threatening situation was further exacerbated by frequent technical faults (e.g. the ship had to adjust the bearing shaft five times during the voyage).

---

72 NA_11: Report about the ship purchase, November 1951.
73 For more information about the events see for example: Johann Smula, "The Party and the Proletariat: Škoda 1948–1953 " *Cold War History* 6 (2006): 153–175.

The authorities immediately responded firstly by replacing the deputy for political affairs on the ship by a more "competent", conscious, and mature member of the Communist Party. Secondly, they agreed on replacing some crew members to build a politically reliable team that would absolutely guarantee the proper fulfilment of all tasks. The age limit for new crew members was set up from 30 to 35 years.[74] However, before these measures could be put into place, the Republika—on her way back from China to Europe—crashed in a typhoon.

The authorities ex-post claimed the ship's state could have allowed (sic!) for the completion of her voyage to Europe had she not been hit by a strong typhoon on the night of 17 to 18 August, 150 miles from Shanghai. The typhoon caused extensive damages: some ship plates were unfastened and one plate on the stern broke through due to corrosion.

> So when the water percolated the ship and could not be pumped easily, the captain had to call for a help. The closest ship, the British steamer Eastway, then accompanied the Republika to the mouth of the river Yangtze, where she was taken over by two Chinese towboats.[75]

One of the seafarers described the accident as follows:

> We arrived there safely, but on the way back, when we were loaded with ore and other unit goods, a very bad typhoon struck and practically destroyed the ship. [...] Those days between 17 and 19 August 1952, we can say that all of us were born again, you see. We almost kicked the bucket. [...] So we were hobbling towards the shore. The ship from Hong Kong accompanied us in case we'd sink, to be rescued. That's because sharks turned up, that's interesting, sharks all around. As if they felt good food on the way. Well, the towboats arrived, took us aboard and started pumping the water, the ship was full of water and could sink at any moment.[76]

In the end, the damaged Republika was moved to the dockyard in Shanghai. The crew was not injured (except for three slight injuries),[77]

---

74 NA_12: Situation on the ship Republika, 28 July 1952.
   Whenever the authorities were willing to admit other than political problems, they would argue that the seafarers had been too old to cope with the separation from their families or with another way of life.
75 NA_12: Situation on the ship Republika, 28 July 1952.
76 M. R., * 1930, ship master, 40 years in the COS.
77 NA_13: Report about the Republika crash, 26 August 1952.

and the cargo was re-loaded to the ship Kyma (Greek flag). However, the international circumstances did not allow for arranging the necessary repairs in a short period of time. Beside this, problems with the ship's classification arose.

Lloyd's Register classified the ship as first class,[78] but the classification expired in July 1951. The Greek owner negotiated to postpone the obligation to examine the ship by one year, i. e. until July 1952. When the ship underwent partial repairs in Norway, the Lloyd's Register authorities extended this term by another two months, until the end of August 1952.[79] But instead of performing the repairs during these two months, the Czechoslovak authorities organized the voyage to the PRC as a primary political task.

After the accident, "extensive repairs had to be carried out based on the expertise of the classification company's inspectors". The Chinese side was willing to allow inspectors to travel from Hong Kong to Shanghai, however, Lloyd's Register "rejected sending a representative to Shanghai".[80] The company either feared the safety of the British representative travelling during the Korean War to the territory of communist China, or simply attempted to impede the operation of ships from communist states as a kind of embargo. Still, this event is a very vivid example of how the Cold War interfered with "normal" economic life.

To solve the situation, Lloyd's Register proposed to make only essential repairs in Shanghai and move other works to a different harbour where

---

[78] Maritime classification societies determine the standards for construction and operation of ships. The classification does not guarantee the ship's safety itself, but it is used e.g. as a guideline for the premium insurance rates, suggesting that the ship is reliable and suitable for transport. The first and the oldest classification society is Lloyd's Register ("the Society for the Registry of Shipping was set up in 1760"). "From 1768 the Society used A1 to indicate a ship of the highest class. From 1775 A1 was used and is now famous as a symbol of quality". /"Lloyd's Register, A Brief History of Lloyd's Register," http://www.lr.org/en/who-we-are/heritage/brief-history/ (as of 4 November 2014)./ According to the available documents, the majority of Czechoslovak ships was registered by Lloyd's Register, and in some cases also the Polish and Soviet registers (e.g. when a ship was built in Poland, or for various other, including political, reasons).

[79] NA_7: Report on the classification repairs of the ship Republika, 7 July 1953.

[80] Ibid.

they had a representative (the closest were either Hong Kong or Japan). But the Czechoslovak authorities viewed this solution as too costly and refused to send the ship to Japan for political and economic reasons.[81]

The documents strongly imply that this time the Czechoslovak authorities ran into real trouble. Having considered all the possibilities and gained assurance from the Shanghai shipyard that it would carry out all the necessary repairs (including the technically difficult repair of the crankshaft on the main machine),[82] the Ministry of Foreign Affairs decided to complete all the repairs in order to gain first class classification in Shanghai. To this purpose, on 13 October 1952, the ship appeared on the Soviet ship register, the only register that had inspectors in the PRC.[83] Consequently, Lloyd's Register struck off the ship from its list and withdrew her class as a result of the missing inspection, which violated the classification rules.

The ship anchored in Shanghai and the authorities still strove to find a place where the repairs would be faster. Because of this, they opened negotiations with Soviet partners, as repairs in the Soviet Union were supposed to be provided from six to nine months from the moment of the delivery of material. They entered into negotiations despite the fact that it was highly risky to transport the ship in view of her condition and the Korean War. As the negotiations protracted, Soviet dockyard capacities were filled and the repair of the Republika was promised for the last quarter of 1953 at the earliest. This fruitless endeavour clearly illustrates the precarious situation in the shipbuilding industry within the socialist bloc at that time. Having no other alternative, the Czechoslovak authorities finally decided to carry out repairs in Shanghai; the works did not begin until April 1953[84] (nearly nine months after the accident).

---

81 Ibid.
82 Due to technical problems, in the end it was necessary to order a new shaft. As it could not be made in the PRC, and the delivery from the Soviet Union or Czechoslovakia would have taken about a year and a half, the new shaft was made by a British supplier who offered the most advantageous conditions in terms of price and delivery time. /NA_7: Report on the classification repairs of the ship Repu-blika, 7 July 1953./
83 Ibid.
84 Ibid.

It was clear that the ship would not bring profit for a rather long period. And moreover, it would not be able to fulfil her "political" task—which was apparently the main reason for this investment. Thus, the Ministry of Foreign Affairs strove to make up for the losses and intended to have other repairs carried out than just those caused by the typhoon (and covered by insurance), namely the deficiencies and defects caused before the accident. However, as the Czechoslovak Ambassador in Beijing reported, this intention was unrealistic:

> I believe that comrades from Čechofracht are aware that this ship is well-known in the capitalist shipbuilding and insurance circles, including its state on setting off. The Chinese and Soviet friends warned us in signs, but still quite clearly that speculations over a higher insurance pay-out than the actual damage caused by the typhoon would be dismissed. It is hard to prove that a plate is torn when even a layman can see that it is completely rusted through. Let the comrades admit that they have bought an old ship which may still serve but which requires care.[85]

As mentioned above, there was no other realistic alternative but to carry out the repairs in the PRC dockyard. Still, the official argumentation would not admit these facts and would highlight the advantages of the solution as well as the PRC dockyard's professionalism and claim that it had enough skilled workers and all other facilities like every other shipyard in capitalist countries.[86] Needless to say, the review was greatly exaggerated, especially regarding the heavy dependence of the PRC on technological support from the Eastern bloc.[87]

Negotiations over the ship's repair, of course, involved also a proper propagandist commentary:

---

85 NA_9: Letter from the Embassy in Beijing for the Foreign Trade Ministry, 27 September 1952.
86 Ibid.
87 Shu Guang Zhang, "The Sino-Soviet Alliance and the Cold War in Asia, 1954–1962," in Melvyn P. Leffler and Arne Westad Odd, eds., *The Cambridge History of the Cold War, Volume I* (Cambridge: Cambridge University Press, 2010), 355, 371.

The repair of the ship Republika is not only a technical and commercial issue. Both the Czechoslovak General Consul and the ship master received affirmation from the Chinese comrades, workers, and other staff of the Shanghai shipyard about their absolute commitment to perform timely and conscientious repairs. Feeling honoured at being chosen for this task, they will treat our ship as if she was their own. The shipyard workers gave us their solemn promise to commemorate with their work the deceased comrade Klement Gottwald.[88]

The repairs were very time-consuming, accompanied by difficult material deliveries (materials had to be mostly transported from Czechoslovakia; if Chinese material was used, it subsequently had to be refunded to the PRC). Beside this, Czechoslovakia had to buy numerous products from capitalist countries, for instance rescue boats, aluminium boat stairs, compasses, or a shaft and bronze propeller.[89] Regardless of the initial assurances, "the dockyard had passed from foreign capitalists and specialists into the hands of the PRC that had no experience with work of such an extent, and on such a large ship as the Republika".[90] While Republika's first voyage led to the PRC as "a political task of high priority" without necessary repairs, after the accident she fell into the hands of a grossly incompetent company. This fact could not be outweighed even by the favourable price[91] and apparent benefits that Czechoslovakia would not have received had it had the ship repaired in a capitalist country.[92]

The price was estimated to 10.23 million Czechoslovak crowns, out of which only about 0.3 million were recovered from the insurance for the

---

88   NA_7: Report on the classification repairs of the ship Republika, 7 July 1953.
     Klement Gottwald was the first Czechoslovak "workers' president". He was elected president four months after the communist coup d'état in 1948; he died eleven days after Stalin's death in 1953.
89   Ibid.
90   Ibid.
91   The Chinese side had exceptionally set a lower rate for repairing the ship Republika, namely 9.500 JMP per 1 rouble (JMP = jin-min-pi currency/yuan, non-convertible thus re-calculated through the rouble in this kind of business relationship) instead of the official rate of 6.754 JMB per 1 rouble. This exchange rate concession was set as strictly confidential and wholly exceptional. Czechoslovakia saved about three million crowns in this foreign exchange. /NA_7: Report on the classification repairs of the ship Republika, 7 July 1953./
92   NA_9: Letter from the Embassy in Beijing for the Foreign Trade Ministry, 27 September 1952.

damages caused by the typhoon. The rest of the amount, almost 10 million crowns, was the price for the classification (1st) by the Soviet register.[93] It was a rather high price: to construct a new ship of this type would have cost about 21 million, and repairs were supposed to cost about 30–40 per cent of the purchase price according to what was then the Soviet experience (in our case the repair costs were approximately 50 per cent). Nevertheless, it was argued that the costs would return from the revenues in three years' time (two years, if the revenue was calculated in capitalist currencies).[94]

In the end, the Republika was under repair in the Shanghai Kiangnan Dockyrd for almost two years. Regarding the proclamations about Chinese workers treating the Republika as their own ship, it is highly paradoxical that beside the delay and other difficulties surrounding the repairs, cases of sabotage (though only to a smaller extent) occurred. But it would be mere speculation to claim that these sabotages were directed against the property of the Czechoslovak state or that they were to express workers' protests against the PRC ruling elite. Finally, on 14 June 1954, the Republika was delivered through a commission handover and on 15 June the Soviet Ship Register's Shanghai inspector edited the ship's documents.[95] Thus the Republika could set out on her next voyages, which lasted until 1962.

3.5 The top secret protocol on cooperation in shipping with the People's Republic of China

Thinking about all the obstacles, financial losses and costly repairs that the Republika had to face since its operation, I come to the conclusion that she was in the first place purchased to cooperate with the PRC in the maritime field (albeit behind the scenes). The purchase may even have served as a "cover-up" to encourage the development of maritime transport in a landlocked country. Only fifteen days before signing the purchase contract for the Republika, the Minister of Foreign Affairs fully

---

93 NA_7: Report on the classification repairs of the ship Republika, 7 July 1953.
94 Ibid.
95 NA_14: Letter from the Consulate General in Shanghai to the Ministry of Foreign Affairs, 19 June 1954.

agreed that ships purchased by the Chinese side would sail under the Czechoslovak flag.[96] This agreement concerned mainly the purchase of ships by the PRC under a Czechoslovak "cover", but the timing of the two events suggests that the negotiations made with the PRC and the purchase of the Republika cannot be treated separately.

After negotiations lasting about one year, on 23 July 1952, the Central Committee of the Communist Party of Czechoslovakia approved the cooperation with the PRC in the maritime field. At that time the Republika embarked on her first voyage, less than a month before the typhoon. Following this approval, in November and December 1952, the negotiations between the Czechoslovak Republic and PRC delegations took place in Beijing. A few months later, both parties closed the negotiations by signing a top secret Protocol on the Development of Maritime Transport between Czechoslovakia and the People's Republic of China, dated to 11 June 1953.[97]

The Protocol stated[98] that the Czechoslovak company Čechofracht was to conduct the negotiations for ship purchases under its name but on behalf of and at the risk of the PRC. Once a ship was overtaken by Čechofracht, it was registered in the Prague Ship Register. Ideally, the ship master would be a Czechoslovak citizen; if necessary a foreign captain was also acceptable for both parties. The ships were operated according to Czechoslovak laws and regulations. During the first ninety days after a ship's takeover, a top secret arrangement between the two parties would be signed confirming that ship's real owner was the PRC.[99]

---

96 NA_22: Cipher from the Czechoslovak Embassy in Beijing for the Ministry of Foreign Trade, 21 January 1952.
97 The text of the Protocol was finally approved on 27 January 1953; the Czechoslovak government approved it on 25 March 1953. /NA_15: Report on negotiations between Czechoslovak and PRC specialists on the transfer of PRC merchant ships into the Czechoslovak Ship Registry, under the Czechoslovak flag, 26 February 1953./
98 The Protocol mentioned those arrangements important for the further development of this cooperation as well as the mutual cooperation in the field.
99 NA_16: Secret protocol concluded between Czechoslovakia and the PRC on shipping cooperation, 11 June 1953.

Regarding the cargo, the ships in this "secret" ownership would primarily transport goods between the PRC and Europe (mainly European socialist countries). The Protocol stated that the PRC would decide which goods from Europe should primarily be loaded and shipped. For transports from Europe to the PRC, the Protocol stated a priority for transporting goods as specified in the trade agreements between the PRC and Czechoslovakia.[100] This last point seems to be the major advantage for Czechoslovakia that stemmed from the cooperation with communist China, as it helped to form a strong business partnership throughout the whole decade of the 1950s.[101]

Beside this, the Protocol defined the rules for financial rewards for services—a fee that equalled three per cent of all expenses, including the costs for the classification repairs (with the exception of those classification expenses paid in Chinese ports). The provision from maritime fright paid to Čechofracht was to be arranged separately for each individual case. The rates for maritime transport to other destinations than the PRC were to be determined by the Chinese side.[102] Čechofracht was allowed to put proposals for maritime tariffs to the Chinese side with respect to the changing conditions on the international maritime market. But these were only proposals without any obligations for the Chinese party. As the PRC bore all earnings and risks following from the ships' operation, the Czechoslovak side could not influence the tariffs at all. This raises the question why Czechoslovakia decided to enter such a business. The reasons were most likely political, following from the Cold War context, and the country's subordination to the interests of the Soviet Union.

The Protocol was kept top secret, mainly because its disclosure would have had a profoundly negative impact on Czechoslovak international

---

100 Ibid.
101 Some figures on the PRC–Czechoslovakia foreign exchange: in 1950 the total export to Czechoslovakia reached $9.24 million and imports $1.12 million; the following year, the export numbers were six/fold and import numbers about twenty/fold; in 1952 export to Czechoslovakia increased to $48.9 million and imports to $48.8 million and the amount continued increasing until 1959. /Zhang, *Economic Cold War*, 284./
102 NA_16: Secret protocol concluded between Czechoslovakia and the PRC on shipping cooperation, 11 June 1953.

relations. Later, when the fleet had grown, and the public had learnt about its existence (for instance, newspapers reported on some of the vessels), it was necessary to present a story explaining the origins of the Czechoslovak fleet, though in general, very little information was made available. Of course, it had to be the "right" story serving socialist propaganda. For example, Czechoslovaks could find the following explanation in a picture publication from 1989 (note that the existence of the Protocol was concealed):

> An extensive exchange of goods with the Far East, especially with the People's Republic of China, could not be—given the political and economic discrimination against China—provided properly when using ship tonnage on the free market. [...] Negotiations resulted in the conclusion of an extensive cooperation in the field of maritime transport. [...] In 1953 Čechofracht concluded a purchase agreement for the Czechoslovak merchant fleet.[103]

This reasoning differs slightly in the only book on the history of the COS published after 1989 by Zdeněk Bastl (which, however, does not meet the requirements for a historical publication, mainly for its poor historiographical work and missing bibliography). It states the main facts that "on 11 June 1953 the Protocol on the Development of Maritime Transport between Czechoslovakia and the People's Republic of China was signed, on whose basis the Chinese partner ran its ships under our flag and formally in our [Czechoslovak] ownership".[104] No further comment, no further explanation.

The main (or the most curious) omission here is the fact that Zdeněk Bastl did not mention the basic information stated in the Protocol[105]— about the running of the ships, rewarding, rights, and responsibilities. His reasoning attempts to present the Czechoslovak shipping business not only as something exceptional (and in a sense it indeed was exceptional), but as an "ideal" world presentable only through seafarers' hard

---

103 Machota, *Československo na mořích a oceánech*, not paginated, part of Historie československé námořní dopravy [History of Czechoslovak shipping].
104 Bastl, *Padesát let Československé námořní plavby*, 9.
105 I cannot dismiss the possibility that Bastl's information about the Protocol's existence was based only on "shared knowledge". However, as the former CEO's economic assistant of the COS director he probably had a copy of the document at his disposal, or he saw it and read it during his time with the company (until the mid-1990s).

work, high expertise, company's good economic results and reputation all over the world, and devotion to the profession, ships and the enterprise. Bastl's narrative does not leave aside the great injustice when the fleet's operation was terminated and describes this loss for the people and country. To gain a more complex picture of the maritime business in the context of the socialist state and economy, the following sections will explore 1) the political and economic environment as a "ground" for developing mutual Czechoslovak–PRC cooperation in the maritime field; 2) basic information on ship operation in this "joint" business in the 1950s.

3.6 Communist China's ship with a Czechoslovak communist hero's name

3.6.1 The political-economic context of the transactions

The year 1953 brought some alleviation on the international scene mainly because of the Korean War truce and Stalin's death. The decade between 1953 and the Cuban missile crisis in 1962 was a period of great hopes "of reversing the Cold War confrontation", while "the peril in its turning into real war" was always present. This "first détente" grew mainly out of Khrushchev's "belief that the Soviet Union could afford to reduce its reliance on military power and benefit from a demilitarization of the Cold War". The détente acquired its concrete form in July 1955, when "Khrushchev met President Dwight D. Eisenhower in Geneva at the first summit conference since the beginning of the Cold War".[106]

As for the Soviet bloc countries, after Stalin's death critical voices started to ask for changes in economic and social policy, the so-called New Course. The exaggerated prioritization of the heavy and defence industries burdened individual economies to such an extent that they no longer met the population's needs—the situation led to unrest, thus jeopardizing the ruling communist power. Economic collapse occurred also in Czechoslovakia at the end of the first Five Year Plan (1953). As

---

106 Vojtech Mastny, "Soviet Foreign Policy, 1953–1962," in Melvyn P. Leffler and Arne Westad Odd, eds., *The Cambridge History of the Cold War, Volume I* (Cambridge: Cambridge University Press, 2010), 312, 317, 318.

a result, instead of introducing another five-year plan, two consolidation plans for 1954 and 1955 were launched. The conceptual economic changes aimed to increase living standards and tackle the worst economic problems by reducing military expenses in the new international situation.[107]

Regarding the economic sphere, since 1956 the economic policy of the countries in the Council for Mutual Economic Assistance, including Czechoslovakia, had partially returned to the priorities set in the early 1950s. But this "return" occurred in parallel with the investment activities and increased living standards. During the second Five Year Plan (1956–1960), economic development in Czechoslovakia was characterized by relatively high increases and annually balanced macroeconomic variables.[108] Good economic results were achieved thanks to increased investment, labour, and costs of raw materials. The Communist Party was so optimistic and enchanted by the economic situation that it declared the triumph of socialism in Czechoslovakia in the year 1960. This victory was also codified in the 1960 Constitution (Act 100/1960 Coll.): it changed the name of the state from the Czechoslovak Republic to the Czechoslovak Socialist Republic and anchored the Communist Party's leading role in society and state in law.

Considering the change of the political and economic environment, Czechoslovakia naturally did not develop its own ocean shipping after signing the top secret Protocol with the PRC. Until 1959 it did not purchase any other ship on its account and operated only the repaired Republika. Economic and political priorities were aimed at different areas of trade since fleet development did not seem to bring noticeable benefits. Regarding the Czechoslovak cover for the PRC's ships, all the legal and organizational measures were adopted. As the next step the PRC started to purchase ships under the Czechoslovak flag. These purchases took place between 1953 and 1959 and deserve a special attention.

---

107 Průcha, *Hospodářské a sociální dějiny Československa II, 1945–1992*, 291.
108 Ibid., 300.

3.6.2 The first "coated" ship Julius Fučík[109]

The ship with the communist hero's name announced in the title was a French ship originally named Volta. She was purchased in Marseille on 8 January 1954; on 15 February 1954 she was renamed Julius Fučík in Gdynia and sent on her first voyage on 3 March.[110] The purchase of the vessel was under negotiation at least from mid-1953,[111] when the Cold War's most restrictive and stringent measures were about to end. Thus this transaction also illustrates the restrictive mechanism imposed by the Coordinating Committee for Multilateral Export Controls (COCOM), including possible circumvention methods.[112]

In the case of the Julius Fučík, COCOM would not approve the transaction if Czechoslovakia paid for the ship in goods.[113] But in fact, France had probably little interest in importing Czechoslovak goods, which were no longer competitive on Western markets after the first post-war years (the negotiated price for the ship was £385,000, i.e. approximately 4,526,000 Czechoslovak crowns[114]). In addition, France was interested in gaining foreign currency. In order to reach this aim, the following procedure was arranged: Czechoslovakia would pay the price in £ to

---

109 Julius Fučík was a Czech communist journalist; in 1942 he was arrested by the Gestapo and in 1943 sentenced to death. For more information about Julius Fučík see the chapter "Ship memoirs".
110 NA_17: Letter from the Czechoslovak Minister of Foreign Trade to the PRC Ministry of Communications, 24 March 1953.
111 A written record of the purchase dated 6 November 1953 exists; but at this time the ship was already prepared for delivery and issues of payment had been negotiated in a detail. /NA_18: Information for the Czechoslovak Embassy in Beijing, 6 November 1953./
112 Ships belonged to the third group of COCOM embargoed goods (next to weapons and items related to nuclear energy). This group included commodities which "although nominally civilian, have military potential". /Congress of the United States, Office of Technology Assessment, Washington, D. C., "*Technology and East-West Trade*," http://ota-cdn.fas.org/reports/7918.pdf (as of 26 November 2014), 155./
113 NA_18: Information for the Czechoslovak Embassy in Beijing, 6 November 1953.
114 Note that the price in Czechoslovak crowns is more than a half lower than the price of the Republika purchased two years earlier. Even this price comparison itself says a lot about the changing embargo measures and Western business interests.

France, which would then send the money to the seller in the domestic currency.

The mechanism of COCOM circumvention in this case looked as follows: 1) the Czechoslovak Foreign Trade Ministry would prepare a list of Czechoslovak goods to be exchanged with France; 2) both parties would prepare a common protocol listing the Czechoslovak purchases from France (in which embargoed and non-embargoed goods were not listed separately); furthermore, the protocol would state—again all together—payments in goods and in £. Thus it would be impossible to pair individual items of debit and credit, and the payment for the ship in £ would be concealed;[115] 3) to deceive the Americans, the French authorities would arrange an official visit of Czechoslovak representatives mainly to deal with the goods delivered in exchange for the ship. These three steps were sufficient to reach COCOM consent for granting the French with an export license for the delivery of the ship to Czechoslovakia. The deadline for "the definite decision was extended several times suggesting that the French authorities had not reached the agreement easily".[116]

The Julius Fučík's operation required an additional contract specifying some issues of the first Protocol on cooperation, confirming that the ship's real owner was the PRC. Both sides were again bound by the contract that was kept secret for the safety of the crew, ship and cargo.[117] This document brings important information on transport tariffs.[118]

---

[115] NA_18: Information for the Czechoslovak Embassy in Beijing, 6 November 1953.
[116] NA_19: Letter from the transport department of the Ministry of Foreign Trade to the Czechoslovak Embassy in Beijing, 19 January 1954.
[117] NA_20: Protocol on operation of the ship Julius Fučík, 9 July 1955.
[118] Line shipping (liner tariffs) is based on the regular connection between certain ports; tramp shipping (tramp tariffs) is operated without a designated shipping area.

Tariffs from Europe to the PRC:	- liner, defined for a given time period; - average recurrent costs of all ships in operation under the Czechoslovak flag, considering the international transport market's average rate.
Tariffs from the PRC to Europe for Czechoslovak recipients:	- tramp; based on the average rate on the international tramp market at shipment time.
Tariffs from the PRC to Europe for other recipients:	- calculated according to the agreement between Czechoslovakia and the PRC).[119]

Table 2: Description of transport tariffs used in cooperation with the PRC

Beside this, it was agreed that Czechoslovakia would pay the freight fee 25 per cent in £ and 75 per cent in Czechoslovak–Chinese clearing.[120] As foreign exchange was essential for the Czechoslovak economy,[121] the arrangement seems to have been disadvantageous. Still, Czechoslovakia had the advantage of paying the major part of the costs in clearing and thus saving on the foreign exchange, whereas (mainly capitalist) countries used the method of time charter. The measure was reasonable also because some recurrent costs had to be paid in foreign currency (bunkering, supplies, spare parts repair services, transit fees in some canals, etc.), and Chinese suppliers could not always ensure these goods and services.

Nevertheless, Czechoslovakia mainly strove to prevent the export fees to the PRC from exceeding the prices of the chartered ships. At the time of signing of the secret protocol on the operation of the Julius Fučík

---

119 NA_20: Protocol on operation of the ship Julius Fučík, 9 July 1955.
120 NA_21: Letter from the transport department of the Ministry of Foreign Trade to the Czechoslovak Embassy in Beijing, 14 April 1954.
121 Failing the project of economic autarky within the Soviet bloc (or countries of the Council for Mutual Economic Assistance), Czechoslovakia had to buy some commodities, especially raw materials and also technologies in Western countries. With regard to the declining competitiveness of Czechoslovak production on Western markets, it was difficult to obtain a sufficient amount of foreign currency for foreign trade. Therefore, the supply of foreign currency into the economy was essential.

(7 July 1955), only the Republika was cruising under the Czechoslovak flag, so the average costs used for the price calculation could have been higher than the world rate. Therefore, while negotiating the price, it was decided that the calculation for transports from Europe to the PRC would draw on the Chipolbrok liner rates.[122] But the Chipolbrok rates would entail that Czechoslovak recipients had to pay higher rates than for ships chartered on the world market,[123] thus losing the net profit achieved by the Julius Fučík's operation that had to be passed on to the Chinese party.[124] Actually, the savings on freight tariffs constituted the main benefit of the maritime cooperation with the PRC at that time. Despite this drawback, both parties developed this cooperation to suit their interests—as will be shown in the next section.

3.7 Flourishing cooperation with communist China

3.7.1 The People's Republic of China's activities

Shortly after signing the protocol on the operation of the Julius Fučík, in April 1954, a new Finnish ship was contracted.[125] Though the ship was still under construction, the purchase contract was signed on 14 May.

---

122 NA_21: Letter from the transport department of the Ministry of Foreign Trade to the Czechoslovak Embassy in Beijing, 14 April 1954.
123 Given the scope of this book and the available resources, it is not possible to further discuss the Chipolbrok (Sino–Polish shipping joint venture) and its rate policy. It could have been influenced by the mutual position of the two partners, and perhaps the stronger negotiating position of the Polish side. Another factor was the payment of the rates in clearing, roubles, or in another less beneficial and inconvertible currency. In sum, the Chipolbrok rates were not advantageous in this case.
124 NA_21: Letter from the transport department of the Ministry of Foreign Trade to the Czechoslovak Embassy in Beijing, 14 April 1954.
125 Finland was not a COCOM member, but it "did not wish to jeopardize important trade links with the West, particularly the USA". Still it managed to realize necessary business in the context of the embargo: through the US Embassy in Helsinki, in rare cases "the matter had to be taken to the Pentagon". Only in one case (exports of computer technology) "Finnish businessmen were taken to court for violating the technology embargo". /Pekka Sutela, "Finland's Eastern Trade: What Do Interviews Tell?" in Gertrude Enderle-Burcel et al., eds., *Gaps in the Iron Curtain* (Kraków: Jagiellonian University Press, 2014), 82./ As for shipbuilding, Finnish companies exported ships to the Soviet Union, which was a very profitable business. /Ibid., 80./ Therefore it is no surprise that after the decision to buy a new ship, the PRC contracted it in Finland, too.

The PRC decided to construct the ship in Finland and in the meantime, a takeover contract was formally concluded "though the Chinese side remained the real owner".[126] The ship was delivered in November of the same year and named Lidice.[127] The Chinese side expressed a decisive request that the ship should be in Chinese ports at least by the end of the year 1954 since it carried very important strategic material.[128]

Very soon it became apparent that the successful operation of the ship required more than just her purchase. In July 1955, the Czechoslovak authorities noted that although the ship's operation was "smooth and successful", the lack of trained crews reduced her efficiency (it was necessary "to have more members on the board"). This was supposed to improve by employing Chinese crews. Another serious problem was the situation around the Taiwan,[129] which caused that ships could only go to southern Chinese ports. Furthermore, suitable cargo for ships like the Lidice and the Julius Fučík was not always available. Finally, "the need to maintain absolute secrecy" caused "some problems such as the speed of accounting, etc."[130]

Meanwhile, higher transport rates were approved (from 1 July 1955), i.e. from 25 to 35 per cent paid in £, and the Czechoslovak–Chinese clearing changed as well. The increased rate favoured the PRC, thus reflecting the Chinese effort to earn more convertible money from the cooperation. At the same time, it shows the weaker position of Czechoslovakia in the partnership.

To facilitate administration and decision making, the so-called Liaison Committee was formed. The first meeting was held on 2 August 1955,

---

126 NA_23: Letter from the Ministry of Foreign Trade to Prime Minister Viliam Široký, 12 October 1954.
127 NA_40: Ship's basic parameters.
128 NA_24: Letter from the head of the transport department of the Ministry of Foreign Trade to the Foreign Trade Minister, 23 November 1954. Unfortunately information which "strategic" material the ship carried is not available.
129 This contemporary complaint reflects the situation of the Taiwan Strait Crises (1954–1955). US interests to defend the Republic of China in Taiwan in the case of a communist invasion, and Mao Zedong's effort to unify the country escalated the situation.
130 NA_25: Preparation for negotiations between the Foreign Trade Ministry and the PRC Ministry of Communication about the operation of the ships Fučík and Lidice, 1 July 1955.

to enable the representatives of both parties to express their interests. Most importantly, the Committee discussed ordering of a new ship from Japan. Furthermore, the PRC's proposal to buy a tanker ship in Western Europe was approved by the Committee, with the plan to visit the key shipbuilding firms in Finland, Sweden, Norway, England, France, Italy, and Lebanon in the nearest future and find real opportunities to buy oil tankers based on personal meetings.[131]

The agreement illustrates once more that economic interests often won over political ones and that the socialist countries considered the Western embargo, as well as the COCOM arrangements, permeable. Most probably, the personal meetings were aimed at something more than finding opportunities for buying tankers and agreeing on the price and delivered conditions; in fact, the adjective "real" implied secret negotiations about the restrictions given by the embargo and their possible circumventions. Finally, despite the plan to buy two or three tankers, Czechoslovakia bought only one tanker named the Ostrava on the PRC account, as late as in 1959.[132]

Actually, after the purchase of the Lidice (1954), no ships were purchased for the next four years on the behalf of the PRC to sail under the Czechoslovak flag. Considering that the negotiation process took on average a year, there is a three-year gap when the PRC took no steps towards developing its fleet. How come the gap was so long when the initial conditions had not changed—the embargo remained in existence, and foreign trade between the PRC and European partners was on the increase?[133]

One likely explanation could be the PRC's shift in focus on the cooperation with Poland, especially considering the fact that in September 1956, the joint PRC–Polish company ordered four motor vessels in Yugosla-

---

131 NA_26: Report from the first meeting of the Liaison Committee held in Prague, 2 August 1955.
132 The ship was taken over in Pula shipyard in Yugoslavia on 15 April 1959. /NA_27: Letter from Čechofracht for the Foreign Trade Minister, 27 April 1959./
133 Foreign trade (export and import in total) increased in various East European countries between 1954 and 1958 as follows: East Germany by 43 per cent; Czechoslovakia by 70 per cent; Hungary by 13 per cent, Poland by 53 per cent; calculations based on the foreign trade turnover in millions of $. /Zhang, Economic Cold War, 284–285./

via, and in March 1957, it signed the contract for two new tankers from the same shipyard.[134] Despite the scarce official documentation that would confirm this new tendency with "hard" data, it seems reasonable that the PRC focused its cooperation to Poland, a country with a long maritime tradition. The cooperation with Poland would thus not bring problems with a shortage of skilled seafarers and offered smoother management.[135]

The cooperation with Czechoslovakia was not renewed until 1958, when the Dukla vessel was purchased. The Chinese side interpreted it as an act of intensification of the cooperation.[136] The ship was built in an East German shipyard[137] based on the PRC order, and then, in March 1958, it was formally taken over by Czechoslovakia in the same way as the previous ships, in accordance with the Protocol from 1953.

In November 1958, the PRC purchased yet another ship, the Mír. The construction of the ship was commissioned in the Yugoslav shipyard in Pula. The documents do not indicate who ordered the ship, but the process was probably the same as in the case of the ships constructed in East Germany, where it was the PRC who had placed the order. But at the moment of delivery, a conflict flared up because the Chinese and Yugoslav parties could not reach an agreement on who should receive the ship. The Chinese side claimed that the original contract bound the Yugoslavs to deliver the ship directly to the PRC. In contrast, the Yugoslavs found direct delivery to China undesirable for political reasons.[138]

---

134 "Chipolbrok History," http://www.chipolbrok.com.cn/en/gsls.asp?historydate=1950 (as of 17 September 2014).
As this is the official Chipolbrok website, the data should be only indicative. Still, it represent a certain guideline for trends in the cooperation between the PRC and Poland in maritime business.
135 I cannot exclude that this PRC attitude may have been motivated politically, considering the situation among states under the Soviet influence. Without any reliable sources, it nevertheless remains only speculation.
136 NA_28: Letter from the Ministry of Foreign Trade to the Prime Minister Deputy Comrade Jankovcová, 11 November 1955.
137 NA_29: Letter from the Foreign Trade Ministry for the Rudé právo newspaper, 20 March 1958.
138 After the Soviet-Yugoslav rift in 1949, the relations between the two countries did not normalized until Stalin's death in 1953. This normalization process "allowed Yugoslavia to play an important role in the process of liberalisation that

In such circumstances, the Czechoslovak Ocean Shipping company came into play to solve the difficult situation by "covering" the business and became the ship's recipient. This solution would settle the Sino–Yugoslav dispute.

The task to taking over the ship from the Yugoslavian deliverer was, however, quite risky for Czechoslovakia, especially if the transaction had been revealed. That would not only have led to a deterioration of relations with Yugoslavia, but also (most likely) worsen the relations of Czechoslovak foreign policy as such. Since the relevant ministries (foreign trade, finance) had not been informed about the "true nature of things", it would have been striking that the ship was bought outside of the plan. Thus the top secret business with the PRC in the shipping industry was at risk of being revealed. Finally, the Minister of Foreign Trade proposed to meet the Chinese party's requirements. The minister pointed out that otherwise the Chinese side might get the impression that Czechoslovakia was no longer interested in cooperation in the shipping trade.[139] This decision indicates that Czechoslovakia was interested in the joint business probably for two main reasons: 1) to keep the best possible relations with the PRC; 2) to profit from this by building up its own fleet.

The takeover of the Mír took place in 1958; still, the tension between Yugoslavia and the PRC (or Yugoslavia's concerns about the cooperation) could not have been insurmountable, as already in 1959, the PRC commissioned another ship from Yugoslavia, which was later trans-

---

swept in Poland and Hungary in 1956" and deteriorated the relations between the Soviet Union and Yugoslavia once again. By the end of the 1950s, Yugoslavia became the leader of non-aligned countries; and the rift began to gain momentum again when it shifted from the purely ideological sphere to that of political relations. /Svetozar Rajak, "The Cold War in the Balkans, 1945–1956," in Melvyn P. Leffler and Arne Westad Odd, eds., *The Cambridge History of the Cold War, Volume I*, (Cambridge: Cambridge University Press, 2010), 219–220; Bakešová, *Čína ve XX. století*, 71–72./ Visible cooperation with the PRC in the time of the Sino–Soviet rift could seriously worsen already bad relations between Yugoslavia and the Soviet Union.

139 NA_30: Report from the Ministry of Foreign Trade for the Politburo of the Central Committee of the Communist Party of Czechoslovakia about the transfer of the Chinese ship under the Czechoslovak flag, 19 June 1958.

ferred under the Czechoslovak "coat" as the tanker Ostrava.[140] In the same year Czechoslovakia took over one more ship—the Orava, originally operated by the Sino–Polish shipping company Chipolbrok (named Żeromski).[141] It was built and put into operation in October 1957. However, some technical deficiencies affected the ship's financial results. Since the PRC's cooperation with Poland was based on the principle of sharing the profit and covering the losses in the same proportion, the Polish partner refused to operate the ship.

Two years later (1959), the Czechoslovak Ministry of Foreign Trade approved taking over the Orava, as the Sino–Czechoslovak cooperation was based on a different principle (the profits and losses belonged to the real owner of the ship[142]) and the Chinese side had no other options for operating the ship.[143] Thus, if the vessel was unprofitable, the Chinese party would suffer the consequences whether it would operate her together with the Chipolbrok or with Czechoslovakia. This episode shows that within these bilateral relationships, the Polish partner probably played the strongest part in the negotiations.

The Orava was the last ship purchased (or overtaken) by Czechoslovakia on the PRC's account in this decade. In sum, after signing the secret Protocol on the cooperation, the PRC financed six ships. What follows is a different viewpoint on this joint venture, based on the analysis of the Czechoslovak activities.

---

140 NA_31: Letter from the Foreign Trade Ministry to the COS director, 7 May 1959.
141 The name can refer either to the Polish novelist and dramatist Stefan Żeromski (1864–1925), or to Kazimierz Chwalibów Żeromski, commander of the Lithuanian forces in the Battle of Kushliki between Polish-Lithuanian and Russian forces in 1661 (one of the battles of the Russo–Polish War in 1654–1657). Taking into account the historical context of the 1950s when the ship was named, the first option seems to be more probable.
142 At the very beginning of the cooperation, the Chinese bore the risks and losses; but then the COS operated only ships in the PRC's ownership (Republika I, initially the only Czechoslovak vessel in the joint venture, was under repair in the years 1952–1954).
143 NA_37: Technical condition of the ships Duk a and Orava, 8 April 1960.

3.7.2 Czechoslovak activities in fleet development

Parallel to the PRC activities, Czechoslovakia independently developed its own part of the fleet. One of the documents from 1958 refers back to the moment when Czechoslovakia intended to buy two new ships from Yugoslavia but finally the Politburo of the Central Committee of the Communist Party of Czechoslovakia did not approve the purchase.[144] This probably occurred in the first half of 1957 or earlier because the decision-making process was considerably slower in a centrally planned economy. I suppose that the Politburo's rejection to purchase the two new ships stemmed from the lack of financial resources or from the need to use them elsewhere. By 1957, the extensive economic boom was over, and since the mid-1950s, the adopted economic mechanisms based on the Soviet pattern urgently required a substantial revision. There was a call for a new system of planning and financing presented on two major meetings, at the Communist Party conference in June 1956 and then during the meeting of the Central Committee of the Communist Party in February 1957.[145]

Within this wider economic policy, the government made important decisions on building the fleet: on 19 November 1956 the Politburo of the Central Committee of the Communist Party of Czechoslovakia decided

---

[144] NA_30: Report from the Ministry of Foreign Trade for the Politburo of the Central Committee of the Communist Party of Czechoslovakia about the transfer of the Chinese ship under the Czechoslovak flag, 19 June 1958.

[145] Průcha, *Hospodářské a sociální dějiny Československa II, 1945–1992*, 379.
Thus the first attempt to reform the economic system was initiated—the so-called Rozsypal reform (named after its main author). The reform's principles were: to strengthen perspective planning and determine the basic directions of economic development; to decentralize the sphere of enterprises and strengthen the material incentives both for enterprises and individuals. In the end, the reform failed. Some economists (and mainly Kurt Rozsypal himself) could not even admit that the failure had been caused by the system's inability to adapt to the changes in external and internal conditions of real development (central planning mechanism, absence of any market principles). They explained the failure by external factors, mainly by the conflict with the PRC and a subsequent cancellation of large contracts given by other countries of the Council for Mutual Economic Assistance, the Soviet Union in particular. /Zdislav Šulc, *Stručné dějiny ekonomických reforem v Československu (České republice), 1945–1995* [A Brief History of Economic Reforms in Czechoslovakia (Czech Republic), 1945–1995] (Brno: Doplněk, 1998), 25–29./

not to build a large Czechoslovak fleet and rejected all the plans for purchasing ships (with the exception of highly advantageous offers). However, several months later, in June 1957, the Foreign Trade Ministry submitted the proposal and argued that shipping could increase the efficiency of the national economy in the foreign trade area as required by the Central Committee of the Communist Party resolution from 1957.[146] The argumentation drew on the calculations and experience with operating the three ships in the past two and a half years (the Republika and two ships purchased on the PRC account), proving that the economic return of a ship investment was either 4.5 years when used for services that would be otherwise paid to capitalist providers or 8.5 years when calculated in Czechoslovak crowns.

After the proposed purchases (six ships till 1960 and another two until 1963), Czechoslovak foreign trade was to use the shipping tonnage provided as follows: 12.4 per cent by Czechoslovak ships; 22.6 per cent by ships from socialist countries; and 65 per cent by ships from capitalist countries (because the Soviet bloc countries probably could not meet all the transport requirements with their current capacities). Although the responsible ministries (finance, transport, the State Planning Committee) approved the proposal, the fleet extension was again rejected. The purchase of eight ships was to increase the current range of trade from 4.7 to the above mentioned 12.4 per cent;[147] nevertheless, the vast majority of transport would have to be arranged with capitalist ship owners. Thus, with respect to other economic problems on the national level, an investment into new ships did not seem to be as important.

The Czechoslovak authorities always approved the purchase whenever the ship delivery was to be paid in exchange for Czechoslovak goods instead of foreign exchange. One example could be the ship later named Kladno, which was commissioned in Japan and delivered in 1959. Her price of 26 million Czechoslovak crowns was covered by the delivery of Czechoslovak malt goods.[148] In sum, by the end of the

---

146 NA_34: Material for the Politburo of the Central Committee of the Communist Party of Czechoslovakia, 13. June 1957.
147 Ibid.
148 NA_35: Material for the Politburo of the Central Committee of the Communist

1950s, the shipping joint venture operated eight ships and faced new challenges, especially the need for better management of the entire business. In consequence, a specialized company was established in 1959, as I will reveal in the next subchapter.

3.8 Czechoslovak Ocean Shipping Ltd.

It was the Politburo of the Central Committee of the Communist Party of Czechoslovakia who took the first step in establishing the international company for shipping transport on 7 January 1958. The main intention was to reinforce the existing cooperation in the shipping area and achieve a new, closer, and more flexible form of cooperation that would meet the needs of international conditions and those of China,[149] who remained a stronger partner in the interaction.

These conditions were probably driven by two variables: 1) the fact that the Chinese party financed almost the entire business including the risks and benefits, and this position entitled the PRC to making decisions; 2) Czechoslovak interest on maintaining (and developing) the cooperation since it was considered financially advantageous. Looking at the rates of ensured shipping transport (more than 80 per cent constituted capitalist tonnage[150]), this benefit does not look as advantageous because it covered only a small portion of the transport fees spent in foreign currency. I assume that the company was established to engage with the shipping business and to eliminate the operational problems that had emerged during the course of the 1950s. Another key factor was the intention to further develop the Czechoslovak part of the common fleet, which had not been supported so far.

Following the negotiations in December 1958, both parties agreed to establish an international joint stock company, Czechoslovak Ocean

---

Party of Czechoslovakia, 3 August 1957.
149 NA_36: Letter to Antonín Novotný, President and General Secretary of the Central Committee of the Communist Party of Czechoslovakia, 23 January 1959.
150 NA_34: Material for the Politburo of the Central Committee of the Communist Party of Czechoslovakia, 13. June 1957.

Shipping (COS),[151] which initially employed 54 workers from Czechoslovakia and 13 from the PRC[152]. The agreement about the formation of the COS was signed on 9 March 1959 (and the company entered the Czechoslovak Commercial Register on 1 April 1959).[153]

The company was established by a top secret protocol[154] between both parties, in the form of an "international joint-stock" company, where the adjective "international" meant communist China. But even the form "joint-stock" was a "fake". The intergovernmental protocol on the company's foundation clearly stated that the joint-stock official form of the company was only fictitious, as this company would issue no shares, and neither part would insert capital. The vessels were to remain in the ownership of whichever contracting party had transferred them into the company. The company's profits and losses would be distributed according to the earnings and risks related to each ships and her owner.

The company's management was twofold: two general managers with the same rights and responsibilities directed the company based on a mutual agreement and followed the instructions given by the higher authorities of their respective governments. Problems and disagreements were to be solved by the Liaison Committee or by the Board of Directors, whose representatives had been selected by the governments of the Czechoslovak Republic and the PRC. Prague and Beijing were to take turns in organizing the meetings once a year. All the ships used the

---

151 The first preliminary approval on this kind of cooperation dates to 30 July 1958, during the course of the negotiations of the Liaison Committee meeting. /NA_41: The 17th meeting of the Liaison Committee held on 30 July 1958./
152 NA_38: Meeting report from the Board of Managers meeting, 2–16 April 1959. The company's organizational structure was: general directors—deputies of general directors—secretariat—cadre (personnel) group—company control—business-operational group, technical-operational group—main economic group. With some changes, this company's structure was valid until the 1980s.
153 NA_39: Meeting record on negotiations between the Czechoslovak Foreign Trade Ministry and the PRC Ministry of Communications, 11 December 1958.
154 The agreement on the COS foundation stated that only the company's management would know of the real ownership of the vessels. Other employees, crew members, and even captains were to believe that the COS is an international company with foreign capital participation. /NA_39: Meeting record on negotiations between the Czechoslovak Foreign Trade Ministry and the PRC Ministry of Communications, 11 December 1958./

Czechoslovak flag, and their home port was Prague.[155] But out of the eight ships operated in 1959, only two were in Czechoslovak possession.

The protocol on the formation of the COS includes one important arrangement for shipping fee payments. As mentioned above, the costs were paid partially in £ (25 per cent in 1953, 35 per cent in 1955), and the rest in Czechoslovak–Chinese clearing. From 1959 onwards, the rules were set as follows: 45 per cent in £, and 55 per cent in rouble clearing.[156] But even under these conditions, the cooperation was still advantageous for Czechoslovakia, considering the fact that the freight costs for shipping services in cooperation with the PRC were cheaper than the rates of other ship owners, and that the majority of the transport was still provided by capitalist companies. But this proportion was to change soon, and Czechoslovak ships were to be operated in time charters for foreign ship owners in the upcoming decade, mainly from the 1970s onwards. But before moving to these periods of independent business, let us have a brief look at the financial results in the 1950s.

---

155 Ibid.
156 NA_32: Protocol on the running of the joint company based on the previous agreement from 9 March 1959, article 4.

3.9 Financial results in the 1950s

	1952	1953	1954	1955
Czechoslovak ships[157]	1	1	1	1
PRC ships	0	0	2	2
Total DWT	10,865	10,865	26,474	26,474
Total GRT	6,592	6,592	17,333	17,333
Completed voyages	1	0	19	17
Profit for Czechoslovak partner (crowns)	− 2,035,000[158]	unspecified loss because of repairs	− 587,000[159]	
Profit recalculation ($)[160]	− 101,750	N/A	− 29,350	

Table 3: Financial results 1952–1955

For the first years of the Sino–Czechoslovak cooperation, the Čechofracht files (the partner organization in Czechoslovakia) reveal some fragmentary information on the overall results of the joint venture for the Czechoslovak side. Even after the completion of the Republika repairs in the second half of 1954, shipping was still not profitable. There are three mutually interrelated reasons for such a development: 1) political aspects often prevailed over economic considerations; 2) a lack of experience with the shipping trade; 3) unrealistic overheads in the plan; when the plan did not reflect real recurrent costs and underestimated them, after comparing the revenue and expenditure, the company showed a loss.[161]

---

[157] Information on the number of ships and their tonnage is based on the files on individual ship parameters in the National Archive /NA_72: Files of individual ships./ Number of ships is stated as of the end of the year.

[158] NA_134: Decision on the approval of the annual report for the year 1953 in Čechofracht, 15 March 1954. The loss resulting from the Republika repairs after the typhoon negatively influenced the total economic performance of Čechofracht.

[159] NA_133: Protocol on the approval of the annual report for the year 1955 in the foreign trade company Čechofracht, 16 March 1956.

[160] More on the recalculation see the note 323.

[161] Ibid.

For the second half of the 1950s, the data about economic results is even more fragmentary.

	1956[162]	1957	1958[163]	1959[164]	1960[165]
Czechoslovak ships	1	1	1	2	3
PRC ships	2	2	4	6	7
Total DWT	26,474	26,474	49,084	92,509	106,103
Total GRT	17,333	17,333	33,153	61,809	70,559
Completed voyages	20	N/A	17		51
Amount of goods transported (tons)	N/A	N/A	137,830	316,716	452,699

Table 4: Financial results 1956–1960

Between 1956 and 1959, profits reached about 1.2 million Czechoslovak crowns (1956) and 1.5 million crowns in 1959; no data is available for the years 1957 and 1958.[166] In 1960, the company reached a substantial profit of 10.4 million Czechoslovak crowns. Despite the fact that after the transfer of the share of the profit belonging to the Chinese partner (around 6.1 million paid in transferable roubles and £3.7 million) the net profit for Czechoslovakia was around 0.6 million Czechoslovak crowns,[167] (roughly $30,000), the second half of the 1950s confirmed that operating merchant ships could be profitable. In particular, this was because using its own ships instead of time charters of tonnage from outside the Council for Mutual Economic Assistance was more advantageous for Czechoslovakia. On the other hand, political aspects, which still prevailed in the cooperation during the 1950s, must not be over-

---

162 NA_137: Annual report on economic results in 1956.
163 NA_136: Annual report on Čechofracht economic results in 1958.
164 NA_135: Annual report on economic results in 1959.
165 NA_73: Annual report on financial results in 1961, meeting record, 22 February 1962.
166 It may be possible that this information will become available in the National Archive in the next years with the organization of individual fonds.
167 NA_132: Protocol from the 3rd COS Board Meeting held in Beijing from 11 to 23 April 1966.

looked. Since the maritime business in post-WWII Czechoslovakia was initiated mainly for political reasons, the company Čechofracht and later Czechoslovak Ocean Shipping could rely on the fact that potential losses would be covered by the state budget. Thus they could use this initial period to build up a fleet and set up a maritime business that would bring high profits to the state in the next two decades.

4 1960s: From the Caribbean Crisis to the mutiny on the ship Kladno

This chapter is roughly framed by two political events: the Caribbean Crisis in 1962 and the Prague Spring in 1968, which were both inscribed into the history of the ship Kladno. The former event was closely related to the Cold War and the rivalry between the superpowers, and the latter event represented an important attempt to democratize the ruling communist regime in Czechoslovakia. The chapter begins with the Caribbean Crisis, and then goes on to describe the basic features of the Czechoslovak economy in the first half of the 1960s as a basis for understanding the Czechoslovak involvement in the development of the shipping joint venture. The chapter will then deal with the rupture in the mutual cooperation with the PRC, which contrasts with the Czechoslovak effort for expansion in the shipping business. The next section details the independent Czechoslovak business, dealing mainly with the economic reform related to the Prague Spring, and explores the strategy of shipping development considered at this time. The chapter ends with the events of 1968 as they were experienced on Czechoslovak vessels, mainly on the Kladno and the Košice.

As already mentioned, the ship Kladno came close to the centre of the Caribbean Crisis, in which the world reached the threshold of the outbreak of a nuclear, total war.[168] The main impetus for its triggering was the Soviet Union's "decision to install offensive nuclear missiles in Cuba secretly [...] to save the Cuban revolution from an American attack".[169]

---

168 This conflict was preceded by the second Berlin crisis in 1961, triggered by Khrushchev's effort to transform West Berlin in a free and demilitarized city (Khrushchev speech in November 1958). This transformation would mean the exclusion of the Federal Republic of Germany from NATO structures. A change in the status of West Berlin would solve the problem of the continuous outflow of the East German population into West Germany. Khrushchev also initiated talks with the United States on limiting weapons of mass destruction. The United States did not concede to these requests; as a "response" the Berlin Wall was erected on 13 August 1961. Western democracies (the United States primarily) thus consolidated the bipolar division of the world and the Soviet sphere of influence in Europe.

169 Mastny, "Soviet Foreign Policy, 1953–1962 " 331.

The successful installation of the missiles in the vicinity of the United States would also yield benefits for the Soviet Union and give it an upper hand in the Cold War. The missile transport and installation was prepared in great secrecy; however, the construction of the missile sites was discovered by the Kennedy administration on 15 October 1962.[170] The United States responded with a naval blockade starting on 22 October. The blockade was termed a "quarantine", since the word "blockade" would assume a state of war.[171] At this time, the ship Kladno was approaching Cuban shores and estimated to reach the blockade area on 27 October. In the end, the Kladno was stopped with a group of Soviet cargo ships in front of this zone.

After weeks of negotiations and precarious moments, the crisis was peacefully solved after Khrushchev publicly declared withdrawing the missiles from Cuba on 28 October. On 2 November 1962, the Czechoslovak Ambassador to Moscow was informed that the Soviet leadership had instructed its twenty ships with civilian cargo, which were waiting at the blockade line, to sail to Cuba. The Czechoslovak authorities were recommended to give the same instruction to the Czechoslovak ship masters.[172] Based on this decision, the Kladno reached the island. The US blockade of Cuba was revoked on 20 November 1962.

During the crisis, yet another ship was close to its focal point—the Lidice anchoring in Matanzas, one of the eleven ports to which the secret Soviet cargo had been delivered since August. The Lidice's ship master Antonín Fojtů met a Soviet master of one of the ships carrying military material:

---

[170] David Holloway, "Nuclear Weapons and the Escalation of the Cold War, 1945–1962," in Melvyn P. Leffler and Arne Westad Odd, eds., *The Cambridge History of the Cold War, Volume I* (Cambridge: Cambridge University Press, 2010), 394.

[171] John F. Kennedy, Presidential Library and Museum, "Cuban Missile Crisis," http://www.jfklibrary.org/JFK/JFK-in-History/Cuban-Missile-Crisis.aspx (as of 2 December 2014).

[172] Karel Sieber, "Češi na prahu třetí světové války," [Czechs on the Verge of World War III], *Lidové noviny*, 20 October 2012, 19–20.

> He was an elderly man, and he confided to me that he was a nervous wreck and that he wanted to have a word with a colleague. We were drinking vodka and chatting. He said he did not believe this could have a happy ending. Later, I realized he knew what the Soviets had sent to Cuba and he could not imagine that this could be possibly sent back.[173]

Against the background of these extremely severe Cold War crises threatening the whole world, the Soviet bloc states were dealing with their own serious problems. In Czechoslovakia these were mainly economic difficulties. The third Five Year Plan (1961–1965) proved to be unrealistic again, mainly for the following reasons: 1) economic policy misconceptions, 2) an unjustified atmosphere of success in relation to building socialism when planned tasks had been assigned, 3) the gradual improvement of international policy after the Caribbean Crisis, which led to the reduction of discriminatory measures against socialist states; as a consequence, Czechoslovakia was gradually losing its monopoly position as a supplier of machines and investment units for the countries of the Council for Mutual Economic Assistance. These countries developed their own industrial capacities or cooperated with Western partners. Since Czechoslovakia could hardly compete in machinery exports with Western companies in terms of technical level, delivery times, and sometimes also price and credit conditions,[174] exports decreased, undermining the economic situation. After its second reduction, the third Five Year Plan collapsed within two years and the economy was managed by annual consolidation plans. The growing economic problems, i.e. the collapse of the planned socialist economy, created the need for an economic reform. Preparatory works on the reform started in 1963 and its principles[175] were approved in January 1965.[176] All reform efforts

---

173 Ibid., 20.
174 Průcha, *Hospodářské a sociální dějiny Československa II, 1945–1992*, 314.
175 "The economy was to continue to be guided by central development plans and, at the same time, measures were to be taken to reduce the degree of bureaucracy and decentralise the planning system with planning autonomy for enterprises in all economic sectors, except banking, on the basis of business profitability accounting. The market mechanism was to be incorporated in the control of the individual economic processes". /A ice Teichova, *The Czechoslovak Economy, 1918–1980* (London – New York: Routledge, 1990), 151./
176 Průcha, *Hospodářské a sociální dějiny Československa II, 1945–1992*, 319.

ended with the 1968 invasion of Czechoslovakia by Warsaw Pact troops.

4.1 Czechoslovaks need more ships

Despite this economic situation, which was definitely unfavourable to the expansion of the marginal transport sector, Czechoslovakia was intensively developing its commercial merchant fleet in the first half of the 1960s. This somewhat paradoxical finding cannot be explained purely by non-conceptual planning and management of the national economy. The materials of the highest Party bodies imply a certain strategy behind this development; they include mainly considerations that using national shipping would be advantageous when transporting goods that did not bring high profits, such as politically motivated goods or support for Third World countries. Czechoslovakia may also have been developing its fleet more intensively in connection to an altered foreign trade structure, announced already in 1957. Due to the decreasing competitiveness of Czechoslovak production (mainly engineering) on its traditional markets, this strategy focused foreign trade on "overseas less economically developed countries".[177] These exports would become significantly more costly after the freight charges of Western ship owners.

Beside this, from the very outset of the Czechoslovak shipping business, the country had taken into account the possibility that its ships would carry "special" cargo, mainly weapons and military equipment, as noted in the previous chapter. Although one of the main arms supply deals executed in the 1950s (guns for the Algerian National Liberation Front) was leaked and caused extensive political troubles on the international scene, transports would henceforth be not only politically desirable but also economically effective. Generally speaking, the efforts to develop the fleet were instigated not only by economic factors, but the

---

[177] The following countries were listed: Egypt, Syria, Lebanon, Iraq, Iran, Yemen, Turkey, Pakistan, Afghanistan, India, China, Vietnam, Burma, and Indonesia. /NA_34: Material for the Politburo of the Central Committee of the Communist Party of Czechoslovakia, 13. June 1957./

responsible authorities also considered using it for "special" or political purposes.

The COS as a whole entered the 1960s with an optimistic assumption that the company would operate twenty vessels in 1965, with two thirds owned by the PRC and one third by Czechoslovakia.[178] At this moment Czechoslovakia ran three ships and the PRC seven. In conformity with this plan, but in a certain discrepancy with the previous decision from 1956[179] that there would not be a big fleet the Politburo of the Central Committee of the Communist Party decided to extend the maritime fleet from three ships to six in 1962.[180] Contrary to the PRC, Czechoslovakia fulfilled the investment plan by purchasing four new ships on its own account by the end of 1965: the Pionýr (1960), the Jiskra (1963), the Košice (1963), the Republika II (1964[181]), and the Brno (1965).

In this period, the ships operated by the COS were used for connection with the Far East (with the PRC above all) and in destinations such as Cuban, the Levant, or the Baltic. The COS also discussed, and later realized, a possible use of ships on the route to/from India. In addition, the company considered the purchase of various special ships (e.g. tankers for the transport of fish oils from Scandinavia or small vessels for carrying lumber to Western Europe, mainly to England). The implementation of these proposals was hindered by the bad economic situation of the Third Year Plan, and a solid economic analysis of these proposals was missing.[182] Still, once the COS was established, its Czechoslovak management not only fulfilled political tasks but also strove to use its transport capacities as effectively as possible. While Czechoslovakia was extending its business plans in shipping, the PRC decreased its activities in the joint venture.

---

178 NA_44: Protocol from the 2nd meeting of the COS Board of Directors held in Beijing, 31 March–13 April 1960, article E.
179 NA_34: Material for the Politburo of the Central Committee of the Communist Party of Czechoslovakia, 13. June 1957.
180 Based on materials from 1965. /NA_45: Letter from the Ministry of Foreign Trade for Antonín Novotný, President and General Secretary of the Central Committee of the Communist Party of Czechoslovakia, 1 June 1965./
181 Republika I was sold for scrap in 1962. /NA_47: Ship's basic parameters./
182 NA_43: Board Meeting Records from 1963 (12 April, 7 June, 9 August, 15 November).

4.2 The People's Republic of China does not need more ships

At the outset of the decade, the PRC invested the last ship into the COS—Orlík. Originally, it was a ship built for the Sino-Polish joint venture, named the Frederyk Chopin, put into operation in November 1959 as one of the eight ships ordered at the turn of 1959/1960.[183] Within approximately half a year, the ship was transferred to the Sino–Czechoslovak joint venture as a formal purchase between the COS and China National Transport Machinery Beijing.[184] The ship served for the transport of cargo between the PRC, the Far East and Europe (or India), headed by a Chinese ship master during the first two years of operation. It appears that the Orlík became part of the joint venture mainly because the PRC required transport capacities.

Nevertheless, at the beginning of the 1960s, the Chinese side was keeping its participation in the COS in stagnation. It corresponds with the gradual reduction of CHINCOM arrangements traceable back to 1957. In May 1957, CHINCOM participants "met to consider adjusting the control system". And in June 1957 "British and French governments informed the United States that they would begin trade with China".[185] The PRC profited from these changes in international relations, becoming a more self-confident power.

Thus, for example, when Czechoslovakia offered its assistance in renting capitalist ship capacity for the transport of grain from Australia or Canada to China in 1961, the PRC denied having any problems when negotiating these rents because of the COCOM/CHINCOM embargo. China stated that certain difficulties lay in the effort of the capitalist ship owners to set maximum prices for the transport. The two sides agreed on the PRC's request to release the ship Kladno for the import of 12,000 tonnes of wheat from Australia to Northern China. But the Chinese side

---

183 "Chipolbrok History," http://www.chipolbrok.com.pl/strona.php?id=25 (as of 8 Se-ptember 2014).
184 NA_48: Letter from the Ministry of Foreign Trade to Antonín Novotný, President and General Secretary of the Central Committee of the Communist Party of Czechoslovakia, and Viliam Široký, Prime Minister, 25 March 1960.
185 Richard T. Cupitt, *Reluctant Champions. U.S. Presidential Policy and Strategic Export Controls* (New York, London: Routledge, 2000), 115.

did not use the offer of other ships for such transports—the Orlík, the Mír and later the Dukla.[186] This could be explained by the PRC's need to run these three ships under the Czechoslovak flag for other cargos. Unfortunately, with incomplete records, this assumption cannot be further verified. Another reason could lie in the ever expanding cooperation in the field between the PRC and Poland. The Sino–Polish cooperation seems to have been more important for the PRC than the Sino–Czechoslovak business (regarding the scope of business, Polish tradition, and capacities in the field, etc.). With a certain degree of speculation, the Sino–Soviet rift has to be taken into account as an important variable in the PRC decision-making process, since Czechoslovakia firmly sided with the Soviet Union in the conflict.

The stagnation in the development of the COS was primarily related to ship purchases on account of the PRC. Contrary to this, transport activities ran quite satisfactorily. In addition, the establishment of Beijing's subsidy agency in Guangzhou and a new agency in Szczecin can be perceived as a visible effort to develop the company's activities. The management emphasized mainly these issues: improvement of management, mobilization of all employees' activities, revenue increases, costs reducing, and efficiency. To reach the goals, the Board of Directors asked for speediness in the turnaround of ships, shorter stays in ports, strengthening of technical equipment and economic control, and better supplies for vessels.[187] Still, these goals were hardly to be fully achieved considering that the two states which collaborated in the COS had centrally planned economies, i.e. economies that did not work on market principles. Moreover, the final results were distorted by the sustained effort of both contracting parties to defend not only economic but also political interests,[188] which could, at times, flatly contradict. One of these political tasks which did not bring economic profit was, for exam-

---

186 NA_49: Telegram from the Czechoslovak Embassy to the Ministry of Foreign Trade—Assistance for the PRC in wheat transports from Australia and Canada, 15 March 1961.
187 NA_46: Protocol from the 4th COS Board Meeting held in Beijing from 2 to 15 April 1962, 7–8.
188 NA_58: Letter from the Ministry of Foreign Trade for the Prime Minister Viliam Široký—Agreement on ships operation under the Czechoslovak flag, 27 July 1955.

ple, a short-term exploitation of the Czechoslovak flag for passenger ships of communist China.

4.2.1 Covering of passengers ships for Indonesian-Chinese immigrants

In the early 1960s, the PRC needed passenger ships for the repatriation of Indonesian-Chinese immigrants. These migrants were often driven back to the PRC by material factors (higher income, better career than in Indonesia), but also by the new Chinese nationalism, which had been growing since the establishment of the PRC in 1949. Another important impetus was that "Indonesian policies aimed at marginalising ethnic Chinese". Between the 1950s and the 1960s, nearly half a million of these people returned to the PRC,[189] many of them on ships. Three of these ships were given to the Chinese side under the COS auspices. The PRC decided on a close cooperation with Czechoslovakia probably for pragmatic reasons—in the case of any problems, the losses would be minimal for China.[190]

The first passenger ship of the PRC was purchased from a Greek ship owner. Initially, considering alleviated embargo measures, the PRC intended to purchase passenger ships in capitalist states on its own account. However, this plan proved to be unrealistic mainly for administrative reasons given by embargo impacts and because of high prices demanded by the sellers. For these reasons, the PRC decided to once again use the "covering" Czechoslovak company as a buyer to complete the business with the Greek owner. Thus Czechoslovakia bought the ship Mariana (renamed the Slapy) with Romanian Constanta set as the place of delivery. The ship sailed off from Europe for Whampoa under the Czechoslovak flag on 21 August 1960. According to an additional request, the Czechoslovak flag remained on the ship also during her re

---

[189] Wang Cangbai, "Guiqiao. Returnees As a Policy Subject in China," *Newsletter of International Institute of Asian Studies*, Spring 2009, http://www.iias.nl/sites/default/files/IIAS_NL50_07.pdf (as of 15 November 2014).

[190] As already mentioned, the cooperation with Poland should have been more important for the PRC. The PRC had begun to cooperate also with Romania and Albania; but here the PRC acted as a supporting partner. Thus Czechoslovak help seemed to be the most advantageous for the transport of the required ships.

pairs in the Hong Kong shipyard.[191] Czechoslovak authorities finally decided not to ask for the negotiated one per cent commission from the ship's purchase price, i.e. £2,650 in total. The official reasoning was twofold: 1) the Czechoslovak party was only involved in the negotiation in the final stage, thus most of the work had been done by the Chinese comrades; 2) Czechoslovakia wanted to help the Chinese partner with their goal of speeding up the transfer of Chinese settlers from Indonesia by decreasing the final costs of the operation.[192] This decision can be considered also politically motivated (providing support to a partner within the socialist bloc), or as a gesture encouraging the development of mutual relationships with the PRC in the shipping industry.

Since the purchases of passenger ships were costly, the PRC decided to transform its cargo ships, which were used for transporting goods in coastal waters in the North of China, into passenger vessels. As it was almost impossible for the Chinese party to move these ships from the North to the South with its own crews and flag, the PRC appealed for "Czechoslovak help" again. Above all, they were aware that the "Chiang Kai-shek clique" were arresting ships and carrying out reprisals against Chinese crews.[193]

This request of the PRC was beyond the scope of the Protocol on the Development of Maritime Transport; thus it was sent for approval to the Czechoslovak President Antonín Novotný (also the Secretary General of the Central Committee of the Communist Party of Czechoslovakia) and to Prime Minister Viliam Široký. The Foreign Affairs Ministry's authorities recommended fulfilling the PRC demand because of "a spirit of mutual cooperation in maritime transport [...] and the difficulties the Chinese party faced when repatriating the settlers from Indonesia".[194] Then the appropriate authorities decided to satisfy the needs of the PRC. No-

---

191 NA_50: Letter from the Ministry of Foreign Trade for Antonín Novotný, President and General Secretary of the Central Committee of the Communist Party of Czechoslovakia, and Viliam Široký, Prime Minister, 3 November 1960.
192 NA_51: Ministry of Foreign Trade billing information on the purchase of the ship Slapy, 14 January 1961.
193 NA_50: Letter from the Ministry of Foreign Trade to Antonín Novotný, President and General Secretary of the Central Committee of the Communist Party of Czechoslovakia, and Viliam Široký, Prime Minister, 3 November 1960.
194 Ibid.

body considered it a dangerous task; nobody took into account the fact that there were justified concerns that the Chinese crew could be endangered, and that Czechoslovak seafarers would face similar dangers if the secrecy of the deal was broken. These men were simply sent to accomplish the task in the interest of the state. Fortunately, they managed to sail through.

In this way, the Czechoslovak seafarers transported two ships. The ships were not formally taken into the COS ownership, the only obligation of the Czechoslovak part was to provide the necessary documents for the ships, organize the transfer, and provide a crew. The PRC ships were renamed the Labe and the Odra (Czech rivers). They were not recorded in the Prague Ship Register; the transaction was illicit. The recurrent costs were paid by the PRC.[195]

The transports were executed by a 25-men crew under captain František Cibík's command. The crew flew from Prague on 28 December 1960 and landed in Beijing on 30 December. The Czechoslovak flag was first hoisted on the ship Odra (anchored in Tsingtao, at an emergency anchorage outside the harbour) on 5 January 1961 at 14:00; at 21:00 the ship set out. She arrived on 19 January 1961 at 8:00, with a delay caused by stormy weather during the voyage. The same day the Odra was handed over to the Chinese partner and the Czechoslovak flag was lowered at 18:00. The next day the crew was transported back from Tsamkong to Tsingtao by a special plane. On the ship Labe, the Czechoslovak flag was raised up on 23 January; at 15:00 the ship left the harbour. This transport lasted until 2 February 1961. Both Chinese and Czechoslovak parties made arrangements to keep the transports in the greatest secrecy, providing them with a minimum of workers. Arrival and anchorage of the ships and crew transport were arranged by the Chinese Navy.[196] The Odra was in Czechoslovak "ownership" for 14 days and the Labe for 13 days. These passenger ship transfers represent the last extraordinary activity in the shipping cooperation with the

---

[195] NA_52: Letter from the COS Director to the Deputy of the Foreign Trade Minister, 5 October 1960.
[196] NA_53: Letter from the COS Director to the Deputy of the Foreign Trade Minister, 6 February 1961.

PRC. The whole joint venture shipping business was dissolved within four years.

4.3 "Why do you yield to US imperialism?"[197] (end of cooperation with the PRC)

Similarly to its initiation, the termination of cooperation in shipping between Czechoslovakia and communist China was also strongly influenced by international politics, specifically the Sino–Soviet rift and the second war in Vietnam. Since Czechoslovak foreign policy was directly dependent on Soviet strategy, Sino–Soviet relations were an important variable in the cooperation. Between 1958 and 1962, these relations worsened for several reasons: 1) Khrushchev's proposition "to build a joint submarine flotilla and a military radio station on China's soil" was rejected by the PRC; 2) in response, the Soviets refused to support the Chinese nuclear programme and withdrew their experts from the PRC; 3) the Soviets repeatedly criticized communist China in international forums allies of the Soviet Union. Further deterioration of the Soviet Union–PRC relationship was caused by the Caribbean Crisis because Mao Zedong was highly offended when he had not been consulted on the matter. After the termination of the crisis, Mao Zedong accused Khrushchev of betraying the Cuban revolution. Then, in September 1963, "the Chinese began publishing a series of polemical articles detailing Soviet violations of Marxism". In 1965, the problems escalated up to the point where Mao Zedong perceived the Soviet threat from the North to be as serious as the US threat from the South, i.e the threat related to the US involvement in the Vietnam War.[198]

The origins of this conflict can be traced back to 1946 (and also to the War in Vietnam, 1945–1946): after the French capitulation in the first war in Indochina (1946–1954), the territory was divided into Cambodia, Laos, North Vietnam (led by Communists and supported by the Soviet

---

197 Paraphrase from the document on the end of the cooperation. /MZV_1: Telegram from the Embassy in Beijing—diplomatic note, 29 July 1965./
198 Sergey Radchenko, "The Sino-Soviet Split," in Melvyn P. Leffler and Arne Westad Odd, eds., *The Cambridge History of the Cold War, Volume II* (Cambridge: Cambridge University Press, 2010), 350, 351, 356, 364.

Union and its allies) and South Vietnam (supported by the United States). North and South Vietnam were divided along the 17th parallel with the intention of unifying Vietnam after democratic elections. However, this did not happen. The conflict between both parts escalated in the period 1955–1959 into the North Vietnamese decision to enter war in January and the resulting directive on the war from May 1959.[199]

In 1961, President Kennedy sent 400 Special Forces soldiers to Vietnam. He believed that these forces "represented the kind of 'flexible response' capability the United States needed to counter the Communists".[200] For the further course of events, the incident between the United States and North Vietnam in the Gulf of Tonkin was of major importance. The first attack in the Gulf was carried out by three North Vietnamese Torpedo boats on 2 August 1964 against the US destroyer Maddox. It resulted in the destruction of the torpedo boats. The second incident occurred on 4 August. Although the whole operation undertaken by the United States was triggered by "mistake" (it appears that on that day no North Vietnamese ships were in the area),[201] based on these events Lyndon Johnson asked Congress "for a resolution authorizing him to take all necessary measures to repel an armed attack against the forces of the United States and to prevent further aggression". This measure became known as the Tonkin Gulf Resolution.[202] It served as a legislative basis for military actions in Southeast Asia without a formal declaration of war.

Later this conflict would cause the gradual termination of cooperation with the PRC in the shipping field. However, the first ship (the tanker Ostrava) was signed over to the PRC possession without any direct link to the geopolitical situation. Her takeover by Chinese management was

---

199 Chen C. King, "Hanoi's Three Decisions and the Escalation of the Vietnam War," *Political Science Quarterly* 90:2 (Summer 1975): 239–259, http://vi.uh.edu/pages/buzzmat/vnarticles/chenhanoi3decisions.pdf (as of 21 November 2014).
200 Maurice Isserman, *Vietnam War* (New York: Facts on File Inc., 2003), 36.
201 "Later it would be suggested that an inexperienced and jittery sonar man aboard the Maddox had mistaken the sound of his own ship's rudder for onrushing enemy torpedoes, while freak weather conditions led to misinterpretation of radar readings". /Isserman, *Vietnam War*, 53./
202 Ibid., 54–55.

initiated by the Chinese party in February 1965 because of a lack of goods suitable to be transported on the tanker between the Black Sea and the People's Republic of China. The Ostrava's running had only a minute benefit for Czechoslovak foreign trade because Czechoslovakia had no available commodities suitable for overseas tanker transport. In addition, at this time the PRC could operate the Ostrava either under its own flag for cruising along the Chinese coast or under the Albanian flag within the PRC–Albanian shipping company.[203] This possible partnership strongly resonates with the fact that during the 1960s "Albania closely allied itself with Mao Zedong's China".[204] Thus the Ostrava's operation represented mainly a form of Czechoslovak assistance for the PRC in overcoming the embargo. Czechoslovak business or political interests were not threatened by the Ostrava's withdrawal.[205]

Other steps in terminating the cooperation were actually more influenced by international politics. The severe disruption of the cooperation with the Chinese side occurred in connection with the Vietnam War. It was triggered when the Sino-Czechoslovak management negotiated a common approach for those Chinese vessels cruising under the Czechoslovak flag in the Vietnam area in case they were stopped or attacked by the Americans. The instructions were as follows:

1) To obey the call to stop the vessel after the warning shot; not to deviate the ship from her course under any circumstances; to report the incident immediately to the Prague CCS headquarters and the Beijing branch.

2) To lodge a protest against a forcible ship detention after the entrance of foreign armed forces onto the ship: to present (on request) the ship documents and enable inspection of the ship and cargo; then to continue in the journey as planned.

---

203 NA_54: Letter from the Ministry of Foreign Trade to Antonín Novotný, President and General Secretary of the Central Committee of the Communist Party of Czechoslovakia—Handover of the tanker Ostrava, 27 March 1965.
204 Rajak, "The Cold War in the Balkans, 1945–1956," 220.
205 NA_54: Letter from the Ministry of Foreign Trade to Antonín Novotný, President and General Secretary of the Central Committee of the Communist Party of Czechoslovakia—Handover of the tanker Ostrava, 27 March 1965.

3) In the case of the ship being detained and dragged away, to ensure that any crew member will not leave the ship. To strive for establishing a connection with the nearest Czechoslovak diplomatic mission with the aim of releasing both the ship and the cargo. To impede the ship from being dragged away by passive resistance.
4) In the last resort, to destroy all encrypted and confidential documents on the ship.

The dispute between the COS directors escalated already in the case of the very first instruction. The Chinese director disagreed with the ship being halted and inspected by US marine troops. Furthermore, he stated that in such a case the Chinese crew would not obey the order given by the Czechoslovak ship command. This dispute between the Czech and Chinese management was escalated to ministry level. On 12 July 1965 the Czechoslovak Deputy Minister of Foreign Affairs invited the PRC chargé d'affaires to discuss the matter.

Although speaking in a gentle tone and using diplomatic phrases, the chargé d'affaires basically held the same opinion as the Chinese director. The chargé d'affaires deemed the US "pirate" actions were primarily aimed to reduce or even to prevent assistance for the Vietnamese people. He added that in case of poor resistance, the American aggressors would spread their activities. Thus the PRC could not allow the Americans to do everything they wanted (to stop ships, inspect them, and even drag them). This Chinese attitude, however, represented a big problem since Czechoslovakia, whose flag was hung on the PRC ships, bore all political risks in this case. The Chinese side did not make any concessions to this opinion, accepting no compromise, not even a proposal that the problem areas would be approached only by ships with a Czechoslovak crew. Keeping this stance was, according to China, "a fundamental question of the struggle against imperialism", and the Czechoslovak instructions were apparently in contradiction with this struggle.[206]

Both countries exchanged diplomatic notes—Czechoslovakia sent its note on 7 July and the PRC responded on 29 July 1965. The PRC rep-

---

[206] MZV_2: Report about the visit of the PRC's chargé d'affaires to the Ministry of Foreign Affairs, 12 July 1965.

resentatives worded their note in a very strong spirit, "Why do you not dare to bear the responsibility in this situation and lead the political fight against US imperialism? In blunt terms, you are scared that the US would be angry with you".[207] In the conclusion of the note, the Chinese side did not offer any alternative or compromise; they asked Czechoslovakia to change their opinion. If Czechoslovakia did not accept this offer, the PRC would have to take over the three PRC ships with a Chinese crew (the Dukla, the Orava, the Julius Fučík) under its own flag.[208] Two days later the PRC representative Ju Chang repeated the PRC's negative response to all Czechoslovak proposals for a solution. However, he also suggested a concrete solution: the PRC would take over the ship Dukla from 4 August and the two other ships afterwards. The Dukla takeover was important mainly because the ship should have set off for Haiphong.[209] Formally the takeover was processed through a sales contract between Czechoslovakia as the seller and the PRC as the buyer (the contract was signed on 5 August 1965).[210] The Julius Fučík and the Orava were transferred in the same way as the Dukla when they were approaching the Chinese port of Whampoa/Guangzhou in September 1965.

After this transfer, three more Chinese-owned ships (the Lidice, the Mír, the Orlík) continued to be operated by the COS. They were cruising in the Far East area (Shanghai, Dalian, Guangzhou, Singapore, Malaysian ports, Java, etc.) and also on the shipping lane between China–Durrës (Albania) or Constanta (Romania).[211] They did not approach the Vietnam War area, where there was a high probability of checks by the US military units.

In December 1966, about a year and a half later, also the remaining three Chinese ships were passed to the PRC. On 20 December 1966, the Czechoslovak Ministry of Foreign Affairs issued a diplomatic note to

---

207 MZV_1: Telegram from the Embassy in Beijing—diplomatic note, 29 July 1965.
208 Ibid.
209 MZV_3: Telegram from the Embassy in Beijing for the Ministry of Foreign Affairs, 31 July 1965.
210 MZV_4: Telegram from the Ministry of Foreign Affairs for the Embassy in Beijing, 5 August 1965.
211 NA_55: Log books from the Lidice, the Mír , the Orlík I.

the PRC's Ambassador terminating both the 1953 Protocol the Development of Maritime Transport and the 1959 Agreement on the Establishment of the COS. To justify the termination of the contracts, the Czechoslovak authorities stated that the reasons which had initiated the collaboration were no longer valid. The main purpose of the cooperation was to allow the purchase of ships for the PRC and their operation under the Czechoslovak flag during a time when the PRC had faced grave problems in shipping because of the embargo and blockade. This situation, as stated by the Czechoslovak authorities, had changed, and the PRC both purchased ships and operated them, even in European capitalist ports.[212]

Beside this, no other ships had been purchased for the joint venture for the last six years, which was interpreted as a Chinese loss of interest in the further development of cooperation in the industry with Czechoslovakia.[213] The Chinese chargé d'affaires accepted this note on 27 January 1967.[214] Having been concluded with a three-month notice period, both contracts thus ceased to be valid in March 1967. The ship Lidice was handed over on 2 February, the Orlík on 16 February and the Mír on 21 March 1967.[215]

While negotiating the notice of the contracts, the two parties also discussed some political issues. The Czechoslovak party insisted on the statement that the reasons for the notice were just of a factual nature—the PRC no longer needed Czechoslovak assistance in the industry.[216] From the PRC's side, the notice on the contracts was seen as the next step "to breaking the friendship between the two countries, a proof that

---

[212] MZV_6: Information for the Czechoslovak Embassy in Beijing—diplomatic note, 25 November 1967.
[213] MZV_5: Draft of the note for the Chinese Embassy in Prague, 28 January 1967.
[214] MZV_6: Information for the Czechoslovak Embassy in Beijing—diplomatic note, 25 November 1967.
[215] NA_56: Log books from the Lidice No. 44; the Orlík I No. 25; the Mír I No. 27.
[216] For example, during the company's annual meeting in 1964 the Chinese party stated the current tonnage of COS ships basically met the needs of the goods exchange between the two countries. /NA_57: Protocol from the 6th COS Board Meeting held in Beijing from 4 to 18 April 1964, 8, item VII./

the Czechoslovak government were continuing to support the Soviet revisionists, consorting with US imperialism".[217]

The handover of the second part of the ships was not provoked by a special impetus, as was the case of the ship transfers in 1965, which were triggered by the political context of the Vietnam War. Still, it is extremely unlikely that in this case the political aspect did not play any role, especially after taking into account a wider political context, mainly the Sino–Soviet rift and the fact that "the relations between China and Eastern European countries were inseparable from the Sino–Soviet relationship". At that time not only Czechoslovakia but also Bulgaria, Hungary, Eastern Germany, and Poland "took the Soviet side".[218] In these international policy circumstances may lie the main reason for why Czechoslovakia decided to stop cooperating with the PRC in the shipping industry. This decision, however, did not result in stopping shipping activities, rather on the contrary.

4.4 The last third of the 1960s—the development of an exclusively Czechoslovak shipping

To avoid any misrepresentations, all the changes in the running of the COS in the second half of the 1960s should not be explained by political reasons only. The period from 1965 to 1967, when the ships in Chinese ownership were transferred to the PRC and removed from the operation of the COS, was also the period when the economic reform in Czechoslovakia was being put into practice. Its main principles included replacement of the current directive planning and bureaucratic tools of economic management with basic market economy principles and greater autonomy for companies. From then onwards, companies would bear the consequences of both good and bad economic results. These changes could have given further impetus for the termination of the cooperation with the PRC since the interests of both parties were entirely

---

217 MZV_7: Record about the audience of the PRC's chargé d'affaires in Prague, 27 January 1967.
218 Li Fenglin, "Paper," in Xiaoyuan Liu and Vojtech Mastny, eds., *China and Eastern Europe, 1960s–1980s: Proceedings of the International Symposium* (Zürich: Forschungsstelle für Sicherheitspolitik, 2004), 32.

divergent by then: Czechoslovakia was interested in economic reform, while PRC's Great Cultural Revolution caused the collapse of the Chinese economy and a huge loss of cultural heritage.

Preference of the economic aspects of fleet operation on the Czechoslovak side can also be documented by investments into new ships in the second half of the 1960s. In 1965, the COS operated six ships; five years later, it operated a ten-ship fleet (five new ships were purchased during that time and one sank in 1969). The first investment of this period was in 1966 the ship Vítkovice built in Glasgow. The construction of this first Czechoslovak bulk carrier was negotiated in exchange for otherwise unusable outstanding claims in Guinean ore. Thus Czechoslovakia obtained a ship necessary for transports of raw materials essential for the Czechoslovak steel industry.[219] Later, the Vítkovice was frequently chartered by capitalist ship owners, thus generating a high profit in foreign currency. With her capacity of 41,203 DWT, she was the largest ship in the Czechoslovak fleet until March 1990, when the ship Tatry (66,088 DWT) was purchased.

The most important development in the conception of Czechoslovak fleet operation was perhaps an intention to run passenger transport as a complementary activity to cargo ships. The idea was initiated by the 1967 decision to buy four ships of the Blaník type. This investment directly corresponds with the implementation of the economic reform measures as mentioned above. At the turn of 1968/1969, the company had at their disposal 33 passenger seats on six ships suitable for this service, and it planned to extend it up to 57 seats. The COS intended to offer rather regular voyages to/from Cuba, which were intended mainly for Czechoslovak specialists working in Cuba and their families. Moreover, the company considered offering tourist trips to Cuba. This plan, however, entailed two difficulties at that time: 1) the poor transport and supply situation in Cuba; 2) problems with the coordination of the exact dates of tourists' stays on the mainland and the rotation of ships in Cuban ports, which were not known in advance.

In addition to the trips to Cuba, the management planned to execute occasional passenger routes to exotic destinations (for example, Brazil)

---

219 NA_59: File of the ship Vítkovice I.

and trips around the world via Japan on the ships Košice and Vítkovice. For their length, these voyages were suitable for private persons unlimited by standard vacation periods (pensioners, journalists, filmmakers, people visiting their relatives abroad, etc.).

In 1968, the net profit yield of this passenger transport was 240,000 Czechoslovak crowns (71 passengers); in 1970 160 passengers brought 430,000 crowns of profit. After adjusting the two other ships for passenger transport in 1971, the profit of this service was planned to increase to 1.4 million Czechoslovak crowns per year.[220] However, because of the August 1968 invasion and the related termination of all reform activities and introduction of stricter conditions for travelling abroad, these plans were not met. As passenger transport still represented only a supplementary service at the end of the 1960s, it did not significantly affect the final financial results of the company's running as they are stated below.

---

220 NA_65: Material No. 28 from the director's meeting, 4 April 1969. (Data on passenger transport profits is quoted from relevant annual reports.)

4.5 Financial results in the 1960s

	1961	1962	1963	1964	1965
Czechoslovak ships[221]	3	2	4	5	6
PRC ships	7	7	7	7	3
Completed voyages	58	58	63	88	78
Total DWT	105,893	95,028	125,049	138,977	106,460
Total GRT	70,578	63,986	82,448	93,345	72,756
Amount of goods transported (tonnes)	511,465	437,794	469,238	849,000	713,951
Total net profit (crowns)	9,033,000	14,785,000	27,909,000	28,320,000	35,286,000
PRC share (clearing)	5,499,574	6,779,798	11,090,478	8,892,609[222]	4,584,123
PRC share (£)	52,878	9,733	274,005	277,404	329,184
PRC share (£) recalculation to crowns[223]	1,057,561	194,660	5,480,100	5,592,472	6,636,360
Net profit for Czechoslovakia (crowns)	2,946,914	7,810,542	11,338,422	13,834,919	24,605,517
Net profit for Czechoslovakia ($)[224]	147,346	390,527	566,921	691,746	1,230,276

Table 5: Financial results 1961–1965[225]

---

221 When exact information on ship parameters is not stated in annual reports, information is included based on individual ship parameters files in the National Archive /NA_72: Files of individual ships./ Number of ships is stated as of the end of the year.
222 Financial compensation in Sino–Czechoslovak clearing was substituted with payments in convertible roubles; in the table recalculated to Czechoslovak crowns.
223 The figures on financial compensation in the years 1961–1965 are based on the following sources: 1961 – NA_46: Protocol from the 4th COS Board Meeting held in Beijing from 2 to 15 April 1962; 1962 – NA_128: Protocol from the 5th COS Board Meeting held in Prague from 29 April to 12 May 1963; 1963 – NA_57: Protocol from the 6th COS Board Meeting held in Beijing from 4 to 18 April 1964; 1964 – NA_129: Protocol from the 7th COS Board Meeting held in Prague from 17 May to 4 June 1965; 1965 – NA_130: Protocol from the 8th COS Board Meeting held in Beijing from 11 to 23 April 1966.
224 Having no other information, I have calculated with the average 22 crowns, being aware that it is a sort of underestimation. More on the recalculation see the note 323.

	1966	1967	1968	1969	1970
Czechoslovak ships	7	8	8	8	10
PRC ships	3	0	0	0	0
Completed voyages	66	61	63	60	70
Total DWT	145,723	122,311	122,311	125,231	137,115
Total GRT	96,793	80,842	80,842	84,192	94,816
Amount of goods transported (tonnes)	653,845	821,000	705,714	680,000	863,000
Total net profit (crowns)	23,133,000 −6,939,900	47,700,000 [226]	84,802,000 [227]	81,305,000 [228]	70,290,000
Net profit for Czechoslovakia (crowns)	16,193,100 [229]	cooperation with the PRC terminated			
Net profit for Czechoslovakia ($)	809,655	2,385,000	4,240,100	4,065,250	3,514,500

Table 6: Financial results 1966–1970[230]

---

225 Figures in the table are based on these documents: 1961 – NA_73: Annual report on financial results in 1961, meeting record, 22 February 1962; 1962 – NA_74: Annual report on financial results in 1962; 1963 and 1964 – NA_75: Annual report on financial results in 1964; 1965 – NA_76: Annual report on financial results in 1965, Record on shipping; NA_77: Annual report on financial results in 1965, Record on the fulfilment of planned task; NA_78: Annual report on financial results in 1966, Results of voyages accomplished in 1966 (the document includes comparative data on 1965).
226 NA_81: Annual report on financial results in 1968, 24 February 1969.
227 NA_82: Annual report on financial results in 1969, 25 February 1970.
228 Ibid.
229 The protocol from the bilateral meeting dealing with the results in 1966 is not available; the profit share is very roughly estimated according to the number of ships of both parties within the fleet. The Czechoslovak profit would be probably even higher taking in mind that the PRC ships were handed over in the first quarter of the year.
230 Figures in the table are based on these documents: 1966 – NA_79: Annual report on financial results in 1966, Report for the Ministry of Foreign Trade; NA_78: Annual report on financial results in 1966, Results of voyages accomplished in 1966; NA_86: Annual report on financial results in 1966, Statement of the Minister of Foreign Trade on COS results in 1966; 1967 – NA_80: Annual report on financial results in 1967, 15 February 1968; 1968 – NA_81: Annual report on financial results in 1968, 24 February 1969; NA_85: Annual report on financial results in 1968, Statistics on shipping in 1968; 1969 – NA_82: Annual report on financial results in 1969, 25 February 1970; 1970 – NA_83: Annual report on financial results in 1970.

The figures from the first half of the 1960s shows that despite rather similar number of ships operated (ten in 1961, then nine, eleven, twelve, nine) the profit still increased. The final results reflect the good performance of Czechoslovak ships: in 1961 Czechoslovakia operated three its own ships representing 30 per cent of the fleet which contributed approximately 30 per cent to the final profit. Three years later, five Czechoslovak ships (41 per cent of the fleet) earned almost 49 per cent of the company's total profit. These optimistic results led the Czechoslovak management and its superior ministries toward further fleet development which was planned to consist of 10 ships. It is clear that having in mind the performance of the Czechoslovak ships, the company was not particularly threatened by the termination of the Sino–Czechoslovak shipping cooperation (this statement leaves aside political and ideological reasons for ending the cooperation).

In the second half of the 1960s then we can see a sharp grow of profits: between 1966 and 1968 the profit doubled each year, i.e. from 20 million Czechoslovak crowns to over 80 million while operating seven ships in 1967 and eight ships up until 1969. It was the first "boom" in Czechoslovak shipping; the second will come in the mid-1970s. For 1967, the important information is that the ships' operation in Cuba contributed to the final profit with more than 70 per cent. This was influenced by extensive trade between the two countries, following the Cuban political and economic reorientation towards the Soviet Union and Eastern bloc countries. The extensive trade exchange was one side of the coin; the other was the serious problems in the cooperation since the mid-1960s, as Cuba did not keep its trade commitments and its indebtedness to Czechoslovakia increased. Still, the scope of the trade remained such that it could rather easily provide sufficient transport opportunities.

Later in the 1960s, when Cuba as a destination was gradually losing its significance for Czechoslovak shipping, the ships were used with a rather high efficiency in the Levant, India or Iran and Iraq. In 1970, the COS even chartered three foreign vessels for individual voyages to fulfil some of its tasks.[231] This closely relates with a reported boom on the

---

231 NA_84: Annual report on financial results in 1970, Evaluation of the activities of the commercial department in 1970, 17 February 1971.

shipping market.[232] This boom continued during the first years of the 1970s. And the ships' good performance was not interrupted even by the events of 1968. Nevertheless, these were important moments of Czechoslovak history and need to be discussed here in greater detail.

4.6 1968: "We dreaded that they would requisition our ships"[233]

The political and social movement of the year 1968 was raising hopes of change and democratization of the ruling regime across the whole Czechoslovak society. Around April 1968, the Communist Party leadership (or rather, its reformist fraction) basically lost control over the political situation and Party leaders succumbed to pressures from society. This political development was faced with great resistance from the "Warsaw five" (the Soviet Union, Poland, East Germany, Bulgaria, Hungary). They were afraid that Czechoslovakia would break away from the Eastern bloc, from Soviet influence, and mainly from the communist regime, which would then significantly threaten the regimes in these states.

This "fear" finally led to the invasion of Czechoslovakia by Warsaw Pact armies on the night of 20–21 August. After 13 days, on 3 September, the National Assembly reintroduced censorship and enacted laws necessary to "restore order". An agreement for the "temporary stay" of Soviet troops in Czechoslovakia was signed; the reformist Communists were dismissed. Further steps and measures of the so-called normalization process are described in the next chapter. I will now present what Czechoslovak seafarers were doing in the aftermath of the invasion, and how they experienced the August events abroad, cut off from home, from their closest family and friends.

Based on available resources, I can describe in greater detail the August days as they occurred on the ships Košice and Kladno, and partially on the Vítkovice. As for the situation on the five remaining ships of the fleet, I can present only fragmentary information. No reports about the

---

232 NA_83: Annual report on financial results in 1970.
233 Paraphrase from the interview with M. R., * 1930, ship master, 40 years in the COS.

behaviour of the crew or the situation on board during the invasion are available for the ships Pionýr and Republika II—the first one was being unloaded in the Cuban port of Cienfuegos and the latter was being loaded in Malaysia.[234]

The situation on the ships Blaník, Brno, and Jiskra was rather quiet. The Blaník was anchoring in Cuba at that time. Here the sources reveal several assaults against Party officials after some non-Communists accused the Communists that they—as the Party—were responsible for the situation in their homeland.

> Most of the crew proved to be extremely nationalist during those critical days, demonstrating it in strong attacks against the Soviet Union and other countries whose troops entered Czechoslovakia. The ship's commanding officers condemned the invasion.[235]

After arriving back in Europe, five seafarers from the Blaník emigrated in the Kiel Canal. A similar situation unfolded on the Brno. The ship unloaded buses in Havana in mid-July, and on 23 July she was sailing out to Montreal. She arrived at Bari in Italy on 15 August, thus the crew experienced the invasion in Italy. Within approximately a week after the invasion, 10 seafarers, five wives, and three children from the ship emigrated.[236]

The Jiskra sailed off on the day of the invasion from the Cuban port of Moa to Hamburg. During the voyage some members of the crew manifested anti-Soviet attitudes. The ship's command, however, did not support them. When crew representatives, namely the chief engineer and the chief mate, approached the ship master with a proposal to strike, they were brusquely rejected with a clear and simple rationale: "What does the company pay you for? For strike, or for work? So, quickly, get down to work". Thus the State Security reported that during the August events the situation on the ship had been quiet, "dramatic events" were avoided. Still, the crew clearly stood behind the pro-reform communist leadership of the Party. They declared the arrival of the Warsaw Pact

---

[234] NA_62: Log book from the Pionýr No. 30; NA_63: Log book from the Republika I No. 17.
[235] ABS_1: Letter from the deputy for political affairs on the ship Kladno, 13 April 1970.
[236] NA_64: Log books from the Brno, No. 12, 13.

troops to be an occupation, and sent a supporting telegram to this effect to the Central Committee of the Communist Party of Czechoslovakia.[237]

The Vítkovice sailed out from the port of Colon in Panama on 14 August 1968, loaded with coal cargo for Japan. She arrived at the port of Tobato on 7 September, after the first "normalization" measures were introduced in Czechoslovakia. But the year 1968 on the ship was far from calm. The situation escalated after the August invasion when the former head of the ship's Communist Party group, together with one of the Party members, refused to condemn the invasion. They were labelled as collaborators, excluded by the others, ostracized, attacked. The bitterness of disappointment with the invasion and the end of the reform development in the country concentrated on the ship into an opposition and aversion towards these men. Things calmed down only with personnel changes on the ship and, of course, in relation to the political developments in the country after August 1968.

The time around the invasion was very complicated on the Košice.[238] On 21 August the ship sailed off from Rotterdam to the Soviet Black Sea port of Tuapse. During the voyage the crew tuned into a broadcast of a Schweningradio message from an unknown amateur radio station[239] with a warning to all Czechoslovak ships on the way to Europe not to sail into the ports of socialist countries. Instead of these destinations, they should use the ports of Hamburg or Split. The author of this message is unknown, and so is his/her motivation. In the case of the Košice, the crucial variable was that the ship remained without any connection with the headquarters for about two days.[240] And the ship was approaching Tuapse. The other Czechoslovak vessels were in locations

---

237 ABS_1: Letter from the deputy for politica affairs on the ship Kladno, 13 April 1970. This letter contains also information about the situation on the ship Košice.
238 Unless otherwise stated, the situation on the Košice is reconstructed based on the log book records. /NA_60: Log book from the Košice I./
239 ABS_1: Letter from the deputy for political affairs on the ship Kladno, 13 April 1970.
240 The first management meeting after the invasion took place on 23 August, dealing mainly with the means of communication with ships. /NA_61: Management meeting report—extraordinary meeting held on 23 August 1968./

quite distant from the shores of the People's Democracies participating in the invasion of Czechoslovakia.

On 22 August, the ship master decided shortly before 10 pm to deviate from the original course because of the unclear situation in Czechoslovakia after the occupation and the potential threat to the ship when approaching the Soviet port. The master sent telegrams to the Czechoslovak embassies in Ankara and Bucharest, as well as to the Prague headquarters with an urgent request for instructions. The next day after 4 pm the ship received instructions from the Embassy in Ankara to contact the Czechoslovak Embassy in Bucharest. Thus the ship master decided to sail to Constanta in Romania in order to establish contact with Bucharest and also to bunker (add fuel) and replenish water and food supplies. Two days after the first message not to sail to Tuapse and three days after the invasion, the ship reached Constanta and the ship master called Bucharest. The Embassy officers recommend that he set off as soon as possible from Constanta to Split "where Czechoslovak ships should meet according to the announcement of the legal radio station Šumava OK". Finally, the officers stressed not to sail to Tuapse in any case.

The ship master followed these directions and navigated the ship to Split. On 27 August he obtained two messages: 1) a radio message about the return of Alexander Dubček, First Secretary of the Central Committee of the Communist Party, and other government officials from negotiations in Moscow;[241] 2) a telegram from the headquarters ordering to disembark the wives in Constanta and go to Tuapse. Today it is hard to imagine how the captain felt, what he experienced, what he was afraid of. Given the fact that the ship navigated close to European coasts, he may have had sufficient information about the invasion and subsequent events in Czechoslovakia. At this moment he was obviously more inclined to believe the advice given by the Embassy operating in a

---

[241] From 23 to 26 August 1968, a meeting between top Soviet leaders and the Czechoslovak delegation took place in Moscow, resulting in the signing of the so-called Moscow Protocol. This document, representing a Soviet dictate, was signed by all members of the Czechoslovak delegation, with the exception of František Kriegel. The Protocol confirmed the denial of the Prague Spring, agreement with the occupation and beginning of the so-called normalization.

country not participating in the invasion than the orders given by the company's management operating in occupied Czechoslovakia. Thus he decided to continue the voyage to Split and to consult the situation with the responsible authorities once more there. His decision was driven not only by distrust to the headquarters' instructions, but also by a hidden fear that the ship could be forcibly detained in the Soviet Union. On 29 August the wives disembarked in Split and the Košice set off for Tuapse.

Naturally, the captain was later highly criticized for taking those steps and his decision was labelled as a serious manifestation of right-wing activities. Finally, his refusal to approach the Soviet port of Tuapse in August 1968 was alleged to have caused a loss of almost 500,000 foreign crowns.[242] The ship master remembered the consequences of his decision, too:

> I managed to scrape through it. Since, well. I was on the ship which should have gone to Tuapse. But we did not reach it because they had warned us, also at the Embassy, that we had been occupied by the armies and that they could requisition our ship. So after this, I was not allowed on the sea for two years. The thing was being investigated. They seized my passport, yeah, seized my passport. I was working at the headquarters for two years. I was lucky I could work there.[243]

This confession reflects also some measures imposed during the so-called normalization period. "Normalization" meant mainly a return to the time before the Prague Spring, the suppression of all reformist tendencies and the removal of their representatives from leading positions in the state and Party apparatuses. Before I describe the "normalization" period in greater detail, I will introduce the days of August 1968 as they unfolded on the ship Kladno.

---

242 ABS_2: Information about the economic and political situation in the COS, 2 June 1976.
243 M. R., * 1930, ship master, 40 years in the COS.

4.6.1 Mutiny on the ship Kladno[244]

The ship sailed out on 13 August from Szczecin to Cuba, carrying about 20 tonnes of dangerous cargo mainly for the Cuban army (artillery shells, detonators, fuses, etc.). The crew learned about the invasion on 21 August around 9 am from radio stations in London and Washington. Having heard the information, the crew began talking about the occupation of the country by the Russians, counterrevolution, and shootings in Prague.

Then, the men on the ship polarized into a conservative group and supporters of the reform process. The news about the invasion resulted in a certain state of surprise, disorder, and fear of what was happening at home. The machine crew was directed to stay in peace and fulfil their work duties. The deck crew began to drink and condemn the invasion. They gave vent to their feelings saying that "the Russians were bastards, invaders and the like". The comparison of the different situations in the machine and deck departments clearly shows the importance of the ship's hierarchy: each department acted according to the decision of its superior officer.

At some point after lunch, the chief mate "probably already a bit tipsy" said that the deck crew would not keep the watchman shift and that the ship would not go further to Cuba. One seafarer referred to this moment as the tipping point when the chief mate was "facing the mutiny".[245] The chief mate then said:

> If the ship continues sailing to Cuba, let's give a chance to freely leave the ship to those men who do not agree with what has happened. I am ready to disembark in Bermuda or elsewhere rather than to go to Cuba and hoe coffee trees for Fidel for two years!

The quoted statement is a second-hand testimony, and thus it may be distorted. Yet it vividly conveys the fear of the crew members that they or the ship herself could be captured in Soviet bloc countries after 21 August 1968.

---

244 Unless otherwise stated, the Kladno affair is described based on the witness protocol written by a former seafarer—deputy for political affairs. /ABS_1: Letter from the deputy for political affairs on the ship Kladno, 13 April 1970./
245 The witness's choice of evaluative and critical words corresponds mainly with the "normalization" period, when the statement was given.

The Kladno ship master called for calm and organized a crew meeting the next day in an effort to pre-empt the crisis on the ship. It was actually a very wise and useful decision since preventing panic was of crucial importance at the time. These men were cut off from the actual events in Czechoslovakia, having only limited information about the invasion, about the shooting in places where their loved ones lived. The crew meeting finally decided for a compromise—to continue sailing to reach the vicinity of Cuban territorial waters, but closer to Florida. Then the ship should wait for the final decision of the Czechoslovak Embassy in Havana or the UN representative directly. The situation calmed down. Even those men opposing the decision followed the directives to maintain the ship's hierarchy. Then the chief mate, who had actually been the first to refuse sailing to Cuba, apologized to the master for his misbehaviour. In spite of this, the activities of the chief mate were still termed as mutiny in later documents and investigations. Actually, the term mutiny was a later "input" into the records by the witnesses quoted here.

On 23 August the crew sent a resolution to support the leadership of Alexander Dubček, the First Secretary of the Central Committee of the Communist Party. When the ship arrived in Cuba on 28 August, various skirmishes followed, e.g. one of the Czechoslovak officers took a megaphone and shouted towards Soviet seafarers "Russian fascists". Later, a delegate from the Czechoslovak Embassy visited the ship and informed the crew about the situation in Czechoslovakia. He brought various prints circulating in Prague, film shots from Wenceslas Square, photos of the burning Prague Radio building, etc. This surely did not help to recover the seafarer's composure. Yet the return trip went ahead without any major excesses.

After arriving to the Polish port of Świnoujście in the first half of September, the COS General Director, together with the head of the company's committee of the Communist Party of Czechoslovakia, visited the ship to discuss the situation with the crew. The director expressed his opinion on problems that occurred during the ship's voyage to Cuba. He assured the crew that all measures taken in conformity with the headquarters' directives would be considered legitimate. He added that any acts contradictory to these directives would be strictly condemned and punished, if necessary even by the Attorney General. The witness of this speech assumed that the director was implicitly targeting this "threat" at the chief mate. Indeed, this man was later sentenced to imprisonment. Before the punishment, however, he was promoted to ship master in 1971 and transferred to the ship Jiskra. Then, in 1972, he was convicted of sabotage and sentenced to a three-year prison term.[246] The available documents do not disclose whether this sentence was served, or whether it was a conditionally punishment.

This description of the imposition of punishment indicates that the process of "normalization" in the COS was lagging behind and in some cases one's experience and professional skills were considered more important than political standpoints. This topic is discussed in more detail in the following chapter.

---

246 ABS_2: Information about the economic and political situation in the COS, 2 June 1976.

5 1970s: The transition from ideological tasks to business tasks

5.1 Détente in abroad, "normalization" at home

In the first half of the 1970s, the relations between the superpowers were characterized by a détente, which arose in response to the political changes in the previous decade and the reduced threat of nuclear war. The détente process also responded "to European desires for improved economic relations and reduced political tensions with the Soviet Union and the Eastern bloc".[247] During this time (1971–1974) the two superpowers completed more than 10 pacts on WWII debts but[248] also on strategic arms limitation, shipping, taxes, and grain purchases.[249] One of the most significant achievements of the détente was the Helsinki Process (Helsinki Conference on Security and Cooperation in Europe), whose preparation started in 1972 and culminated by signing the Final Act in 1975. For the Soviet Union, this Act was essential since it recognized the status quo of the power distribution between the East and the West (the first basket). Western states, on the other hand, found the third basket (human rights) particularly important. After the Helsinki conference the human rights agenda indeed started to play a significant role in Eastern bloc countries, which strove to fulfil their aspirations for universal freedom. In the end, the Helsinki process undermined Soviet power.

Yet by the mid-1970s, the link between the Helsinki negotiations and the fall of communism in Eastern Europe was not apparent and the détente lost popularity significantly in the United States. There were two crucial reasons for abandoning the détente: 1) the United States had to pay a

---

[247] Robert D. Schulzinger, "Détente in the Nixon – Ford years," 1969–1975, in Melvyn P. Leffler and Arne Westad Odd, eds., *The Cambridge History of the Cold War, Volume II* (Cambridge: Cambridge University Press, 2010), 374.

[248] President Nixon and the Head of the Soviet Union (the Communist Party General Secretary) Brezhnev signed the framework document for freezing the number of missiles SALT I (Agreement on the Limitation of Strategic Arms) in 1972. In 1972 they also signed the Anti-Ballistic Missile Treaty. /Ibid., 380./

[249] Ibid., 383.

high price for a grain deal with the Soviet Union and perceived it as a "robbery";[250] 2) the Vietnam War finished with a communist victory.

The growing criticism of the détente in the United States primarily drew on the argument that the arms-control agreements had put the United States into a disadvantageous position in relation to the Soviet Union. In February 1976, this decreasing popularity of the détente policy resulted in the decision of President Gerald R. Ford "that officials in his administration would no longer use the word 'détente' to characterize US–Soviet relations".[251] Détente was no longer advantageous for Gerald Ford mainly because he could not convince the American people "that the 1975 Helsinki Conference on Security and Cooperation in Europe (CSCE) was not primarily serving to legitimize the Stalinist division of Europe".[252] In this slow process of erosion, the détente was ultimately frozen after the Soviet invasion to Afghanistan in December 1979. "Describing it as the most serious threat to world peace since World War II, Carter abandoned détente".[253]

While international policy of the first half of the 1970s was dominated by the détente, Czechoslovakia initiated the process of "normalization". [254] Very simply put, this "normalization" was a return to the situation before

---

250 In 1972 and 1973 the Soviet Union purchased about a quarter of American wheat supply, "in part by using commercial credits supplied by the United States", thus causing a steep rise in wheat prices in the United States. /Schulzinger, "Détente in the Nixon – Ford years, 1969–1975," 384./

251 Schulzinger, "Détente in the Nixon – Ford years, 1969–1975," 391.

252 Olav Njølstad, "The Collapse of Superpower Détente, 1975–1980," in Melvyn P. Leffler and Arne Westad Odd, eds., *The Cambridge History of the Cold War, Volume III* (Cambridge: Cambridge University Press, 2010), 141.

253 Ibid., 150.

254 The "normalization" process did not mean the return to normal, but rather contrary to normal; therefore, it is stated in the text either with quotation marks or in the form so-called normalization. Speaking about "normalization" covers: 1) in its narrower scope the period from the invasion in August 1968 until the adoption of the document "Instruction on the crisis development in the Party and society after the XIII assembly of the Communist Party of Czechoslovakia" adopted in December 1970; 2) the whole period of Soviet occupation, i.e. from 1968 to 1989. As for the "Instruction", it became the only permissible interpretation of the Prague Spring events (and their context in between 1967 and 1969). The reform was labelled a counterrevolution in the document. The only achievement of the Prague Spring was the federalization of the state, approved on 28 October 1968, valid from 1 January 1969.

the 1968 Warsaw Pact invasion, with the main objective of eliminating the reformers of the Prague Spring from their leading positions in the Communist Party and in the state, and consequently blocking and totally eliminating all democratic reforms from Czechoslovak society.

A substantial part of the "normalization" process consisted in politically motivated cadre changes—the so-called vetting processes. To justify the Soviet intervention, Communist Party members were interviewed by vetting commissions, which evaluated their activities, especially those executed during 1968, as well as their willingness to submit to the new, "normalized" circumstances. They had to negate their previous condemnation of the Soviet intervention and testify that counterrevolutionary elements had wanted to take matters into their hands. In principle, this constituted an internal vetting of the entire Communist Party, which thus got rid of almost one third of its members.[255] As a result, the Party lost a substantial part of its professionals, skilled and highly educated members, thus causing damage to itself. This phase of the "normalization" process affected also a number of non-Party members—those socially and politically engaged in the years 1968–1969 or those who disagreed with the Warsaw Pact invasion. All those who did not pass the vetting process successfully, whether they were Communist Party members or not, were assigned worse jobs, socially degraded, they or their children were expelled from university, etc.[256]

Certainly, Czechoslovak Ocean Shipping could not escape the wetting process and had to "weed out" the staff, i.e. remove the reformists and employees sympathetic to the Prague Spring democratization process. In the COS, "normalization" was important for ensuring that in the future only loyal employees would be allowed to travel abroad. Nevertheless, as will become clear in the next section, the vetting process in the COS was slightly different from other home organizations in terms of the timing and the need for specialized seafarers.

---

255 Jiří Maňák, *Čistky v Komunistické straně Československa 1969–1970* [Purges in the Communist Party of Czechoslovakia 1969–1970] (Praha: Ústav pro soudobé dějiny AV ČR, 1997), 58.

256 Because of the vetting process, "normalization" became also a chance for younger people to be promoted to leadership positions.

5.1.1 The "normalization" process in the Czechoslovak Ocean Shipping company

Political aspects had always played an important role in staff selection in the COS, especially when choosing those who would be allowed to work abroad. However, at the very outset the requirements on political loyalty and ideological devotion were often overlooked in practise because of the shortage of qualified seafarers. To balance this "problem" some control mechanisms were introduced. Let us briefly look at their history.

To control the political loyalty of the crew, which was not always recruited from Party members, a position of the ship master's deputy for political affairs[257] was introduced by the beginning of the 1960s, the time when the third and fourth Czechoslovak ships were purchased. The model was probably adopted from the Czechoslovak People's Army where the function of the deputy commander for political affairs came into existence as a consequence of the army's politicization and subordination to the Communist Party.[258] The former seafarers pointed out that the same function had existed on the PRC and Soviet merchant ships in order to supervise the crew, ensure political-ideological control, and prevent emigration.

> These guys [ship master's deputies for political affairs] were a weird class. They were mainly in charge of political training. They were filling our heads with Marxism-Leninism. [...] We were all scared by these political guys, 'it shouldn't occur to us that we'd stay there'. Or they threatened us with all those things that capitalists would do to us.[259]

> Well, they could eliminate us. But they had no power over the international bodies in the harbours where we stopped. They had no power abroad, in ports. Still in the ship's hierarchy, they were so-and-so's. I don't know anyone who'd be worth of mentioning, and there were quite a few of them.[260]

On the one hand, these functionaries had to "educate", control and threaten the crew; on the other hand, many of them built a bad reputation in another sense, because of not fulfilling their role, many of them

---

257 NA_66: Directive for the ship master's deputy for political affairs, 24 May 1963.
258 Similarly, the position was introduced also in police forces until 1953.
259 M. S., * 1939, chief engineer, 26 years in the COS.
260 V. S., * 1942, ship master, 26 years in the COS.

took advantage of travelling abroad and making money without any special effort. Because of the benefits, their employment in the COS was often through nepotism,[261] which further limited political and ideological "enthusiasm" of the person.

The position of ship master's deputy for political affairs was abolished in 1967 as a part of the reviving process and political alleviation and it was not restored even under the so-called normalization. Apparently, the main reason for cancelling this position was the negative experience with the activities of these master's deputies. Many of them defiled their role (by drunkenness, black marketeering) and instead of advancing proper personnel policies and trying to politically regulate the life on ships, they executed political work formally and in many cases their personal lives was in sharp contrast with the Party line.[262]

The ship master's deputy for political affairs, however, was not the only "institution" supervising the crew's ideological loyalty. The Communist Party organizations on ships played an important role, too. Between 1968 and 1969, however, almost all Party organizations on the ships dissolved, many members left the Party and a number of seafarers emigrated. Contemporary documents contend that these negative phenomena had occurred mainly because of "the constant pressure of hostile capitalist propaganda" that the seafarers heard abroad. In other words, the effort to "justify" the invasion and the socio-political movement failed and did not disperse the disappointment with the "normalized" state and Party policy.

To "consolidate" the situation after the invasion, the company's director, human resources manager, and the head of the company's Communist Party organization visited almost all the ships to explain the current situation. In the eyes of the "normalization" leadership, some of these visits had a positive impact as they partially reactivated the ship's social organizations, i.e. the Communist Party, the Youth Union, or trade unions.[263] After these first "consolidation" steps, however, it seems that

---

261 ABS_2: Information about the economic and political situation in the COS, 2 June 1976.
262 ABS_3: Manifestations of terror in the COS in the years 1968–1969, 27 May 1970.
263 ABS_4: Analysis of personnel work and its consequences in the COS in the

"normalization" measures in the COS lost their momentum. Even in 1976 an official document prepared by the Federal Ministry of the Interior stated that the "consolidation" process in the COS was slow and still far from completion.[264]

Nevertheless, the impact of the vetting process on COS staff was as follows: 86 persons were crossed out and 12 expelled[265] from the Communist Party.[266] Considering the total headcount of 316 seafarers and 87 people in the headquarters as reported in 1970[267] before the vetting (the "normalization" process in the company was prolonged due to the specifics of its business), the crossed out and expelled employees represented about 24 per cent of all COS employees. This number is rather high taking into account that not all COS employees were members of the Communist Party. If Communist Party members constituted presumably a third of the company's staff, then those who had left the Party represented more than sixty per cent of all the members of the Communist Party of Czechoslovakia in the company. Such numbers confirm that the employees-members of the Communist Party were strong supporters of the Prague Spring and did not change their opinion shortly after the invasion.

Similarly to elsewhere, the non-Party members had to undergo interviews[268] in the COS to show their attitude to the invasion and their loyalty to the "normalized" regime. In the COS, however, those expelled and crossed out from the Party or the punished non-members were not affected as greatly as the rest of the society that sympathized with the

---

period 1968–1969, 12 May 1970.
264 Ibid.
265 Crossed and expelled Party members: these are two forms of the Party purging process. Expulsion from the Party represented the ultimate punishment resulting in discrimination against the former member and his/her family in everyday life. The act of crossing out was a more moderate form of punishment when people ceased to be Party members mainly for their passivity.
266 ABS_2: Information about the economic and political situation in the COS, 2 June 1976.
267 NA_100: Annual report on financial results in 1970, Statistics on shipping in 1970.
268 The COS decided on these interviews during the management meeting in September 1970. /NA_67: Meeting record No. 33 from the director's meeting, 18 September 1970./

Prague Spring and condemned the invasion. For example, as late as June 1975, four ship masters were "only" demoted despite the fact that they were expelled from the Communist Party in 1970. The documents reveal an important practice during the interviews with non-Party members: in some cases the committee concluded that the seafarer could continue serving because of very good political knowledge and the fact that his political involvement had increased. The trick was that the interview did not actually take place and the record of the interview was prepared in advance.[269] The most likely motive for conducting these feigned interviews was the effort to keep professionals in the company. To some extent, it could have also been given by friendly ties between individuals which mitigated the vetting process.

Thus in Czechoslovak Ocean Shipping, the majority of the employees who were supposed to be punished kept their jobs on ships or in the company's headquarters, even in leading positions. The State Security constantly criticized this fact and that "the right-wing wreckers still had considerable influence on the ships because of their activities and engagement in the right-wing opportunist policy in the years 1968–1969".[270]

Some of those seafarers negatively affected by "normalization", especially the ship officers, developed specific mechanisms to reduce the negative impacts of the vetting process to their career. In cooperation with COS management, the relegated masters were for example, embarked in the chief mate function on those ships where the master was a Soviet officer.[271] Because the Soviets did not speak Czech, these men *de facto* took charge of the ship master's position and commanded the ship. However, it should be added that Soviet captains were often incompetent and would receive employment on Czechoslovak ships as a sort of "reward".

---

269 ABS_5: Deficiencies in political and personnel work in the COS, 10 November 1971.
270 ABS_2: Information about the economic and political situation in the COS, 2 June 1976.
271 Ibid.

> The difference [between Czechoslovak and Soviet captains] was that they [Soviets] were poor. Because our captains, although they graduated from the same school, often in Odessa, our captains were significantly [emphasis] more skilled. Essentially. Just take the difference in speaking English. Russian captains were mostly limited in English. They did not need it. And professional skills? I could not evaluate it because I was in the engine room at those times. But I know there were differences. They [Soviets] were rather passive, passive. They left everything to the chief mate. And the chief was always Czech or Slovak—he actually commanded everything, including the documentation. Because Soviets did not speak Czech and all the correspondence [within the ship, with headquarters] was in English.[272]

Some ship masters expelled from the Communist Party got the same job in Slovakia, in Československá plavba dunajská [Czechoslovak Danube Shipping], which ran the maritime business in the Levant (the Eastern Mediterranean) area with "river-sea" ships. As the Slovaks appreciated the federalization of Czechoslovakia as one of the achievements of the Prague Spring, they did not object as fiercely to "normalization" practices. And consequently, the vetting process in Slovakia was not as strict as in the Czech Republic. This different approach enabled some seafarers to get hired in Slovakia.

In some cases, the company's management justified keeping those "unwanted" persons employed in the COS by their irreplaceability and professional qualifications, even when they had not been approved within the vetting process. Their expertise seemed to be often more important for the company then the seafarers' (mainly officers') political and "moral" profile.[273] For the same reasons, cases can be found where seafarers first lost their job because of their "wrong" behaviour in 1968/1969, but several years later got their job back as long as they condemned the invasion.[274]

Despite these small individual victories over the vetting, the "normalization" process also saw significant achievements. The most important one was the re-establishment of the Communist Party groups on ships during 1971. As their leaders had to be politically loyal to the communist leadership installed after the invasion, they were not voted in by the Par-

---

272 M. B., * 1949, chief engineer, 29 years in the COS
273 ABS_2: Information about the economic and political situation in the COS, 2 June 1976.
274 Ibid.

ty members on the ship but appointed by the company's Communist Party committee. In the beginning, the seafarers criticized this non-democratic practice, as they may still have felt encouraged by the previous democratization process. But under the "normalization" authoritarian regime any complaints were pointless. As a result, in 1971 "statements against the Party and the socialist system were no longer heard on the ships".[275]

The "normalization" process, however, did not run only in the form of vetting interviews aimed at checking one's loyalty towards the "normalization" regime. One of the first "normalization" steps was the reintroduction of censorship and the adoption of arrangements to "restore" the order from 13 September 1968 (Acts 126 and 127/1968 Coll.). Then, on 16 October 1968, the agreement on the "temporary" stay of Soviet troops in Czechoslovakia was signed. Since then, the Communist Party's policy changed in response to permanent Soviet pressure. The population gradually became estranged with the Communist Party, contrary to the strong support of the Party's policies during the Prague Spring.

Since personal changes in key management positions occurred across the whole of society, they soon affected all the political, economic, social, and cultural élites and had devastating impacts on the country's future development. As for economic life, reformist policies were gradually abandoned, and the reform was labelled as counterrevolutionary.

As the "normalization" process shaped different economic or social areas of society, it occurred with different speed, and a break with reformist arrangements did not always occur overnight. For instance, the COS general management meeting record from 5 January 1969 stated that the company still followed its Action Programme,[276] especially its eco-

---

275 ABS_6: Letter from the Czechoslovak Consulate General to the Czechoslovak Federal Ministry of Foreign Affairs, 6 November 1972.
276 This document prepared by the COS management followed the text of the same name, the overall Action Programme. It was adopted on 5 April 1968 and represented a conception of how to reform the socialist system, both in its economic, political, and social aspects. Like the general Action Programme, which was retracted after the invasion, the COS Action Programme did not survive. Taking into account the measures given by "normalization" and that the reform efforts were declared counterrevolutionary after the invasion, I as-

nomic tasks and profit creation and distribution.[277] In April 1969, the management still confirmed that "the concept of fleet development is one of the essential parts of the company's Action Programme and its sub-tasks were being fulfilled".[278] A similar statement is included in the meeting record from May. In June 1969, however, the language of official documents changed slightly, and a new task was assigned, namely "to consider once more the company's Action Programme".[279]

The last reference to the reformist Action Programme comes from March 1970, implicitly announcing the end of COS reformist effort:

> The company's Action Programme needs to be partially completed and changed in its sub-sections. The company's director expects comprehensive guidelines [i.e. those prepared by the higher—communist, "normalized"—authority] to be developed in the near future. [...] The Communists in the management were assigned to finalize the company's business development.[280]

The economy of the state returned to the command model of planning, the model in which the central planning body was not able to specifically plan a large number of product types and cater to customers' needs, and thus it could not organize production efficiently.[281] The absent market principles in this model inhibited entrepreneurial activity. As the central planning authorities had no idea about enterprises' capacities, reserves, production possibilities, etc., they resorted to defining "soft" plans which were easy to surpass and receive rewards without any real performance.[282]

---

sume that the relevant company documents were either destroyed or not archived. Fragmentary information confirms that on 19 April 1968, i.e. two weeks after the publication of the Prague Spring Action Programme, the COS director's meeting decided to develop the company's program with an emphasis on two areas: 1) business development (finding new forms of business activities within the industry where it proved to be profitable), economic management in light of the company's much higher independence in the economic sphere; 2) personnel and social policy, i.e. mainly working conditions. /NA_68: Meeting record No 2. from the operative meeting, 19 April 1968./

277 NA_65: Meeting record No. 2 from the director's meeting, 5 January 1969.
278 NA_65: Meeting record No. 13 from the director's meeting, 1 April 1969.
279 NA_65: Meeting record No. 21 from the director's meeting, 5 June 1969.
280 NA_67: Meeting record No. 8 from the director's meeting, 6 March 1970.
281 Ota Šik, *Jarní probuzení – iluze a skutečnost* [The Spring Awaking—Illusion and Reality] (Praha: Mladá fronta, 1990), 76.
282 Not running along market principles, the enterprises focused on gross annual

5.2 The company's performance after the suppression of the Prague Spring

The COS has to adapt its operation to the economic environment of "normalization". However, compared to other domestic companies, it was possible to realistically estimate the required transport performance and set a plan to operate 10 ships (1970 end-of-year figure). Still, the figures show the planned economic indicators increased or decreased mainly based on the actual shipping market situation during a particular year, corresponding to real achievable performance. The common practice at those times was that if the company's results were positive and the majority of the planned indicators were met, the management and workers were paid bonuses. In fact, it was the only motivation for the employees. Otherwise, nobody was interested in the profit since its overwhelming part was paid to the state budget.[283]

The planning authorities and responsible ministries had a special interest in Czechoslovak Ocean Shipping: above all, they pressured the company to earn as much foreign currency as possible; or at least to save this currency by providing transport of Czechoslovak goods. Foreign currency was very valuable for necessary purchases of raw materials and technologies from advanced capitalist states. Because of the decreasing competitiveness of Czechoslovak goods on these markets, foreign currency was scarce. Despite these drawbacks, the COS main-

---

production. When an enterprise grew, a financial bonus was paid to the employees. Under this model, producers never had any problems with sales. Thus they did not determine their production structure according to market demands; instead they concentrated on products with favourable billing prices without considering actual consumer's needs. Preferring production over market needs, they often wasted material, energy, and labour. The companies and employees were not affected because the calculated labour productivity formally increased, and wages increased too. /Šik, *Jarní probuzení – iluze a skutečnost*, 65./

283 For example, tax contributions to the state budget and superior authority, i.e. the Ministry, amounted to 83.8 per cent from the profit in 1980, while in 1979 it was as much as 96.3 per cent. In other years the contributions oscillated between 70 and 79 per cent. /NA_97: Annual report on the financial results in 1980, Report on annual analysis of the company's economic activities in 1980, 5 March 1981./

tained high competitiveness compared to other commodities mainly due to cheap labour,[284] and even achieved profitability.

Under the new conditions at the beginning of 1969, the Minister of Foreign Trade required COS management to quickly prepare a programme aimed at reducing the foreign exchange costs of transport, especially in foreign currencies. Due to the withdrawal of the economic reform, a new conception had to be created to run the operation of seagoing ships. The management of the COS responded that saving opportunities in the transport of Czechoslovak goods had their limits. However, they added, there were wider possibilities in foreign exchange benefits when ships were purchased on socialist markets and ran in time charters for capitalist ship owners.[285]

Further investments into ships reflected the strategy outlined above. From 1969 to 1975, six new ships were purchased in Poland and one in the German Democratic Republic. But their use on capitalist markets was not as straightforward as it may have seemed. As a company in the state's possession, the COS had to perform not only its economic tasks with the best economic results but also political tasks. For instance, it had to provide less advantageous transports on the one hand and transports of very profitable military material on the other (the company had a monopoly in the shipping industry). And only a third of the services were time charters for capitalist ship owners. Therefore the company strove to gradually increase proportion of Czechoslovak goods transported abroad. This ratio increased during the entire decade from about 45 per cent at the beginning of the 1970s to 75 per cent in 1980.[286] These figures include lucrative transports of military materials.

The arrangements of shipping services described here had little to do with the upcoming "normalization" and the strengthening of the communist regime. The use of Czechoslovak vessels was closely linked to

---

[284] In addition, a great portion of maintenance and repair works on Czechoslovak ships were carried out by the seafarers themselves, whereas Western ship owners had to buy and pay for them. The service was either part of their working hours or counted as overtime.

[285] NA_68: Meeting report from the extraordinary operative meeting, 27 February 1969.

[286] The figures are stated based on the financial statements presented in charts at the end of this chapter.

state foreign policy, which—as already mentioned—unfolded within the limits given by the superior power, i.e. the Soviet Union. This is true mainly for the liner transport with **Cuba** from the beginning of the 1960s, when Cuba had to cope with the economic blockade by the United States with the help of socialist countries and mainly the Soviet Union.[287] Although the transports by Czechoslovak ships were not as extensive in the 1970s as in the previous decade, economic cooperation between the two countries continued quite successfully.

In 1971 traffic to Cuba accounted for 38.2 per cent of the COS economic outcome. The company ran three ships to Cuba a year and another three ships in the first quarter of the year 1972.[288] By the end of the decade (1978), however, the Cuba line transports were operated only during a part of the year with only one ship, and its share in the COS profit fell to only three per cent.[289] The situation was similar in the years that followed (four individual voyages in 1979 and in 1980).[290] Yet this decrease of transport services could not be explained by the decreasing volume of trade. Even when the foreign trade interchange with Cuba did not reach the level of the 1960s, the trade and economic relations between the two countries continued to develop in the 1970s.[291] Actually, Czechoslovak ships started to sail on other lines, mainly to the Persian Gulf and India, since these voyages ensured ships' operation at capacity, thereby achieving a higher profitability of the operation.[292]

During the whole decade mainly voyages to/from **Iraq** were of great frequency. The first information on more extensive use of Czechoslovak ships in this destination dates to the turn of 1970/1971, when these transports represented 15 per cent (10 per cent respectively in 1971) in

---

287 Vítězslav Košťák, *Kuba. Obchodně ekonomické sborníky* [Cuba. Business-economic Collections] (Praha: Institut zahraničního obchodu, ČTK – Pressfoto, 1980), 121.
288 NA_69: Management meeting material No. 30, Report on financial results in 1971, 3 March 1972.
289 NA_95: Annual report on financial results in 1978, 5 March 1979.
290 NA_97: Annual report on financial results in 1980, Report on annual analysis of the company's economic activities in 1980, 5 March 1981.
291 Košťák, *Kuba. Obchodně ekonomické sborníky*, 121.
292 NA_91: Report on the performance in 1974 as stated in the company's collective agreement, 26 March 1975.

the total company's economic results. At this time the company reported that the ships mainly transported the military goods.[293] Over subsequent years, the business with Iraq became an integral part of the Czechoslovak ships' employment. In 1979 the volume of transport to Iraq climbed up to 43 per cent of the total COS economic results.[294] Although weapons and military material did not represent the only cargo,[295] the connection between these results and arms supply to Iraq by Eastern bloc countries is evident. Iraq's five largest army suppliers "in the period 1970–90 were the Soviet Union, France, China, Czechoslovakia and Poland".[296]

Transfers of arms, military equipment, and materials took place not only between Czechoslovakia and Iraq, but also in the Levant area and later in India. The Levant geographically covers the Eastern part of the Mediterranean, but COS documents included Libya in this region and used the term when referring to the most important transport lines for Czechoslovak ships in the Mediterranean.

To better understand the motives behind Czechoslovak interests in the Levant and other regions, the role of Soviet foreign policy should not be overlooked, since the Soviet Union predetermined the foreign contacts of other bloc countries to a great extent. Since the 1960s, a new crucial player emerged on the international scene: the so-called Third World which became "one of the major arenas of Soviet-American rivalry". The Soviet Union achieved considerable success in this struggle, as shown

---

293 NA_69: Management meeting material No. 30, Report on financial results in 1971, 3 March 1972.
294 NA_101: Annual report on financial results in 1979, Letter from the COS economic assistant to the Federal Statistical Office, 21 January 1980.
295 In the 1970s Iraq belonged to the three most important Czechoslovak economic partners in the Third World. Iraq invested money from oil production (because of the oil crisis in the 1970s Iraq received a large income) primarily into industrialization and weapons. Czechoslovakia was in a strong position to be an important partner for Iraq particularly in engineering products and "special materials". /Petr Zídek and Karel Sieber, *Československo a Blízký východ v letech 1948–1989* [Czechoslovakia and the Middle East in between 1948–1989] (Praha: Ústav mezinárodních vztahů, 2009), 102./
296 Simeon T. Wezeman and Mark Bromley, "SIPRI Yearbook 2005 – Chapter 10. International Arms Transfers," in *Stockholm International Peace Research Institute* (2005): 417–448, http://www.sipri.org/research/armaments/transfers/publications/yearbook/CH10YB05 (as of 5 January 2015).

in the dramatic increase in the number of countries[297] that had experienced "Marxist-Leninist revolutions, coups or takeovers".[298] In this context, Czechoslovak military exports contributed to this development. Furthermore, the Soviet Union established close relationships with and supported also other, non-Marxist states in the Third World, especially India, Iraq, Syria, North Yemen, Libya,[299] and this list matches almost exactly the main recipients of Czechoslovak military cargoes transported in the 1970s.[300]

The business with the Levant, India and other Third World countries included a foreign trade exchange of non-military commodities, which allowed operating Czechoslovak ships at full capacity. For example, in 1973 five different ships were ordered for transports with India.[301]

> And I saw a huge harbour for the first time. Bombay. Bombay. Twelve million people, jungle. A real jungle. And in India there's that Gate of Victory.[302] And they say that if you walk from the sea into the gate, you will return to India. Well, I walked through that gate, it's near the seafront, to return to India many times. And that saying turned out true cos' then I sailed with another ship, the Sitno, again to India. And again. Then the ship Blaník, and again to India. I started to be unhap-

---

297 For example, North Vietnam and Cuba in the 1950s, later Laos, Ethiopia, Mozambique, Nicaragua, etc.

298 It is more than likely that supplies of arms or other "special" material were carried by Czechoslovak ships to some extent also during the 1960s. Unfortunately, the information on these transports is untraceable. The log books include information on "general cargo" in such cases, and annual reports on the company's results do not mention these services in the 1960s. Still, fragmentary information from the log books confirms this type of transport: for example, in 1964, the ship Kladno carried explosives from Szczecin to Cuba; in 1967 the ship Brno transported the same cargo from Rijeka to Casablanca. /NA_70: Log book from the Brno No. 10; NA_71: Log book from the Kladno No. 15./

299 Mark N. Katz, "The Soviet Union and the Third World," in *Current History* (October 1986): 329–339, http://digilib.gmu.edu/jspui/bitstream/1920/3128/1/Soviet%20Union%20 and%20the%20Third%20World.pdf (as of 10 January 2015).

300 "In the 1970s and 1980s, Bulgaria, Czechoslovakia, and East Germany were the principal Soviet proxies for arms transfers to the Third World". /"Non-Soviet Warsaw Pact Countries in the Third World," *Global Security*, http://www.globalsecurity.org/military/world/int/warsaw-pact-09.htm (as of 10 January 2015)./

301 NA_99: Annual report on financial results in 1973, Situation on the maritime market in 1973, Assessment of the activities of the business department in 1973, 25 February 1974.

302 The narrator mistakenly named the Gateway of India, Mumbai.

py about it, to always go to India. And I've never been to Cuba. Some dudes kept talking about Cuba, Brazil, but I didn't, we sailed to India all the time.[303]

Even though the records of the military cargoes in the 1970s are rather vague, it is possible to retrieve at least some illustrative data. The most accurate information on "special" cargo deliveries dates back to 1973 when five ships in some part of the year carried the following percentage of military cargo: the Blaník 12.04 per cent from the total cargo transported; the Brno 26.11 per cent; the Kriváň 32.84 per cent; the Mír 39.44 per cent (paradoxically, the word "Mír" means peace); the Jiskra 49.93 per cent.[304] In the two subsequent years, the same cargo represented 27 per cent (1974) and 22 per cent (1975) of the total COS transports made by all ships, including bulk carriers that cannot bear unit cargo. Although the data from the second half of the 1970s is not as precise, the available records confirm that at least one ship was regularly transporting these "special" materials to the Levant even in 1980.[305]

The recipient countries of these cargoes are not stated in the documents. The only comment about the destination in the **Levant** area can be found in the documentation of the ship Jiskra. The former seafarers recalled that the Jiskra had carried weapons and military material primarily to Libya.

> We carried, we carried tanks to Libya on the ship Jiskra. For Gaddafi. A few hundred tanks. We made jokes that every farmer there must have a tank to plough his field. There were really many of these tanks. And then we also carried munitions.[306]

---

303 Interview with J. J., 1952–2014, A/B sailor, 18 years in the COS.
304 NA_99: Annual report on financial results in 1973, Situation on the maritime market in 1973, Assessment of the activities of the business department in 1973, 25 February 1974.
305 NA_97: Annual report on financial results in 1980, Report on annual analysis of the company's economic activities in 1980, 5 March 1981.
306 M. S., * 1939, chief engineer, 26 years in the COS. The facts described in this personal testimony have been documented by historians, for example, Libya during 1974 and 1985 is described as "the best customer of Czechoslovak arms factories". /Petr Zídek a Karel Sieber, *Československo a Blízký východ v letech 1948–1989*, 199./

That was the main reason why the Jiskra achieved exceptionally good results[307] and its operation paid off many times compared to all the other ships in the fleet.[308] In September 1980 the ship was sold. Due to the decline in Czechoslovak arms production in the second half of the 1980s, no other Czechoslovak ship was then exploited for transporting "special" cargos to such an extent as the Jiskra.

So far, the information about the voyages and the cargo during the 1970s reflected only unit cargo. Still, it cannot be ignored that the company also ran four **bulk carriers** (five since 1975) and strove to operate them in time charters for Western businessmen. The possibilities of favourable chartering, however, were crucially influenced by the situation in the world maritime market, as will become clear in the next section.

5.2.1 The COS operation within global maritime market conditions

At the outset of the 1970s, when the shipment rates on the international market dramatically decreased (in some cases by 70 per cent), while the cost of ship operation remained high, Czechoslovak bulk carriers still operated in time charters negotiated before 1971, thus generating profit.[309] Since the severe decrease of the world shipping rates continued also in the year 1972, the COS experienced the worst year in the company's lifetime (today we know that several years later the situation deteriorated even more). The decline in maritime rates became most apparent in the operation of the bulk carriers. Although the company's close collaboration with local partners helped to overcome the shortage of foreign goods aimed for transport,[310] the net profit in 1972 represented only 34 per cent of the profit reached in 1971.

---

307 For instance, the ship Jiskra in 1972 operated in the Levant area during the whole year, transporting special cargo. It was the only ship that achieved better results compared to the year 1971 by two million of Czechoslovak crowns. /NA_89: Annual report on financial results in 1972, Document No. 21 for the management meeting, 5 March 1973./

308 For example, the highest reimbursement of invested funds in 1980 was achieved by the oldest ship of the fleet Jiskra, 52.4 per cent. /NA_97: Annual report on financial results in 1980, Report on annual analysis of the company's economic activities in 1980, 5 March 1981./

309 NA_69: Management meeting material No. 30, Report on financial results in 1971, 3 March 1972.

310 NA_93: Annual report on financial results in 1972, Management meeting rec-

The shipping market did not recover until the second half of 1972 when it was encouraged by enormous purchases of US corn by the Soviet Union, and by 1973 the recovery had become evident. In fact, it was the big grain deal that had disrupted the détente process that brought recovery for the shipping market. Even when this commodity shipment between the United States and the Soviet Union had concluded, grain was still perceived as the most important goods on the market and a reliable indicator of future shipping trends. Based on the positive indicators, the COS decided in 1973 to negotiate long-term time charters for the four bulk carriers.[311] Thanks to the long-term contracts, the deterioration of the tariff situation in 1974 did not actually affect the company's economic results.[312]

However, in 1975, the shipping rates decreased again while the recurrent costs in the maritime market substantially increased.[313] This situation reflected the recession years of 1973–1975 with "the peak in business activity preceding the recession"[314] in November 1973. The slump in the market occurring in this period surpassed even the decline from 1972. It was primarily a reaction to the first oil crisis (1973–1974) triggered by the fourth Arab–Israeli War, which had broken out in October 1973. In a short time the oil prices increased fourfold,[315] and the dynamism of the world economy slowed down.

Despite the situation on the world market, the COS managed to meet its planned indicators in 1974, 1975, and 1976 with a year-on-year increase of profits by about nine per cent. The management explained the

---

ord No. 15, 19 April 1973.
311 NA_99: Annual report on financial results in 1973, Situation on the maritime market in 1973, Assessment of the activities of the business department in 1973, 25 February 1974.
312 NA_91: Report on the performance in 1974 as stated in the company's collective agreement, 26 March 1975.
313 NA_92: Final report on the performance in 1975, 23 March 1976.
314 Victor Zarnowitz and Geoffrey H. Moore, "The Recession and Recovery of 1973–1976," *Explorations in Economic Research* 4:4 (October 1977): 471–557, http://www.nber.org/chapters/c9101.pdf (as of 5 January 2015), 471.
315 Roy Licklider, "The Power of Oil: The Arab Oil Weapon and the Netherlands, the United Kingdom, Canada, Japan, and the United States," in *International Studies Quarterly* 32:2 (June, 1988): 205–226, http://www.jstor.org/stable/2600627 (as of 12 January 2015), 206.

company's good results by two variables: 1) a part of the fleet (four ships) was employed in long-term time charters with profitable rates; 2) a new ship was put into operation in 1976.[316] In 1977 the company experienced a profit decrease, reflecting the significant decrease in the profit achieved by bulk carriers, as world rates decreased. An even more dramatic decline occurred in 1978. After that, a slight profit increase in economic results is evident, despite the second oil crisis in 1979.

As a matter of fact, up until 1978 the COS management did not experience any problems in relation to the oil crisis, neither in oil shortage nor in prices. As a solution to the growing costs, especially the fuel prices in 1974, the management adopted various cost-cutting measures, increased transport rates and supplied ships with deliveries from socialist countries whenever possible. Furthermore, some records in the log books attest that ships often bunkered in Trinidad, Kuwait, South Africa, and during 1974 and 1975 even in Italy[317] (Augusta in Sicilia) and Spain (Las Palmas). These purchases of fuel were most probably compensated for higher rates negotiated in the pre-crisis period. In sum, the COS faced the crisis quite effectively because the increased transport fees were reasonable, for instance for military cargoes, and the labour of Czechoslovak seafarers was cheap.

In 1979 the second oil crisis erupted after the Iranian Revolution. The situation deteriorated in 1980 when the Iran–Iraq War started and their oil exports decreased thus "affecting the global supply and the price of oil".[318] The company coped with the oil crisis by fuel deliveries from the Soviet Union. In 1979 these supplies reached a record volume of 10,672 tonnes, representing an increase of the Soviet fuel consumption by 44 per cent in comparison with 1978.[319] The same amount (10,000

---

316 NA_94: Annual report on financial results in 1976, Management meeting record No. 18, 4 April 1977.
317 Italy was the largest importer of Libyan oil until 1974. /Glenda Goldstone Rosenthal, *The Mediterranean Basin. Its Political Economy and Changing International Relations* (Butterworth-Heinemann, 1982), 77./
318 Toyin Falola and Ann Genova, *The Politics of the Global Oil Industry: An Introduction* (Westport: Praeger, 2005), 46.
319 NA_102: Annual report on financial results in 1979, Evaluation of socialist competition in 1979.

tonnes) of fuel was delivered by the Soviet Union also in 1980, covering about a third of the yearly requirement for the ships' bunkering.[320] Here the company used the CMEA (Council for Mutual Economic Assistance) price mechanism where prices were calculated based on the world five-year moving averages. As a result, at the turn of the 1970s and 1980s, the prices in mutual trade among the CMEA countries were lower than world prices. The pricing mechanism, however, led to a raise in CMEA prices even after 1981 when the price level on the world market saw a decline.[321] How all these influences affected the COS's final performance in the 1970s is illustrated by the following tables.

---

[320] NA_97: Annual report on financial results in 1980, Report on annual analysis of the company's economic activities in 1980, 5 March 1981.
[321] Průcha, *Hospodářské a sociální dějiny Československa II, 1945–1992*, 670, 688.

5.3 Financial results in the 1970s

	1971	1972	1973	1974	1975
Ships[322]	10	11	10	11	12
Chartered ships	2	2	2	1	1
Completed voyages	88	91	91	95	N/A
Total DWT	137,115	137,115	156,534	184,416	221,646
Total GRT	94,816	115,134	105,051	125,640	146,236
Amount of goods transported (tonnes)	886,000	887,000	933,000	1,348,000	1,202,000
Total net profit (crowns)	67,787,000	23,113,404	97,000,000	127,072,000	138,300,000
Net profit recalculation ($)[323]	3,081,227	1,055,609	4,409,090	5,775,909	3,286,363

Table 7: Financial results 1971–1975[324]

---

[322] When exact information on ship parameters is missing in the annual reports, it is retrieved from the files about the parameters of the ships. /NA_72: Files of individual ships./ The figures on ships are stated as at the end of the year.

[323] The recalculation of the company's net profit to $ is very rough. The Czechoslovak crown exchange rate became very unclear relatively soon after the currency reform in 1953. At the beginning of 1957, an official coefficient was used to correct the over-valued official (parity) rate. In 1967 the "internal reproductive price equalization" was introduced as a coefficient correcting the crown's official exchange rate in the range 150–275 per cent for free currencies and 25–125 per cent for the transferable rouble. The only information on the exchange rate is available in the annual reports from 1975 (27 crowns per $), 1976 (19 crowns) and 1980 (19 crowns). Having no other information, I have calculated with the average 22 crowns, being aware that it is a sort of underestimation.

[324] Figures in the table are based on these documents: 1971 – NA_88: Annual report on financial results in 1971, Management meeting record No. 15, 6 April 1972; 1972 – NA_89: Annual report on financial results in 1972, Document No. 21 for the management meeting, 5 March 1973; 1973 – NA_90: Report from the extraordinary management meeting, 9 April 1974; 1974 – NA_91: Report on the performance in 1974 as stated in the company's collective agreement, 26 March 1975; 1975 – NA_92: Final report on the performance in 1975, 23 March 1976.

	1976	1977	1978	1979	1980
Ships	12	12	12	12	12
Time chartered ships	1	0	0	0	0
Completed voyages	98	N/A	102	67	108
Total DWT	221,646	221,646	221,646	221,646	234,469
Total GRT	146,236	146,236	146,236	146,236	154,949
Amount of goods transported (tonnes)	1,441,000	1,539,208	1,480,000	1,445,000	1,711,000
Total net profit (crowns)	148,300,000	90,736,000[325]	46,199,000	69,394,968	85,321,000
Net profit recalculation ($)	6,740,909	4,124,363	2,099,954	3,154,316	3,878,227

Table 8: Financial results 1976–1980[326]

What could be concluded about the 1970s is that Czechoslovak Ocean Shipping experienced a remarkable transition from ideological to business tasks, as suggested by the title of this chapter. But it should not be misunderstood as some sort of gradual or chronological transition from fulfilling ideological challenges at the outset of the decade to pursuing business orientation towards the end. I see the transition in the steps taken by the restored conservative communist leadership, which attempted to "normalize" life in the company after the suppression of the Prague Spring and then oriented the COS' activities towards business. At the same time, the title depicts the transition from ideological tasks given by the cooperation with the People's Republic of China in the first half of the 1960s to the company's more business-focused tasks in subsequent decades. In fact, after finishing cooperation with communist

---

325 NA_95: Annual report on financial results in 1978, 5 March 1979.
326 Figures in the table are based on these documents: 1976 – NA_94: Annual report on financial results in 1976, Management meeting record No. 18, 4 April 1977; NA_98: Annual report on financial results in 1976, Material No. 34 for management meeting, 7 March 1977; 1977 – NA_103: Evaluation of economic results in 1977, Management meeting record No. 36, 10 March 1978; 1978 – NA_95: Annual report on financial results in 1978, 5 March 1979; 1979 – NA_96: Annual report on financial results in 1979, report on shipping in 1979; 1980 – NA_97: Annual report on financial results in 1980, Report on annual analysis of the company's economic activities in 1980, 5 March 1981.

China, the profit of the COS increased significantly while running a similar tonnage.

Drawing on what we know about the "normalization" process in the COS, it can be argued that the execution of political (ideological) tasks in the company went almost always hand in hand with business interests. Thus, the "normalization" process imprinted mainly in individual life stories and in the people's disillusion about the possibility of democratizing the communist regime. Disillusion could also explain why the seafarers increased their smuggling and black marketeering activities. Being sorely disappointed with the post-invasion situation, the seafarers simply wanted to "grab what they could". In the course of the 1970s, these activities had reached such an extent that the management pointed out this serious problem in the annual reports on economic results.

With respect to the détente and the international situation, the COS operated in a similarly "normalized" environment. Calmer international relationships enhanced foreign exchange and subsequently offered new transport opportunities. Membership in the Soviet bloc then helped the company to overcome the two oil crises, while benefitting from cooperation with the Third World. Owing to this unique combination of different circumstances, the period from 1974 to 1976 represented three consecutive years when the COS achieved the highest profits in its existence until 1989. The real crisis was yet to come.

6   1980s: From a drop in earnings to fleet renewal

This chapter discusses the final period in which the Czechoslovak Ocean Shipping Company (COS) was run according to a planned socialist economy. The turning point was the revolutionary year of 1989, which people (not only) in Czechoslovakia associated with new hopes for the future. Some of these new expectations were fulfilled, others not.[327] One of the crucial achievements was the transformation of the police force and in particular the abolition of the State Security at the outset of 1990. A powerful repressive body, the State Security had controlled the life and work of people in all professions, especially those who had the "privilege" to travel abroad and stay there. Seafarers (and their families to some extent) also fell into this group.

The State Security's activities are reflected upon in the chapter about seafarers' lives through their own memories. In this chapter, however, I will reveal the State Security's role and function in the shipping industry focusing on the specific interests that the State Security had in the COS and in the shipping trade generally. Furthermore, I will outline the basic features of the COS operations during the decade, starting from elucidating the alarming losses in the first half of the 1980s, and finishing with a summary of the main changes in shipping activities in the second half of this decade. The chapter ends with a discussion of the major plans and intentions with which the COS entered into the era of freedom, democracy, and the market economic environment.

6.1   The company as an object of counterintelligence interests

To better understand the role of the State Security, we need to first explore the actual constitution of this repressive body during the first post-WWII years, including the basic characteristics of the State Security's individual units. After WWII, the Ministry of the Interior established the

---

[327] The book by Miroslav Vaněk and Pavel Mücke, *Velvet Revolutions: An Oral History of Czech Society* (New York: Oxford University Press, 2015, manuscript) captures these hopes in more detail, what the newly achieved freedom brought to the people, and what they are missing today.

National Security Corps by decree on 30 June 1945. These corps incorporated all existing uniformed units, the gendarmerie, as well as uniformed state and municipal police. At the same time this security body comprised other organizationally independent security forces: criminal, intelligence, and state security. The State Security was formed in 1945 as an executive body, i.e. not as intelligence but a component of the security system that was to ensure the protection of the state. In order to fulfil this task, the State Security was authorized to conduct investigations, arrests, search houses, etc. In the first years, the State Security was mainly involved in the investigation of the crimes committed during the Nazi occupation.[328] The Act on National Security 149/1947 Coll. from 11 July 1947 assumed that after solving the key criminal cases from the period of the occupation, the State Security would cease to be a separate unit within the National Security.

Events, however, took another direction. Even though the Act from December 1948 (286/1948 Coll.) issued by the new communist government, reaffirmed the plan to establish a unified National Security Corps, in practice, the Corps gradually became formed by two components: the State Security and the Public Safety. From the very beginning, the State Security was constituted, arranged, and re-arranged several times as part of the Ministry of the Interior. In 1950, the State Security underwent restructuring according to the Soviet model. Finally in 1965, an act[329] was adopted to redefine and enact the actual state of affairs, i.e. that the State Security together with Public Safety formed the National Security Corps.[330]

From the beginning of the 1970s the State Security consisted of fifteen administration organs.[331] Within this system the COS was managed by

---

328 František Koudelka, *Státní bezpečnost 1954–1968* [The State Security 1954–1968] (Praha: Ústav pro soudobé dějiny AV ČR, 1993), 10–11.
329 The Act 70/1965 Coll., replaced nine years later by the Act 40/1974 Coll., valid until 1990.
330 Koudelka, *Státní bezpečnost 1954–1968*, 12–13, 17.
331 Administration Organ I (Main Intelligence), adm. II (Main Counterintelligence for the Fight against External Enemies), adm. III (Main Military Counterintelligence), adm. IV (Management of Monitoring), adm. V (Protection Management of the Party and Constitutional Officials), adm. VI (Management of Executive/Intelligence Technology), adm. X (Main Counterintelligence for the Fight

Administrative Organ XI—Counterintelligence for Economic Protection and the Administrative Organ II—Main Counterintelligence for the Fight against External Enemies, which administered "emigrants and returnees, Czechoslovak citizens going abroad, travel agencies".[332] The collected information was stored, recorded, and processed within the so-called object volume. In addition, the State Security introduced specific object files for individual ships.

Over the years, the files were moved, merged, and shredded; in ship files, for example, only important documents with long-term value were selected, and the rest of the files were shredded after the ships were sold. Thus the oldest preserved documents date to around the mid-1960s. As a result of these activities, today only a single object file, which incorporates information about ships, seafarers, and the company, is at our disposal. Even this incomplete file, however, provides a clear idea of the State Security's interests when monitoring and controlling the COS. The aims of the object file will become even more apparent from the following description:

> The main aim of the object file is to monitor activities of institutions, mainly capitalist, or headquarters and offices of hostile intelligence agencies. In order to protect the state from the enemy, the object file comprises important objects of national economy, military objects, border areas, etc. The operational work on objects is based on gaining thorough knowledge of the operational situation. The prerequisite is to analyse class and political composition of the staff and management and to map hostile elements, vulnerabilities, problems in production, protection of state secrets, distribution of secret collaborators, confidents, etc.[333]

---

against Internal Enemies), adm. XI (Counterintelligence for Economic Protection), adm. VII (Counterintelligence in Bratislava [the capital of Slovakia]), adm. XIII (Computing and Information Centre), adm. XIV (Counterintelligence for the Fight against Extreme and Specific Forms of Crimes), Administration of the State Security Investigation, Investigation Department of the State Security Military Counterintelligence, Management of Passports and Visas, Statistics Department, Department of Foreign Press. /Úřad dokumentace a vyšetřování zločinů komunismu, "Struktura StB," [the State Security Structure in the web Office for the Documentation and Investigation of Communist Crimes], http://www.policie.cz/clanek/struktura-stb.aspx (as of 25 January 2015)./

332 Jan Frolík, "Nástin organizačního vývoje státobezpečnostních složek Sboru národní bezpečnosti v letech 1948–1989," [An overview of the Organizational Development of the State Security Bodies in the National Security Corps, 1948–1989], *Sborník archivních prací* [Collection of Archival Works] 41:2 (1991): 447–510.

333 Marián Gula and Zdeněk Vališ, "Vývoj typologie svazků v instrukcích pro jejich

It clearly follows from this characterization that the object file included almost all information about the company's operation and its employees. The main body of information collected about the employees was actually all the information available: it includes personal and professional curricula; information about family members and their political opinions and activities; work experience and work references; all personal as well as professional offences, which in the shipping sector ranged from information about smuggling, black marketeering, conversion of funds, bribes, to information about alcoholism, infidelities, homosexuality, etc.; of great interest was information about employees' contacts with foreigners or emigrants.

Information collected in the object file covered also a rather complete scope of COS activities. It can be argued that the activities conducted by Administrative Organ II of the State Security went far beyond its framework for action, which was the fight with an external enemy. Its scope of work also included attempts to intervene in economic, political, or cultural decisions of "objects", i.e. various institutions, enterprises, organizations, etc. Given the specificities of the shipping industry, the file included detailed information about ports (customs, control of movement in ports, control of people visiting ships, evidence of seafarers' outgoings, etc.), the whole range of the company's foreign partners (suppliers, ship owners, dockyards, charterers, etc.), the most serious accidents, and the process of delivery of special cargo. Especially important was information about the interests and activities of foreign intelligence services.

The State Security's officers collected the information from various sources, also from interviews with authorized management members (or

---

evidenci," [Development of Files' Typology], *Securitas Imperii* 2 (1994), 117–150.

Other main types of files were: Personal file—introduced after checking a signal of committing or preparing subversive anti-state crime; Group file—for administrating common subversive activities committed by two or more persons; Investigation file—introduced when a subversive anti-state crime was committed or when the object or the interests of the Republic were threatened and the offender was unknown; Observation file—introduced for people who could form a base for enemy activity, or people otherwise dangerous for the socialist system. /Ibid./

from reports written by these managers) who were obliged to provide the information by virtue of their job position, i.e. mainly top management members. These "official" inputs were accompanied by "unofficial" reports, namely those provided by the State Security's secret informants who had infiltrated both the ships and the headquarters. Another source of information about the company was the department for special tasks. This department (usually one person dedicated to special tasks) was primarily established with the aim to protect state secrets; this was by all means the field of the State Security.

Despite the numerous information sources, the State Security's officers constantly struggled when recruiting the necessary number of secret collaborators-seafarers on the ships. They strove to control every moment at every location where the ship was cruising or anchoring. To meet this aim, however, the State Security needed a substantial number of collaborators. What complicated matters most was the fact that seafarers used to spend a few months at home while other men took charge of their working duties on the ship.

To increase the number of secret collaborators, agents, or confidents, the State Security's officers searched and contacted pre-selected "ideologically reliable" men, Communist Party members or loyal people who wanted promotion or other benefits. What is more, the State Security often collected compromising information in order to blackmail suitable candidates and force them into secret collaboration.

Thus, the two main obstacles preventing the State Security from creating their "ideal" network of secret collaborators were the specificities of the seafarers' work, mainly their long-term absence and stays in destinations that the State Security's officers could not access, and the high fluctuation discussed in the chapter "Seafarers' lives and memoirs". In the second half of the 1980s the State Security set less ambitious recruiting goals. In 1986, for example, the responsible officer suggested increasing the number of collaborators among seafarers to at least 30 in order to "cover" 14 vessels.[334] However, this estimation did not calculate with a necessary margin for the periods when some seafarers-collaborators would be at home for holiday. The estimate is also low

---

334 ABS_8: Appendix to the Plan of counterintelligence protection, 7 July 1986.

when compared to the numbers in the previous decade. On one occasion, there is evidence that in 1976 three confidantes and two secret collaborators were on one ship at the same time.[335] Though this disproportion in numbers between the two decades might be accidental, it is more probably a sign of the gradual loosening of control in society in the second half of the 1980s when people stopped, albeit slowly, fearing the "omnipotent" State Security and were less easily convinced to cooperation than in the past decades.

During the whole pre-1989 period, the main task of the counterintelligence was to protect the COS and to prevent: 1) the infiltration of enemy special services into the field; 2) the misuse of the COS as an illegal channel for the transfer of information, unwanted printed materials,[336] weapons, or drugs; 3) the commitment of crimes; 4) the disclosure of state secrets and protecting the state secret holders among the management, both in the headquarters and on the ships (in simple words, control the company's management).

In the State Security's "everyday life", this protection entailed a variety of activities, from "detecting and investigating seafarers' relations with enemy intelligence and counterintelligence bodies" to "detecting illicit enrichment, speculations, smuggling, currency machinations, and bribes". In addition, the State Security was particularly interested in seafarers' contacts with emigrants, foreign workers, church organizations, and religious sects. Equally important was "detecting advocates of right-wing opportunist, anti-Soviet, or anti-communist opinions and eliminating their negative influence on mainly young employees". The State Security also set the task of "investigating and preventing incidents on ships", i.e. various accidents and collisions, and focused finding their

---

335 ABS_9: State Security's officer's business trip to Szczecin, 4 March 1976.
336 The group of unwanted printed materials included not only political, dissident, or democratic texts but also erotic ones (typically Playboy) or pornographic magazines. However strange this may look today, this prohibition was based on the § 205 of criminal law 140/1961 Coll. (endangering morality). Much more absurd was the inclusion of the National Geographic magazine into this group. State Security officers decided that the National Geographic distribution in Czechoslovakia was not allowed because the magazine sometimes contained articles harmful for the state. /ABS_11: Archiving of the file Geograf, 22 October 1985./

perpetrators. In addition, this security body strove to detect preparations and attempts of seafarers, passengers, or other COS employees to misuse their voyage for emigration to capitalist states.[337]

Within the basic scope of the State Security's tasks and responsibilities in COS "protection", the issue of emigration was categorized as counterintelligence protection or the protection of state secrets. The strictly guarded borders and control of citizens' movement formed an integral part of not only counterintelligence protection but also the communist regime as such. Since free movement would cause a transfer of ideas and allow free access to information, the ruling regime could be threatened if it gave its citizens a chance to obtain more complex knowledge about the political, economic, and socio-cultural life abroad, and compare real life with what was claimed by communist propaganda.

However, despite the relative freedom of movement that seafarers had, they did not consider emigration, nor did they actually emigrate, as often as we would expect, or as the repressive bodies expected. Being able to go abroad and return, the value of homeland, one's roots, home and family, gained importance in their lives. In this light, it seems absurd that the State Security feared the possibility that ship masters could emigrate not only with their families when they happened to accompany them on board, but also with the ship and cargo. Military cargo was mentioned explicitly:

> Please, if possible, make arrangements that captains on ships carrying special cargo are not allowed to bring their whole family on the voyage. You can explain it by the risk of explosion or the like. If the ship master emigrated with the vessel, we could hardly justify it.[338]

The "importance" which the State Security assigned to emigration meant that emigration represented one of the most frequent subjects of

---

337 ABS_10: Plan of the main tasks of the counterintelligence protection of the COS in 1986, 6 February 1986.
338 ABS_12: Internal record of the Administration organ II, 28 September 1970.
It was an internal document written as a basis for negotiation between a State Security officer and the COS director. It is necessary to take into account that this record was written in the first "normalization" years when the repressive forces still remembered well a strong civil movement during the Prague Spring. It also serves as a good example how exaggerated the fear that the State Security had of citizen's activities was.

denouncements, whether sent to the company or to the security authorities. Even a suspicion that a man or someone from his family intended to emigrate could result in denying him permission to travel abroad, sometimes temporarily, for several years, which led to a loss of their job. Other frequent subjects of denouncements or anonymous letters had more of a financial character and included offences such as embezzlement or bribery; provisions paid by deliverers were concerned as bribes. Such anonymous letters were written about officers, perhaps because compared to ordinary sailors they had more chances to enrich themselves through commissions from ship suppliers or through fraud. It may not be surprising that another frequent subject of denunciations, not anonymous in this case, were letters through which partners settled their accounts during divorce disputes. These informers—furious ex-partners—sometimes extended the network of the State Security's secret collaborators.[339] Anonymous letters or denunciations give evidence not only of human resentment or anger but also of the power that people attributed to the State Security.

At the turn of the 1970s/1980s, the State Security's activities showed continuity compared with previous periods. Czechoslovak society did not change during the first half of the 1980s, and the policy of "normalization" persisted in a very similar fashion to the 1970s. The outside world, however, started to experience substantial changes during this time. The Soviet Union was increasingly exhausted by the war in Afghanistan; moreover, this conflict contributed to the dramatic deterioration of its relations with the United States. In addition, political unrest in the Soviet bloc began to emerge, most intensively in Poland. These were the key signals within the bloc that promised changes to come.

---

[339] The number of secret collaborators in the COS, both on ships and in headquarters, varied during the time. Having compared the fragmented State Security's documents with the total number of employees, the numbers indicate that from the 1970s about 10 per cent of the headcount were in some way involved in cooperation with the State Security.

6.2 Problems in the Soviet bloc, problems in the COS

The Soviet Union could not accept the idea that it would lose Afghanistan from its sphere of influence. The Kabul pro-Soviet movement, which seized power in April 1978, was especially valuable as a balancing force to the rapprochement between the United States and the People's Republic of China. When in March 1979 the Kabul administration faced rebellion against the revolutionary government in Afghanistan, it asked the Soviet Union for support by means of military intervention. Brezhnev was hesitant about this step as he was still in favour of the détente. But several months later, the internal development in Afghanistan convinced him to decide in favour of invasion. One of the variables in this decision-making process was "deployment of US Pershing and cruise missiles in Western Europe" in December 1979. Finally Brezhnev and the Politburo approved the plan to "save" Afghanistan. A fierce international reaction to the Soviet Union's violent invasion emerged almost immediately, and the policy of détente was torn to pieces.[340]

Still the Soviet Union sought to salvage the détente at least in Europe, trying to convince West European countries about its "peaceful" intentions. The Olympic Games held in 1980 in Moscow were supposed to represent the most important international event in this respect. They took place despite the US boycott, and almost immediately after they ended, a severe crisis erupted in Poland, calling into question the profits the Soviet Union had gained in Europe from the détente. The mobilization of working masses in Poland was, however, of much greater importance than the events in Afghanistan because they threatened the Soviet sphere of influence in Europe. The Soviet Union, whose economy was increasingly exhausted, refused to send its troops to Poland to suppress the crisis. Regardless of the political costs that such a decision would have, the Soviet Union was not strong enough to undertake the invasion. Moscow leaders were well aware that any other decrease in living standards could lead to an internal political crisis. Thus mainte-

---

340 Vladislav M. Zubok, "Soviet Foreign Policy from Détente to Gorbachev, 1975–1985," in Melvyn P. Leffler and Arne Westad Odd, eds., *The Cambridge History of the Cold War, Volume III* (Cambridge: Cambridge University Press, 2010), 89–111, 103–104.

nance of domestic stability was given precedence over maintaining full control over the bloc.[341]

As for Czechoslovak shipping, the Polish events directly affected seafarers' work when strikes took place in ports. Of course, the Czechoslovak State Security used its collaborators to examine what seafarers thought about the Solidarity movement. It received only vague or meaningless answers, or answers the informants expected that State Security's officers wanted to hear.[342] People living under the oppression of the communist leadership were well aware that it could be dangerous to express a true opinion. At this time, however, the political situation in Poland was not really interesting for the COS. The company had to primarily solve problems with the ships' employment and decreasing financial results.

6.2.1 The early 1980s—the worst performance in the history of the COS

The second oil shock discussed in the previous chapter was followed by the 1979–1980 recession, shortly interrupted in 1981 by the US economic boom, and another deep recession in late 1982, which lasted until 1983.[343] To a great extent, this development mirrors the performance of the COS at the beginning of the 1980s. In 1980 the company achieved expected results (net profit 85.3 million of crowns), which were similar to the previous years' outputs. The COS entered 1981 with two more vessels compared to 1980, 14 in total. The profit in 1981 was almost 60 per cent higher than in 1980. The good results can be attributed mainly to charter contracts negotiated for favourable market prices at the turn of 1980/1981.[344]

---

341 Ibid., 107.
342 "When the source [the term "source" was used by the State Security to label their informants] spoke with some workers [in Gdansk], he found that more than 50 per cent of workers were no longer interested in Solidarity. Still Solidarity was not cancelled and had a great influence, especially in decision on workers' remuneration and food distribution". /ABS_7: Situation in the port of Gdansk, 18 November 1982./
343 Luís Aguiar-Conraria and Yi Wen, "Understanding the Large Negative Impact of Oil Shocks," in *Federal Reserve Bank of St. Louis, Working Paper Series*, June 2005, revised February 2006, http://research.stlouisfed.org/wp/2005/2005-042.pdf (as of 11 January 2015), 17.
344 NA_104: Evaluation of economic results in 1981, Management meeting record

In 1982, however, the company experienced a dramatic drop in economic results to less than half of the level achieved in 1981. Primarily, this was caused by the shipping market crisis, the worst from 1945, which was largely the result of the second oil shock crisis. In consequence, only in Europe 1,600 ships were put out of operation and a number of COS business partners faced existential problems. As these companies largely provided employment for Czechoslovak ships on the capitalist market, their difficulties soon caused the losses for the COS. For example, the ship Radhošť on one of her return trips from India to Europe carried a cargo of only 400 tonnes though her capacity was 6,000 tonnes.[345]

The negative economic development on the shipping market had a negative influence even on 1983 results. The year 1983 was the only loss-making year in the entire history of the company before 1989. The COS reached a profit of 10.3 million crowns according to the section on financial results; but it is in fact a modified result which includes a state subvention of 77 million. The real economic output was minus 66.7 million.[346] Although the world economy gradually recovered in the following years, the COS performance did not improved accordingly, reaching approximately the mid-1960s level. But whereas in the 1960s the COS managed to reach these results with 10 ships, in the mid-1980s it operated 14 vessels.

The tenser atmosphere on the international scene together with the new escalation of the Cold War brought further troubles that affected the company's performance. In November 1982, the Department of Transportation of the US Coast Guard published a directive for ships from Warsaw Pact countries, which from now on had limited access to American ports. In practice this arrangement meant that ships under the Czechoslovak flag could not anchor in eleven American ports.[347] In the

---

No. 5, 5 February 1982.
345 ABS_15: Problems of the COS on capitalist markets, 5 January 1983.
346 NA_105: Report on economic results in the 1982, Management meeting record No. 8, 25 February 1983.
347 Ports unavailable to Warsaw Pact vessels: Portsmouth NH, New London and Groton CT, Hampton Roads VA, Charleston SC, Port Canaveral FL, Panama City FL, Pensacola FL, Port St. Joe FL, San Diego CA, Port Hueneme CA,

case of other ports, the United States tightened up the visa policy for Czechoslovaks and announced certain obligations for their ships.[348] The American authorities allowed entrance to available ports only after notification sent seven days prior to entrance, which meant between 10 and 13 consecutive days. In addition, the relevant direction was so complex that any inaccuracy meant shifting the ship on a waiting list and thus losing time. In sum, these measures caused significant economic losses not only because of delays but also because Czechoslovak ships which run in time charters could no longer offer full service that capitalist businessmen required from them. Czechoslovakia in this regard faced stricter rules than Hungary, Romania, and Poland—ships from these countries were assigned only a four-day notification period prior to entering American ports.[349] This measure probably reflected the degree to which Czechoslovakia was perceived to support the Soviet Union's policies.

When building its trade policy, the COS management had to face not only the American restrictions but also obstacles given by Czechoslovak foreign policy, highly determined by Czechoslovakia's membership in the Soviet bloc. As a result, the COS was excluded from operating in South Africa, South Korea, Taiwan, Israel, and Chile.[350] With the exception of Israel, with which the COS did not have any commercial ties, the restrictions limited the employment of Czechoslovak ships and repre-

---

Honolulu HI. /ABS_16: Discriminatory measures given by the US Coast Guard, 2 March 1983, Appendix 9 to Annex A of Shipping Agent Guidelines./
348 ABS_16: Discriminatory measures given by the US Coast Guard, 2 March 1983.
349 ABS_17: Problems of so-called excluded areas in employing Czechoslovak tonnage on foreign accounts, 31 May 1983.
350 These countries were "allies" of the United States or countries supported by the United States. Czechoslovakia in this period strove to further develop its cooperation with North Korea and to normalize its relations with the PRC. In the Lebanese–Israeli war it "condemned" the US–Israeli aggression in Lebanon. /Zdeněk Veselý, *Československá zahraniční politika 1945–1989. Dokumenty* [Czechoslovak Foreign Policy 1945–1989. Documents] (Praha: Vysoká škola ekonomická, 2001)./ In August 1981, the Ministry of Foreign Affairs issued a protest against South Africa's aggression against the People's Republic of Angola. /Pavol Petruf, *Československá zahraničná politika 1945–1992* [Czechoslovak Foreign Policy 1945–1992] (Bratislava: Historický ústav Slovenskej akadémie vied, 2007)./

sented a severe disadvantage in shipping competition. Some business partners cancelled time charters and others required discounts because of complications caused by the new circumstances.[351]

6.2.2 The mid-1980s—a time of slight optimism

All these consequences negatively influenced the use of the COS tonnage during the first half of the 1980s. Whether they stemmed from the economic crisis or from the re-sharpened Cold War, their worst effect became evident in time charters for capitalist businessmen. In response to these changes, during 1984 the company made a change in its shipping conception, shifting emphasis to the transport of substrates and cargos from/to Czechoslovak enterprises. Thus the largest portion of the fleet's usage was dedicated to the transport of apatite from Murmansk, sugar from Cuba, ores from South America, phosphates from Africa and the USA, or seed cakes from India; the ships also delivered iron to Egypt, and special cargos to the Levant and the Red Sea areas. In addition, transports for customers from socialist countries significantly increased, of special importance here was the contract with Hungarian Mafracht that chartered two Czechoslovak vessels for the whole year.[352] In spite of all the conceptual changes, the profit achieved in 1984 was largely given by the transports of military cargos. Without this employment, the demanding planned indicators would not have been met.[353] It can be argued that the same mechanism—armament—on the international political scene, which had positively influenced the shipping market in the 1970s, once again allowed the COS to temporarily recover. As a matter of fact, although Reagan's policy of the arms race was meant to economically exhaust the Soviet Union and its bloc, it paradoxically led to a significant increase in investments spent on the Czechoslovak arms industry, with arms production reaching a peak in 1987.[354] Natural-

---

351 ABS_17: Problems of so-called excluded areas in employing Czechoslovak tonnage on foreign accounts, 31 May 1983.
352 NA_107: Evaluation of the company's economic results in 1984, Management meeting record No. 3, 30 January 1985.
353 ABS_18: Assumptions for economic results in 1984, 30 July 1984.
354 Průcha, *Hospodářské a sociální dějiny Československa II, 1945–1992*, 787.

ly, the development of the arms industry had positive impacts on the transport of highly profitable special cargos.

As for military issues, the state's military policy in shipping deserves special attention. Based on the agreement between the Czechoslovak Federal Ministry of Foreign Trade and the Soviet Ministry of Naval Fleet, in the case of combat readiness all Czechoslovak vessels were to be transferred, including their cargo and crew, to Soviet areas, and fall in the shortest possible time under the command of Soviet naval fleet representatives. In connection with this agreement from 1980, the General Staff of the Czechoslovak People's Army established a special department for naval ships management. In 1985 this department received instructions for using these ships during combat readiness. Related documents confirm that these instructions had been processed from around the mid-1970s, and their final approval was delayed due to problems with data necessary for building a connection between Czechoslovak ships, the Soviet Union's warships and Soviet shore radio stations.[355] Thus, the intense use of Czechoslovak merchant ships for military purposes can be seen as a result of the escalated Cold War and Ronald Reagan's anti-communist policy.

The significant milestone in Reagan's approach toward the Soviet Union was his announcement of the Strategic Defence Initiative in March 1983. The Soviet foreign policy failed to respond not only to this arms race challenge but also to other problems in Eastern Europe, i.e. the democratizing efforts in Poland and soon also in Hungary, where in 1983 non-Party members were allowed participation in elections for the first time. In addition, the Soviet Union was increasingly exhausted by the war in Afghanistan. The important and inevitable change that triggered subsequent democratization steps was the emergence of Mikhail Gorbachev and his relatively young, "Westernized" and "enlightened" group of leaders.[356] As the supreme representative of the Soviet Union from 1985, Gorbachev introduced his policy of *glasnost'* and *perestroika* [political openness and reconstruction] thus allowing the implementation

---

355 ABS_19: Measures for commanding Czechoslovak ships during state combat readiness, undated (according to the estimation based on the content, they may date to the beginning of 1986).
356 Zubok, "Soviet Foreign Policy from Détente to Gorbachev, 1975–1985," 111.

of gradual changes in the economy, and subsequently in the whole of society. Although the Czechoslovak communist leaders at the time attempted to slow down the changes for as long as they could, in the end some changes were inevitable.

6.3 Perestroika and the first (un)successful business attempts in shipping

From 1976, the Czechoslovak economy slowed down for five main reasons, which persisted also in subsequent periods: 1) the concept of a directly planned economy together with the absence of market principles were the most serious impediments to economic development; 2) the Party leaders refused to implement even such measures that could have positive economic impacts within the planned economy, e.g. release the directly fixed prices of subsidized rentals; probably for fear that some economic changes could have a negative impact on people and thus threaten their leading positions; 3) Czechoslovakia failed to adapt to global economy changes related to the oil shocks and subsequent crises, mainly because it was lagging behind in high technology development; 4) the economy did not undergo a turnaround towards higher efficiency and quality of work; 5) the Czechoslovak economy did not benefit from economic cooperation within the Council for Mutual Economic Assistance, except for temporary supplies at prices below the world price level.[357]

The growing economic problems provoked discussion about the need for change, for an economic reform. At that time it was called "improvement of the management system", since the word "reform" was forbidden due to the associations with the Prague Spring. The first attempt to improve the management system was introduced in 1980. Basically it was an attempt to repeat the failed reform from the end of the 1950s.[358] The ruling centre tried to disguise the failure of these first reform steps by designating the improvement of the management system as unfinished, and open to other arrangements and improvements. It formed a

---

357 Průcha, *Hospodářské a sociální dějiny Československa II, 1945–1992*, 674.
358 For a short comment about this reform, see the note 145.

special committee which was supposed to prepare a new reform proposal—Management of the Eighth Five Year Plan (1986–1990). In 1987, however, the basic assumption of this management—the assumption of economic stability—failed.[359]

Changes finally arrived in 1987. Despite a certain degree of resistance, the Czechoslovak communist leadership also had to react in some way to the changes introduced in the Soviet Union after Gorbachev's takeover. After a partial transformation in high-level policy, when the function of the President was separated from that of the General Secretary of the Central Committee of the Communist Party of Czechoslovakia, and the Prime Minister's office changed its personnel, the first liberalization tendencies started to emerge. Still, they were decelerated by the conservative ruling elite that had gained power in the state and in the Party during the "normalization" process. The ideas of *perestroika* and *glasnost'* were threatening their power. By 1987, they had to adopt immediate measures in the economy to avoid the suspicion that the planned *perestroika* in Czechoslovakia had been forced from outside, by the changes in the Soviet Union.

Thus, the Principles for the Economic Mechanism of Reconstruction were adopted very quickly, in the first days of 1987, before the January session of the Central Committee of the Communist Party of the Soviet Union. Finally, these principles were approved in a comprehensive version by the Central Committee of the Communist Party of Czechoslovakia in November 1987. Central planning remained the basic principle of this reform plan. Its influence was meant to "roll over" all the progressive elements in the sub-areas designated within the reconstruction principles.[360] Thus the real *perestroika* in Czechoslovakia did not occur until the 1989 Velvet Revolution, when Czechoslovakia finally made the transition to a market economy.

Still some minor arrangements were made before November 1989, the most important of which was the Act on State Enterprises (88/1988 Coll.). The act removed some barriers of entrepreneurship, introduced

---

359 Průcha, *Hospodářské a sociální dějiny Československa II, 1945–1992*, 699–700.
360 Ibid., 702–703.

self-governance into the management of enterprises, and gave companies a certain degree of autonomy, including the possibility of executing foreign trade transactions.[361] The second important legal arrangement at this time was the Act on Enterprise with Foreign Property Interest 38/1988 Coll. Even though this law concerned only companies established with capitalist partners, the new environment supporting business behaviour gave rise to the idea of re-establishing cooperation with the People's Republic of China in the shipping industry.

6.3.1 Revival of cooperation with the People's Republic of China

A new wave of frequent meetings among important Chinese and East European politicians began in the mid-1980s and aimed to promote mutual relations. As a result, Czechoslovakia signed a number of bilateral agreements with the PRC, all of which affected the economic, cultural, scientific, and other relations between the countries. Czechoslovak export to China experienced a boom that in some ways resembled the successful business contacts with the PRC in the 1950s. The rapid growth of export arose from the interplay of several favourable circumstances. After Gorbachev became the Soviet leader, Sino–Soviet relations greatly improved, and economic ties between communist China and the Soviet satellites were much less influenced by unfavourable political factors.[362] In this atmosphere, and with the need to find employment for Czechoslovak ships, the COS started negotiations about establishing a joint venture in shipping.

The Sino–Czechoslovak joint company named COSSHIP was founded on 1 January 1988, following the signing of the Czechoslovak–PRC business contract during Czechoslovak Prime Minister Lubomír Štrougal's visit to China in 1987. The main aim of this step was to develop mutual trade cooperation.[363] The COS and the China Ocean Shipping

---

361 Based on the Act 42/1980 Coll. about economic relations with foreign countries, the foreign trade activities could be carried out also by other Czechoslovak subjects with permission. /Průcha, *Hospodářské a sociální dějiny Československa II, 1945–1992*, 855./
362 Aleš Skřivan, *Československý vývoz do Číny 1918–1992* [Czechoslovak Export to China 1918–1992] (Praha: Scriptorium, 2009), 265–266.
363 ABS_27: Memorandum to the Czechoslovak–PRC joint venture COSSHIP, 30 March 1988.

Company Beijing established that the COSSHIP would have its seat in Prague, with doubled management functions. Its registered capital was $10 million, and the operational capital was one million $. Both parties shared 50 per cent of the capital, and equally distributed the earnings and losses. The joint venture was exempt from all kinds of Czechoslovak corporate taxes.[364] Czechoslovakia put its ship Orava II into the joint venture, up to now operated by the COS, while the Chinese side provided the ship Funtushan.[365]

The operation of the COSSHIP, however, was far from ideal. To start with, the Chinese employees working in the Prague headquarters were disappointed with low salaries, in addition paid in Czechoslovak crowns while they had expected Swiss francs.[366] On the other hand, Czechoslovaks were frustrated with the Chinese employees in the COSSHIP for low expertise, lack of English language skills and inflexibility.[367] As early as four months after its foundation, the COSSHIP reported serious problems in management, finance, and accounting. The report included the explanation that Chinese employees considered Czechoslovak accounting complicated, did not understand it and refused to understand it; in addition, they were not acknowledged by relevant Czech legislation, and refused to be acknowledged. Since every decision in the joint venture had to be approved by both directors, the problem became more serious. For instance, the COSSHIP business department failed to contract goods for transport in time. The consequence of this bad cooperation in the very first months of the running of the COSSHIP meant that the company reported only losses. For example, the salaries of Chinese employees had to be borrowed from the Czechoslovak side[368] despite the fact that the Chinese partner was supposed to share losses and benefits in the same portion as its Czechoslovak counterpart.

---

364 ABS_24: Documents from the Federal Ministry of Foreign Trade—Proposal for the establishment of the Czechoslovak–Sino joint venture, 13 March 1987.
365 ABS_27: Memorandum to the Czechoslovak–PRC joint venture COSSHIP, 30 March 1988.
366 ABS_25: Findings about the COSSHIP, 19 February 1988.
367 ABS_26: Findings about the COSSHIP, 23 March 1988.
368 ABS_28: The COSSHIP – serious problems in the economic field, 4 July 1988.

Another problem for the COSSHIP was the high surplus of roubles. The accounting unit within the Council for Mutual Economic Assistance (CMEA) countries was the clearing rouble. Earned roubles could be used either for business within the CMEA or exchanged for convertible currency. In view of the deteriorating economic situation in the Eastern bloc, whose countries focused on trading with Western partners, the possibilities of spending in roubles narrowed. Furthermore, the exchange rate of the rouble was overvalued, thus reducing the possibilities of exchanging it: the official rate was 0.6 roubles to $1.0; however, banks refused this exchange rate, since the real rate was 1.2 roubles to $1.0. Thus various internal enterprises were faced with amounts of rouble that could not be spent. For example, up to September 1989 the COSSHIP had identified 0.5 million roubles that could not be disposed of. Czechoslovak foreign trade enterprises solved the problem in some cases by using absurdly expensive transport of Chinese goods by Soviet aircrafts.[369] This example not only illustrates how desperate the situation of the rouble was; it also clearly indicates that such behaviour on the part of foreign trade enterprises led to less frequent use of Czechoslovak ships, whether they were run by the COSSHIP, or by the COS.

After the first year of operation the company achieved a profit of about one million $, the majority of which was generated by the Czechoslovak side, mostly when providing transport for Czechoslovak foreign trade enterprises. When using the COSSHIP, the Chinese partner covered its own transport needs of Chinese goods to Czechoslovakia for favourable rates. In addition, the PRC used the cooperation to take advantage of the expertise and contacts of the Czechoslovak counterpart and to explore the shipping market, its conditions, habits etc., to gain future benefits. One would expect that having thorough knowledge of the market, the PRC could have entered as a competitor onto the European shipping market, since it operated over 600 ships equipped with very inexpensive labour and could push the COS of its business positions.[370] In the end, the COSSHIP terminated its business activities in 1990. At this

---

369 ABS_23: Situation in the COS, further investigations of rouble surpluses, 20 September 1989.
370 ABS_29: The COSSHIP – experience from its first year of operation, 19 November 1989.

time, Czechoslovak enterprises became market-oriented and could no longer invest state finances to cover onerous business. Still the COSSHIP was only a supplementary business. The main shipping activities were executed within the COS and with the approaching revolutionary year 1989, the company was confronted with problems, too.

6.3.2 Facing the realities of the late 1980s

The COS entered into the 1980s with the conception of fleet renewal designed in 1978, and thus based on the realities of the second half of the 1970s, the period after the boom of 1975 and 1976. Even when the year 1978 showed the lowest profit gain within the second half of the 1970s, the plan of fleet renewal calculated with the development of Czechoslovak foreign trade, both with the countries of the Council for Mutual Economic Assistance and with capitalist states. These considerations were based on the forecast for the development of the world economy. The second oil crisis had not been predicted.

The conception followed from the presumption that ships would provide transports for Czechoslovak goods, mainly those which otherwise required capitalist tonnage. In addition, the vessels were to be involved in transports paid in foreign (capitalist) currency. This plan was supposed to guarantee a relatively high profitability of the fleet's operation and at the same time justified the purchases of new ships. The intention was to buy nine ships between 1981 and 1985, two ships per year and the ninth purchase in 1985.[371]

In the subsequent five-year period (1985–1990), the conception of fleet renewal presupposed that the COS would operate seventeen ships in total. In the end, the COS had eighteen ships in operation in 1990, but the purchases were executed in a different sequence than planned, according to the real possibilities and current needs of the company. Primarily, the investments were postponed because of the bad performance in the years 1982 and 1983 and the subsequent standstill period in shipping performance.

---

371 NA_114: Material for the counsel of the Minister of Foreign Trade, Proposal for fleet development until 1985 and prospect until 1990, 20 October 1978.

Unfortunately, no later concept for the fleet development and renewal is available. From the documents we only know that four ships were purchased on a wave of optimism at the turn of 1980/1981. After that, only one used ship was bought in 1986, partially paid from the sale of another ship, the Košice. Up until the end of the 1980s, transport performance was executed with the same fleet composition.

In the period 1988–1989, the COS purchased eight new ships: two from Poland, two from Yugoslavia and four from the PRC as a result of the on-going cooperation between the two countries. Probably these investments were inevitable since at the turn of the 1980s/1990s, five ships were planned to be discharged. Still the new ships were purchased not only in conformity with the planned concept of fleet development but also in conformity with wider state interests. This concerned mainly the new ships of Chinese origin—they were purchased for high prices in exchange for the contract for a thermal power station that the PRC purchased for a high price from Czechoslovakia. During the negotiations, the Chinese representatives allegedly stated that "if they could buy an expensive power plant from Czechoslovakia, in turn we could buy expensive ships from them".[372]

The COS soon faced the fact that four ships from the PRC brought in a loss of $200 per day. The loss was caused not only by the ships' high price, but mainly by the lessening of international tensions, which suddenly caused transports of military cargoes to decrease to a minimum.[373] Once again, the developments in the international community towards peace in the late 1980s, the insolvency of most traditional buyers of Czechoslovak weapons in the Third World, and the decreasing internal budget expenditure on defence led to the decline in certain fields of Czechoslovak military production. In 1988, the conversion of defence industries to civilian production finally began.[374] It was an important change for the conception of fleet running, since originally the four ships were intended to carry military cargos. Considering the high portion of net profit earned by "special" cargos, it is evident that the drop

---
372 ABS_23: Situation in the COS, further investigations of rouble surpluses, 20 September 1989.
373 Ibid.
374 Průcha, *Hospodářské a sociální dějiny Československa II, 1945–1992*, 787.

in military cargo represented a substantial problem for the performance and profitability of the COS.

Within the constraints of still limited business opportunities, the company's headquarters started to look for new ways of ensuring the effective operation of its vessels. One of the options was a bareboat charter, i.e. chartering ships without their crew. The COS was considering operating the ship Mír II in this manner until the end of 1989, with the customer having a preferential right to the purchase of the ship. The transaction was supposed to verify this mode of operation and its feasibility in general, including solutions to, for example, registration problems under the tenant's flag versus registration in Prague as Czechoslovak property; another issue concerned the areas from which Czechoslovak ships were excluded.[375] If they proved profitable, the four "expensive" ships from the PRC were supposed to operate in this manner. Unfortunately, the COS based this plan on the economic boom on the maritime market at the end of the 1980s. By no means could they have foreseen other, more important and more extensive changes that were about to influence not only the company, but also the society as a whole—those triggered by the 1989 Velvet Revolution.

Already in the pre-November 1989 period, the responsible employees in the COS were doing their best to meet the economic challenges of the enterprise and bring benefit to the country. This effort, however, was met with the State Security's displeasure. One of the officers, for example, in his report from 22 September 1989 stated:

> All the activities of the ships' command lead to fulfilment of economic challenges and everything else is subordinated to this task. At the headquarters, the passive approach to the Communist Party is increasingly evident and again, the activities are directed solely to fulfilling the economic indicators, with the main aim to reach profit.[376]

Let us look what the profit was.

375　NA_115: Record from the extraordinary management meeting, 5 July 1989.
376　ABS_30: Assessment of the situation in the COS, 22 September 1989.

6.4 Financial results in the 1980s

	1981	1982	1983	1984	1985
Ships[377]	14	14	14	14	14
Completed voyages	94	122	121	118	131
Total DWT	266,967	266,967	266,967	266,967	266,967
Total GRT	175,355	175,355	175,355	175,355	175,355
Amount of goods transported (tonnes)	1,462,000	1,787,000	1,737,000	1,842,000	1,879,000
Total net profit (crowns)	135,500,000	60,600,000	10,300,000[378]	26,200,000	34,700,000
Net profit recalculation ($)[379]	6,755,000	3,030,000	515,000	1,310,000	1,735,000

Table 9: Financial results 1981–1985[380]

---

[377] When exact information on ship parameters is not stated in annual reports, information is included based on individual ship parameters files in the National Archive /NA_72: Files of individual ships./ The figures on ships are stated as at the end of the year.

[378] The final output includes the subvention of 77 million crowns provided by the Federal Ministry of Foreign Trade. /NA_105: Report of economic results in 1982, Management meeting record No. 8, 25 February 1983./

[379] Having no other information, I have calculated with the average 22 crowns, being aware that it is a sort of underestimation. More on the recalculation see the note 323.

[380] Figures in the table are based on these documents: 1981 – NA_104: Evaluation of economic results in 1981, Management meeting record No. 5, 5 February 1982; 1982 – NA_105: Report on economic results in 1982, Management meeting record No. 8, 25 February 1983; 1983 – NA_106: Evaluation of the company's economic results in 1983, Management meeting record No. 5, 2 February 1984; 1984 – NA_107: Evaluation of the company's economic results in 1984, Management meeting record No. 3, 30 January 1985; 1985 – NA_108: Assessment of the 1985 plan fulfilment, Management meeting record No 3, 27 January 1986.

	1986	1987	1988	1989	1990
Ships	14	12	14	20	18
Completed voyages	146	117	121	149	155
Total DWT	262,616	215,486	231,372	394,373	443,155
Total GRT	172,164	142,524	155,374	263,278	282,491
Amount of goods transported (tonnes)	1,873,000	1,636,000	1,804,000	2,146,000	2,655,000
Total net profit (crowns)	35,200,000	51,300,000[381]	46,400,000	109,000,000	76,400,000
Net profit recalculation ($)[382]	1,760,000	2,565,000	2,320,000	5,450,000	3,820,000

Table 10: Financial results 1986–1990[383]

The results of the 1980s show virtually every possible position—from high profit in 1981, through the years of crisis when the company would have finished with losses had it not been for state subsidies, up to a slight recovery in the late 1980s. In some years the revenue was bolstered by sales of ships.

The 1980s was also a decade when the COS had to solve the issue of settlement with Čechofracht. As explained in the chapter about the 1950s, the Sino–Czechoslovak joint venture was only a red herring for

---

[381] Profit from the sale of two ships positively impacted the final net profit.

[382] Information on the exchange rate when calculating the net profit in $ is stated in note 323.

[383] Figures in the table are based on these documents: 1986 – NA_109: Assessment of the 1986 plan fulfilment, Management meeting record No. 3, 29 January 1987; 1987 – NA_110: Assessment of the 1987 plan fulfilment, Management meeting record No. 3, 28 January 1988; 1988 – NA_111: Assessment of the 1988 plan fulfilment, Management meeting record No. 3, 26 January 1989. From 1989 archive files do not contain annual reports or meeting records; the documents were probably not handed over to the archive. Therefore the information about the financial results in 1989 and 1990 is based on secondary literature, the already mentioned book written by the former economic deputy of the company, Zdeněk Bastl. The most serious imperfection of this source is the fact that Bastl does not mention any source of the information stated. However, when comparing the data about the previous decades obtained from the archive with Bastl's book, both sources comply in approximately 90 per cent. The financial results stated for the period from 1989 to 1998 have a similar level of reliability. /Bastl, *Padesát let Československé námořní plavby*, 98–100./

the fact that the embargoed PRC purchased and ran ships through Czechoslovakia. The Czechoslovak state executed the business through the company Čechofracht. While Čechofracht deposited 180 million Czechoslovak crowns, the PRC deposited the ships into the business, as documents from 1989 reveal. Up to that year, the COS managed to prove that 160 million had already been compensated to Čechofracht, and the remaining 20 million were to be settled. Čechofracht, however, claimed that the remaining amount was 40 million. The matter was planned to be dealt with at the beginning of October 1989 during the meeting of both managements.

At this time Czechoslovak enterprises changed their legal form from "national" to "state" enterprises based on the law about state enterprise 88/1988 Coll. Also the COS was supposed to change its status from that of international joint stock company to state enterprise. As the law stipulated the self-financing of companies and responsibility for profits and losses, with the obligation to pay 40 million to Čechofracht, the COS would start the business with a loss. There was also another possibility of settling the matter: if the COS remained a joint stock company, the future shareholders (banks, insurance companies, etc.) would invest into the shares, and the 40 million crowns would be covered from the sales of the shares. The "resource" giving this information to the State Security however noted that "it is suspicious that when Čechofracht found out that the COS would change in a state enterprise, it immediately asked for its share, although the original contract had not embedded this right".[384] In the end, Czechoslovak Ocean Shipping entered the 1990s as a joint stock company. The next few years brought major changes for the company; the most important of which are outlined in the next chapter.

---

384 ABS_23: Situation in the COS, Further investigations of rouble surpluses, 20 September 1989.

7 Epilogue: Czechoslovak and Czech maritime business after the Velvet Revolution

Even though the most recent period of Czechoslovak shipping after November 1989 lies outside the scope of this book, I will outline at least the decisive milestones and events that influenced the shipping industry's development in democracy and the new market economy. Unfortunately, the available resources are poor in both quantity and quality. The reasons are twofold: 1) some documents are not available because of the thirty-year protection period given by the law on archive resources; 2) most of the documents are still (hopefully) stored with the company but are inaccessible for research because they are part of the company's registry.

Therefore, I base this epilogue mainly on non-archival resources such as relevant legislation, records on the company in the Business Register, and one relevant book which provides the majority of the financial data.[385] In addition, the online archive of TradeWinds magazine has proved to be very useful.[386] In fact, this specialized magazine offers more comprehensive and relevant information about the Czechoslovak/Czech fleet after 1989 than Czech newspapers and websites. What is more, articles published by TradeWinds show what was monitored, i.e. what was important for the professionals in the ocean shipping industry worldwide.

---

385 Bastl, *Padesát let Československé námořní plavby*. The book offers valuable information about the ships' operation; however, it is not highly reliable because it does not support data with references to primary sources. Still, having compared some parts against the available primary sources, I found a relatively high level of compliance and thus find this source valuable to a certain extent.

386 TradeWinds is a shipping newspaper established in 1990 by the NHST Media Group providing business news in the areas of shipping, seafood, and oil and gas. TradeWinds has offices in the United States, Singapore, Shanghai, Oslo, London, Athens, and Bergen. According to its main characteristics, TradeWinds is a market-leading up-to-date news provider offering the very latest information, interviews with key players in the shipping sector. /TradeWinds, "The business of shipping," http://www.tradewindsnews.com/aboutus/ (as of 16 February 2015)./

What we learn from these sources is that after the Velvet Revolution, there were three milestones in Czechoslovak shipping development, namely the privatization of the company, the impact on the split of Czechoslovakia, and transfers of property. Actually, in 1990 and to some extent in 1991, business did not differ too much from the previous decade, and the company was in a rut. In February 1990, a new director was selected, the captain Vladimír Podlena. The updated law about joint stock companies was reflected in the COS's statutes.[387] The management's main effort was to expand business. The company's performance looked as follows:

	1991	1992	1993	1994
Ships	18	18	18	15[388]
Completed voyages	139	139	146	128
Total DWT	443,155	443,155	499,741	427,555
Total GRT	282,491	282,491	310,390	263,058
Amount of goods transported (tonnes)	2,566,000	2,382,000	2,939,000	2,705,000
Total net profit (crowns)	273,900,000	69,900,000	271,100,000	613,000,000
Net profit recalculation ($)[389]	9,289,627	2,473,198	9,298,656	21,300,254

Table 11: Financial results 1991–1994

---

387 After the nationalization of the Czechoslovak economy, joint stock companies were regulated by the Act 243/1949 Coll. It was very brief as this form of business in centrally planned economy was used only for arranging some business relationships with capitalist countries. In the market economy this law was very unsatisfactory, incapable of regulating joint stock running. To solve the situation, a new Act 104/1990 Coll., was adopted and very shortly thereafter, due to the deficiencies of this hastily adopted law, yet another Act was passed, 513/1991 Coll., the Commercial Code.

388 The three oldest ships in the fleet were sold since the company did not want to run ships older than 20 years. /Trond Lillestolen, "Romanian Tankers to Fuel Fleet Renewal at Czechoslovak Ocean Shipping," *TradeWinds*, 24 June 1994./

389 The recalculation to $ for the period 1991–1998 is based on the Czech National Bank data /"Kurzy devizového trhu – čtvrtletní průměry," https://www.cnb.cz/cs/financni_trhy/devizovy_trh/kurzy_devizoveho_trhu/prumerne_mena.jsp?mena=USD (as of 25 February 2015)./

The slump in 1992 can be explained by the slowdown of the world economy and the subsequent decline in global freight rates. A three times higher profit in 1994 compared to 1993 partially came from ship sales.[390] The results also show that the privatization process did not greatly affect the company's performance. Privatization was one of the five main ways of transforming state ownership after 1989.[391] Within the first privatization wave, several financial subjects obtained a major share in the COS; furthermore, individuals invested their vouchers into the company;[392] finally, employees' shares were issued, too. After the first privatization phase, it was clear that Czechoslovakia would split, which could complicate the next privatization steps.[393] In the end, the financial compensation following from the split of the Czechoslovak federation did not directly affect the COS. The company was renamed Czech Ocean Shipping (COS). When the entire privatization process was completed, the company was "largely owned by private Czech investment funds".[394]

Shortly after the declaration of an independent Czech Republic on 1 January 1993, the first post-revolutionary director of the company, Vladimír Podlena, was replaced by another former ship master, Pavel Trnka, who assumed office on 24 March 1993.[395] Apparently, the main

---

390 Ibid.
391 The first was restitution, i.e. the return of property to former owners; the second was the transfer of property from the state to municipalities; the third way concerned the transformation of socialist cooperatives into private cooperatives. Finally, the remaining two means of ownership transformation consisted of small and then large privatization. /Martin Myant, Vzestup a pád českého kapitalismu [Rise and Fall of Czech Capitalism] (Praha: Academia, 2013), 41–45./
392 Voucher privatization is a privatization method in which the citizens had the opportunity to obtain state property. They could buy voucher books with a certain number of vouchers (coupons) at low prices (in Czechoslovakia it was 1,000 Czechoslovak crowns) or received them free of charge. They could then acquire ownership of shares in any privatized company through investing the coupons.
393 Ian Lewis, "Czechoslovak Ocean Shipping Keen to Flag Out Vessels," *TradeWinds*, 27 November 1992.
394 Trond Lillestolen, "COS is Back on Track," *TradeWinds*, 24 December 1993.
395 Business Register Record: Veřejný rejstřík a Sbírka listin, "Úplný výpis z obchodního rejstříku Česká námořní plavba a. s., BXXXVI 39 vedená u Městského soudu v Praze," https://or.justice.cz/ias/ui/rejstrik-firma.vysledky?s

reason for this change in the top-level management was Podlena's disagreement with the board's decisions.[396] At the end of the same year, the newly appointed COS managing director and chairman Trnka optimistically reported a sharp increase of profits in 1993.[397] The company achieved good results also in the following year; this time, however, the income was positively impacted by the sale of some ships.

Let us look briefly at the fleet development up until 1995. In 1990 the ship Tatry (bulk carrier, Panamax type, 66,088 DWT) was purchased and three smaller ships were sold (less than 20,000 DWT in total). The other two ships of the Panamax type were ordered in the same Daewoo shipyard as the Tatry. At first these newbuildings were ordered before 1989 together with the Tatry, but the shipyard accused the COS of not having paid all the financial liabilities and the shipyard resold the ships to Egypt[398] (see more on the deal in the chapter "Ship memoirs"). Since Panamax-type ships were considered an integral part of the conception for future fleet development, the company was interested in extending its fleet by these ships.

The problem lay in the lack of financial capital. At the beginning of the 1990s foreign investors did not consider Czechoslovakia a sufficiently trustworthy partner to be granted a loan. Still the COS needed to take out a loan because its own funds could only cover one Panamax ship. The problem with the lack of credibility could be solved by registering some Czechoslovak vessels, including the newbuildings, abroad, in countries with a mortgage system that would be acceptable to foreign banks.[399] Thus some Czechoslovak ships were registered under the Maltese flag, later also under the Cypriot flag.[400] In addition to Pana-

---

ubjektId=411847&typ=UPLNY (as of 21 February 2015).

396 Trond Lillestolen, "Management Reshuffle at COS Hits Daewoo Deal," *TradeWinds*, 5 February 1993.

397 It reported a profit of 200 million ($6.7 million) in 1993, up from 69.8 million of crowns in 1992. /Trond Lillestolen, "Romanian Tankers to Fuel Fleet Renewal at Czechoslovak Ocean Shipping," *TradeWinds*, 24 June 1994./ We see the reported figures correspond with the resources quoted in the chart.

398 Trond Lillestolen, "National Navigation Takes Up Bulker Option," *TradeWinds*, 15 June 1995.

399 Trond Lillestolen, "COS Is Back on Track," *TradeWinds*, 24 December 1993.

400 It is said that this form of registration was advantageous also for tax reasons but I cannot confirm the information with any solid data.

max-type vessels (the Tatry, the Beskydy, and the Šumava), the COS purchased one smaller ship, the Svitava, from a Romanian shipyard in 1995.[401]

Today we know that the turning point in the company's life was the year 1995, when all shipping activities began to cease. After the privatization of the COS, the chairman Trnka reported that the company had no intention to invite foreign shareholders into the COS. Still, he admitted such prospects for 1995 or 1996.[402] And that is exactly what happened. Around December 1995, some reports, at that point not confirmed, suggested that 69 per cent of the stake in the COS had been purchased through the Harvard Group and Stratton Investments by the Bahamas-based investor Michael D. Dingman and the exiled Czech investor Viktor Kožený.[403] This takeover of such a substantial share proportion was a critical moment that changed the future course of the company.

Today Viktor Kožený is perceived as the man who deprived or even robbed the Czech Republic (and its seafarers) of a prosperous maritime fleet for his personal gain and profit. Nevertheless, there is little reliable information about Kožený's business plans to draw any final conclusions. The issue is that if Viktor Kožený could purchase the majority of shares, someone else (companies, banks individuals) had to sell him those shares. Most probably the main cause therefore lay in the privatization process, which was faster than the development of necessary legislation that could regulate the process effectively.

The changes were finally confirmed in February 1996 with the information that Dingman and Kožený were in control of about 85 per cent of the COS. Again, we may only speculate whether Viktor Kožený purchased the majority in the COS with the primary aim to sell the ships almost immediately or if he intended to run the shipping business. The transaction brought the investors profit since they had paid for the COS shares less than what the net value of the company was. However, TradeWinds observers stated that it was "an open question" what the

---

401 The delivery of the ship was probably a part of a settlement from the period of the Council for Mutual Economic Assistance.
402 Trond Lillestolen, " COS Is Back on Track," *TradeWinds*, 24 December 1993.
403 Trond Lillestolen, "New Investors Take Over COS," *TradeWinds*, 15 February 1996.

investors would accept for the shares now, i.e. after approximately two years from the moment the deal had been reported for the first time. Some specialists assumed that Kožený and Dingman would sell the assets soon.[404]

There are some indicators that at least at the beginning, Kožený and Dingman entered the COS "with the view that shipping has good potential for a high payoff". This intention is supported also by the fact that in 1997 the COS ordered four 26,000 DWT newbuildings in a Chinese shipyard, which was the biggest investment in the whole COS history. TradeWinds experts, however, added that the COS was the only company to have ordered this type of vessel (bulk carriers, type Seafarer 26), which was otherwise not very successful with customers. They also drew attention to the low market rates for bulk carriers and expressed fears that there was a surplus of these ships on the market. Still the COS was confident in running the bulker segment.[405]

The belief was based on the fact that Czechoslovak seafarers, engineers, and other experts were rated as some of the best professionals in this field. On the other hand, in its insistence on this high self-image, the management overlooked the current changes in the shipping market. It seems as if they were convinced that if they could successfully operate on Western markets during the socialist economy, they were skilled enough to operate in a market economy. If these are not mere speculations, then the management ignored/disregarded one important difference, i.e. the fact that in the past the company held a monopoly in maritime transport and its losses were balanced with state funds.

In the same year when the order for four bulk carriers of 26,000 DWT was placed, Kožený asked the US-based American Marine Advisors, which earlier that year had refinanced the COS, to conduct a tender for the sale of the company's ships.[406] The deal was concluded with the Rotterdam-based Van Ommeren, which agreed to pay nearly $200 million. But because the rates began dropping from the moment this deal

---

[404] Trond Lillestolen, "Czech Ocean Keeps the Handysize Faith," *TradeWinds*, 24 April 1997.
[405] Ibid.
[406] Trond Lillestolen, "COS Ships Sold at a 'Discount'," *TradeWinds*, 23 October 1997.

had been announced in October 1997, by February 1998 the business would bring Van Ommeren a loss of around $40 or $50 million. Thus this Dutch company exercised its cancellation rights, and took over only four bulk carriers,[407] while dropping the remaining eight ships, including the four newbuildings from China.[408]

In the end, the remaining ships were sold to the German owner Egon Oldendorff and Danish owner Clipper for a very low price, less than $60 million for the last six vessels. The chairman Trnka said: "I feel like a general who has lost his army", and he added that the ships "were sold at holocaust prices".[409] He was perhaps right if evaluating the deal only through the prism of the value of the vessels. This lamentation, however, did not reflect the shipping market conditions of that time. Van Ommeren's withdrawal from the deal complicated the search for a new buyer—these are clear indicators that the time was highly unfavourable for selling the ships. Of course, I cannot exclude that the business was influenced by some speculations or efforts to artificially further reduce the price.

To make the picture complete, the following table offers a summary of the financial results during the last four years of the COS shipping business.

---

407 Geoff Garfield, "Dry Cargo Slump Spoiled COS Deal," *TradeWinds*, 12 February 1998.
408 Geoff Garfield, "Race for COS Ships Stops Dead," *TradeWinds*, 19 February 1998.
409 Trond Lillestolen, "Czechs Bet on Comeback Cash," *TradeWinds*, 7 January 1999.

	1995	1996	1997	1998
Ships[410]	13	12	10	11
Completed voyages	121	95	96	74
Total DWT	433,335	274,978	218,723	235,128
Total GRT	261,413	464,962	378,980	405,077
Amount of goods transported (tonnes)	2,804,000	3,077,000	3,315,000	2,425,000
Total net profit (crowns)	362,200,000	434,100,000	1,069,300,000	− 2,352,700,000
Net profit recalculation ($)	13,647,839	15,993,073	33,753,689	− 72,877,365

Table 12: Financial results 1995–1998[411]

Having sold its fleet, the COS did not finish its activities in the shipping business completely. In the first years after the sale it concentrated on providing ship management activities for a third party,[412] including for example, Van Ommeren. But this service rapidly shrunk to the management of only four vessels on which the company could not survive. To solve the problem, the COS extended its business activities by real-estate investments in Prague.[413]

After selling the last ship Jan Želivský, the chairman Trnka made a rather desperate attempt to "salvage" the shipping business. He asked some Czech entrepreneurs to invest in rebuilding the Czech maritime fleet. In the beginning he intended to raise between $20 to $25 million of Czech crowns to buy four or five used (seven or eight years old) bulk

---

410 The chart includes the number of ships at the end of the year, i. e. including all purchases and sales within the year; 11 ships in 1998 is the situation before the final sale.
411 The data in both charts in this chapter is based on the Bastl, *Padesát let Československé námořní plavby*, 88–89, 99–100. The information about the number of ships and their tonnage is calculated from the file on ship parameters. /NA_72: Files of individual ships./
The economic performance in these years included also income for the ships' sales; thus the net profit row does not show the real profit earned by shipping services.
412 Trond Lillestolen, "Cash Drought Delays Czech Bulk Comeback," *TradeWinds*, 3 June 1999.
413 Geoff Garfield, "Bulkers Owners Target Handies," *TradeWinds*, 22 July 1999.

carriers.[414] The entrepreneurs, however, were not interested. Maybe their attitude answers the question of whether shipping business could survive in the Czech Republic in market conditions. Looking at today's shipping business environment, it is clear that it could not run without substantial changes to its operation, a modern conception of shipping services, and sufficient foreign capital.

As a reminder of past successes in the field, the COS administrative building can still be found in Prague. It is a small white building, which from 1980 was used as the COS temporary headquarters before a more representative building could be built. And in front of the building, there still stands the old admiralty anchor that the seafarers from the ship Blaník pull out of the Caribbean Sea in 1976 (I took a photograph of the anchor on 8 March 2015).[415]

---

414 Trond Lillestolen, "Czechs Bet on Comeback Cash," *TradeWinds*, 7 January 1999.
415 NA_131: Management meeting record No. 10, 23 April 1976.

8 Seafarers' lives and memories

My father was a seafarer. Before his death in 1994, he asked us to scatter his ashes into the sea. At those times, the Czech Republic was still not a European Union member, nor a Schengen Area member, so it was rather difficult to transport the ashes across the borders to the sea. The borders were still controlled, although randomly, and it proved impossible to arrange my father's last wish in an official way. Thus, we decided to arrange this unusual transport crossing only one border—that with Poland. To some extent, it was also symbolic since Czechoslovak seafarers considered the Polish ports of Szczecin, Gdynia, and Gdansk the "home" ports. The first part of this "mission impossible" was successful. We arrived near the town of Kołobrzeg, where we took advantage of the bad weather and boarded a small excursion boat. Far in the open sea, my husband secretly fulfilled this important task, and scattered my father's ashes into the Baltic.

My three-year-old daughter was present at this last farewell and later on when we explained this symbolic act to her, she promised me to scatter my ashes in front of the ŠkoFIN building, where I was working at that time—a commercial open-plan building in a suburb of Prague. It was so absurd and funny!

Now, when I am writing about seafarers' lives I recall this story again—the majority of people would find it absurd to be scattered next to their place of work. But for seafarers, the sea is the most desired place for their "final rest" because many of them cannot imagine being without this element in their life, nor in their afterlife. The sea captivates many of them for its power and magic. Thinking about the interviews with seafarers I conducted, I cannot find a better comparison for this attachment to the sea than that of drug addiction. But the addiction metaphor cannot be applied to everyone who has ever spent some time (working) on the sea, as the "hard" data in the company's records clearly illustrate. The turnover of seafarers proves to be relatively high and deserves special attention.

Although a seafarer's job offered various benefits (mainly the possibility to travel, which was otherwise limited by the communist regime), the company had to deal with the turnover of employees quite frequently. For instance, in 1974 the reported turnover was 10.5 per cent (60 men) of all the employed seafarers; surprisingly, this number was interpreted as a successful result, since the turnover had been estimated to 15.8 per cent based on previous experience.

Even more interesting than figures themselves are the actual reasons for quitting a seafarer's job. More than half of those who resigned from their job stated family reasons. Specifically, they had to take care of their elderly or sick parents, construct a house, or return to their partners. Furthermore, most of the seafarers' wives could not bear the long-term separation. It is significant that three quarters of these men had been employed at the COS for less than two years. Less frequent reasons for leaving their job (or getting fired) can be ordered from the most to the least common as follows: 2) disciplinary reasons (emigration in the family, customs offences, crimes committed in Czechoslovakia, offenses committed on ships, cadre reasons, meaning weak political reliability or loyalty); 3) health reasons; 4) emigration; 5) death; 6) retirement.[416]

But some seafarers quit the job simply because it did not fulfil their expectations. After the first few months aboard, they realized that exciting adventure suddenly turned into hard work, and that many destinations were uninteresting, mainly non-Western countries. Especially boring were the endless days and weeks waiting in the roadstead. Beside this, the first cruise also entailed the first experience of work on a tilting ship (in some cases entries in log books speak about ships titled by thirty or forty degrees).

> But we set off on the Atlantic from La Manche to the beloved Bay of Biscay. And you know, as I was still hungry, I had a good breakfast. Well and then I went up to the fore to button up the cars, you know what I mean, don't you, to fasten the ropes. Among them there were also hops, smelling all over the hold, and my stomach was wedged in there. [...] So of course, I ran up on the deck without any pressure, and I let it go into the ocean. In the meantime I bumped into the boatswain, who says: 'Hey, go and fetch the steward. Have a beer and bread with pepper'. Bread with pepper for the swinging. I completely fooled my stomach. Well, I downed perhaps more than one pint that morning. [...] And since then I had to weigh up what I ate for breakfast. Cos' it wasn't worth eat-

---

416 NA_138: Material No. 25 for the management meeting held on 21 March 1975.

ing heavy stuff. I mean, at the beginning. Later on, I didn't mind. But not everyone was keen on it.[417]

Some men got discouraged by these moments, others did not. Some men decided for other life priorities, others became "addicted"—addicted to the sea, ships, and seafarers' work. This chapter concentrates on the second group, on the men for whom the sea and ships became probably the most important thing in their lives. They were the men who with their hard work helped to build and run the Czechoslovak fleet and create its fame.[418] Bearing in mind the importance of every man on a ship, in the next section, I will draw an outline of the professions and comment on what they consisted of.

8.1 "Work on the sea is simply different"[419] (an overview of seafarers' professions)

This section explores the area of human work, the most essential element for the safe and successful operation of a ship (aside from the ship's condition and quality). I will start by introducing the scheme of individual ship departments and then describe the professions within each department including their qualification.

How did the seafarers come to find their job, considering that it was rather exceptional in a landlocked and communist country? Quite surprisingly, most of the seafarers reported that the main impetus for their decision to work on vessels was coincidence (whether it was newspaper advertisements, the recommendation of a friend or acquaintance, staff recruitment in certain enterprises, etc.). After this first step and fulfilment other necessary requirements, a man could occupy one of these positions in the ship's hierarchy:

---

417 J. N., * 1943, boatswain, 30 years in the COS.
418 The good reputation of Czechoslovak ships and seafarers in the world cannot be supported by "hard" data or resources; to a large extent this assumption is based on the seafarers' subjective feelings. On the other hand, narrators reflected that Czechoslovak ships in most cases received very good rating (e.g. interview with J. N., * 1943, boatswain, 30 years in the COS) by the Lloyd's Register which is—given the Register's reputation—confirmation of quality.
419 Paraphrase from the interview with J. K., * 1946, chief cook, 22 years in the COS.

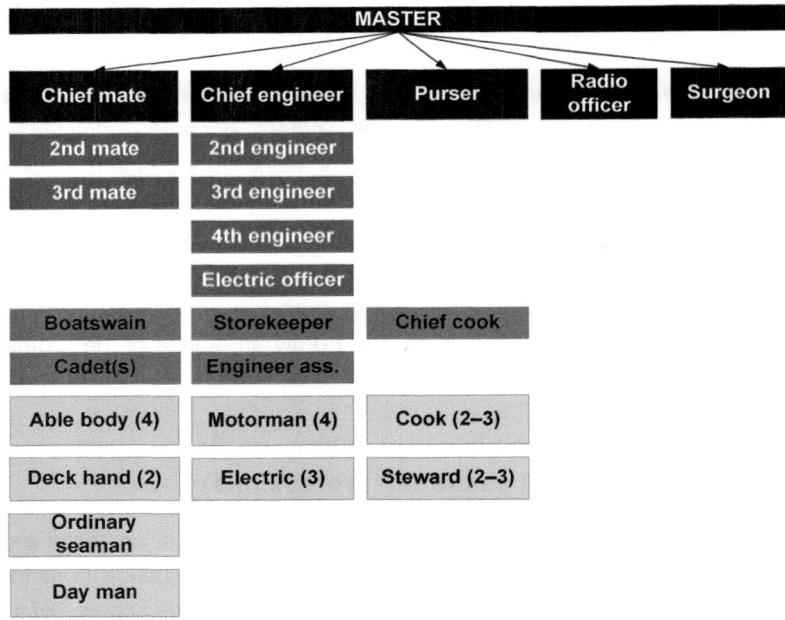

Figure 1: Ship hierarchy

This scheme is outlined based on the crew list from 1981, the ship Bratislava.[420] The numbers in parentheses indicate the number of workers in each category; when no number is specified, only one man was in charge of that position. As for the cooks, two men set out on that particular voyage, as well as three stewards. No cadets undertook this voyage; they are included in the diagram to offer a complete overview.

The schema generally corresponds with the situation on Czechoslovak ships in the 1960s, 1970s, and partially even the 1980s. Originally, in the first years of ocean shipping (the first half of the 1950s) more than fifty crew members sailed on the ships, including jobs such as carpenter or stoker. But with the introduction of modern technology, the crew (mainly lower positions) was reduced.

What did these ship professions deal with more specifically? Starting with the most "visible" men on the ship working on deck, I will move to

---

[420] NA_140: File about the ship Bratislava's collision, crew list, 1981.

the "hidden" group in the engine room. Then I will comment on the professions providing necessary services (cooks and stewards) and conclude with two specialized professionals—radio officer and doctor.

8.1.1 Seafarers working on the deck

A great part of the deck crew members were recruited from the Czechoslovak Elbe Oder Shipping [Československá plavba labsko-oderská] Vocational School. They completed a bargee apprenticeship and started working on barges, sailing on the rivers connecting Czechoslovakia with the seas—the Elbe, the Oder (and the Danube in Slovakia). At this school they gained necessary knowledge for their future seafaring profession, e.g. how to operate the ship devices, moor, or navigate. Later—when some graduates entered Czechoslovak Ocean Shipping (COS)—they gained more expertise working on ocean ships. After completing their practice and passing examinations, they could be gradually promoted from the third rank ("deck hand") to "ordinary seaman". Then they could aspire to the first rank of "able body" seaman and finally to the highest function—boatswain.

When a man wanted to be promoted to the officer's position, he needed relevant education: after graduation from high school, students could be admitted to a maritime academy abroad.[421] Theoretically, it was possible for a man to be promoted from the lowest to the highest position in the ship hierarchy—that of the master: higher education wasn't necessary until the boatswain position and apprenticeship on the ship was enough. Only once a man became a boatswain, he could start studying at a specialized high school (the above mentioned Elbe Oder Shipping Vocational School offered such a programme of study) and apply for the third educational level—the academy. After graduating from the academy, such an officer started with a cadet position and then, having fulfilled the

---

421 Czechoslovaks mainly studied in the former Soviet Union—with Odessa as the main location, Kaliningrad and Klaipeda exceptionally; Poland—Szczecin, Gdynia; Bulgaria—Varna. More (incomplete) information is available on ship masters (113 in totals): in the post-WWII period about 58 per cent of the students graduated in the Soviet Union; 37 per cent in Poland; the rest in Bulgaria and Yugoslav Rijeka. /Námořní plavba, "Námořní školy," http://www.namornip lavba.cz/cnp/2436.html (as of 20 February 2015), [web about the COS history, page Naval Academies]./

required practice and exams, he could get promoted. The mechanism of promotion to senior positions depended on education and work experience in all the ship's departments.

However, in reality this "great leap" from a deck hand to a ship master was unlikely to happen; seafarers studying at the academy had to interrupt their work, and earned less, while the company had to look for substitutes on the ships for several months or years. Thus, the company offered the possibility of studying at a university abroad mainly to graduates from various high schools, with either a general or technical specialization.

> I finished the high school there [...] and came across something in our library [...] a book *The Sea Calls for the Brave*.[422] So I thought, 'Hey Peter, you're brave, so march out of here to the sea'. I applied for the COS. [...] But as there was no reply coming from them, I went for technology in Brno, as I'd have had free living there, at my grandma's. [...] And when the technical university accepted me, the company replied that they accepted me, too.[423]

When this man continued describing the circumstances of his application for the COS (getting employment and studying with the support of the company), he also touched upon the issue of unequal opportunities, or some selectivity when choosing the people who should work abroad. The communist state's effort strived to control its citizens, keep them behind strictly guarded borders and let only the "reliable" ones (loyal to the regime) travel abroad. Thus before being admitted to the company, every man had to go through a complicated process examining his "reliability".

> Of course, in those times they checked me and interviewed me at home, and I had references, that's the way it went at those times. One had to be reliable and couldn't have any political problems. I even had to go through an interview at the local authority so that they could see, what sort I am.[424]

---

422 Vojmír Šimonek, *Moře volá odvážné* (Praha: Práce, 1959).
423 P. K., * 1944, ship master, 36 years in the COS.
424 M. S., * 1939, chief engineer, 26 years in the COS.

> I realized when self-critiquing myself that in that selection there could have been a boy captivated by seafaring since childhood, really keen on it, and that I overleapt him just because of my communist references. In a way it was something like self-pity that I took a job from someone.[425]

> Obviously, it entailed long rigmaroles of inspections. I was interviewed by caretakers and the like. It all resolved after three quarters of a year by a telegram one day, and then I set off.[426]

Similarly to all other institutions at that time, the COS had a politically oriented personnel department responsible for checking loyalty to the Communist Party and acquiring, processing, and evaluating information on all the employees,[427] including the applicants.[428] On the other hand, available resources indicate that the COS personnel department was not always successful in this effort because it was facing a permanent shortage of maritime professionals, especially officers; thus one's expertise was often put above his political loyalty. As a result, the political situation on ships was "bad" from the communist perspective; one State Security document even notes that "it is no exception that only one Communist Party member works on the ship and lives almost in illegality".[429] (See more on the issue of Communist Party membership below in the section "The impacts of the communist regime on ocean shipping").

Returning to the description of the ship's crew and its duties, let's expand on this overview starting from the highest rank, the ship master. He performed his duties in accordance with the Czechoslovak laws and regulations as well as international conventions and practices.[430] As for

---

425 J. V., * 1964, A/B sailor, 6 years in the COS.
426 Interview with I. P., * 1950, doctor, 13 years n the COS.
427 Vladimíra Hradecká and František Koudelka, *Kádrová politika a nomenklatura 1969–1974* [Personnel Policy and Nomenclature 1969–1974] (Praha: Ústav pro soudobé dějiny, 1998), 117.
428 I am considering here the situation after the Warsaw Pact armies' invasion to Czechoslovakia in 1968, during the so-called normalization when the Communist Party strengthened its leading role in society (see more in the chapter dedicated to the 1970s). As for the 1950s and 1960s, political issues and ideological correctness were assured not only by the head of the Communist Party group on a ship but also (mainly) by the ship master's deputy for political affairs. The activities of these persons varied in accordance with the current political situation (i. e. tougher in the 1950, moderate in the 1960).
429 ABS_36: Evaluation of the situation in the COS as of 31 August 1989.
430 The most important was the International Convention for the Safety of Life at

the deck department, the ship master had a deputy called the chief mate, who supervised the ship's technical condition and cargo (he prepared plans of loading and unloading, performed calculations to ensure the ship's stability, etc.). The 2nd mate managed and maintained all the navigational aids and devices, including maps; he was responsible for the navigation bridge and navigation cabin; before the ship left the port, he outlined courses for the entire journey; when a doctor was absent on the ship, the 2nd mate also provided first aid. The 3rd mate took care of the entire rescue and fire-fighting equipment on the ship. Beside this, all the three mates took turns in guard duties held on the bridge.[431] During this service they monitored the ship's position, direction and speed; they recorded all the data into maps and log books. They could not change the direction and speed without the captain's approval, unless forced to urgently deal with unexpected danger.

The lower positions working in the deck department were sailors of three qualification levels under the boatswain's direction. The boatswain managed the day-shift of the deck crew and was responsible (to the chief mate) for the ship's overall maintenance (with the exception of machinery). As for sailors, they spent a great portion of their time painting the corrosion that the ships suffered due to the sea water and salty environment. Apparently, a good boatswain can be recognized from a distance—by the ship's appearance. The sailors in the deck department also had to secure the cargo, moored and unmoored the ship during

---

Sea (SOLAS) issued by the International Maritime Organization (first issued in 1914 as a response to the Titanic sinking in 1912). The Czechoslovak Socialist Republic became an IMO member on 1 October 1963. In the domestic context, the fundamental Act was 61/1952 Coll., On maritime navigation.

431 The working hours of the services; the officer served accompanied by sailors; a similar regime was valid for the engine department. Sentry duties held during the cruising:

chief mate	08:00–12:00	20:00–24:00
2nd mate	04:00–08:00	16:00–20:00
3rd mate	00:00–00:04	12:00–16:00

Services held in roadsteads and ports (with the main task of overseeing the ship's loading and unloading):

chief mate	08:00–16:00
2nd mate	16:00–24:00
3rd mate	00:00–00:08

manoeuvres in ports (the boatswain dropped the anchor). They also worked with wood, glass, or prepared and adjusted the ship's winches and booms. Together with the appropriate officer, they keep watch.

8.1.2 Seafarers working in the engine room

Engine staff did not need any "special" education. The lower positions were performed by graduates from various jobs from machinists to mechanics and machine operators from vocational schools or secondary technical schools. Once they became familiar with the ship's engine and other devices and had served on ships for some years, they could aspire to the storekeeper position (a petty-officer function rank). The officer positions required a diploma from technical universities as well as considerable experience.

> It was six of us, all cadets sent to a machine. Unusually high number. But they needed new people then. They even made an exception for machinists graduating from Czech schools [this narrator graduated from Brno Technical University], that they didn't have to go for two-year service but just for one year. And after that they could take an exam at the Ministry of Transport to become the 3rd officer. [...] Some guys went for just one or two ships and managed to take advantage of this exception that year, because after that it was no longer possible. At that time, I was sailing my second ship Orlík somewhere in Tunisia. They didn't want to bring me ashore by plane because of the exams, they told me to wait until arrival in Poland. But of course we got delayed, so we arrived in Poland on the day of the exams. And that's why I couldn't take advantage of the exception and had to board the third ship as a machinist cadet. It was the ship called Vítkovice, where I finished my years of practice. I think it was fair to go through the cadet position, and that everyone has to start from scratch on the sea. However, those who studied at naval schools did just half of the practice. And at those times of exception, it was enough for them to do just a half a year of practice to take the exams, just one voyage. But this shows then in practice.[432]

As for daily duties executed in this department, the chief engineer was solely responsible for the machinery section and did not hold a watch duty. He was directly subordinated to the ship master, directly superior to the crew of the entire engine department. He was responsible for the operation, function, and repairs of all machinery equipment as well as for keeping the wastewater clean. Other engineer officers (the 2nd, 3rd,

---

432 J. T., * 1951, 2nd engineer, 19 years in the COS.

4th) shared responsibilities for machinery sub-sections and took turns in holding watch duty in the engine room to check that the machines were running correctly. Beside these men, an electrical engineer was responsible for the operation of the entire electrical equipment; he was directly subordinated to the chief engineer (and superior to the electrician).

The storekeeper had a similar position in the engine room as the boatswain on the deck. He supervised the engine crew to ensure that the main tasks were carried out smoothly (including the necessary repairs). Not only did the crew have to often repair the main motor driving propeller and auxiliary engines producing electric power; they also dealt with the whole range of machines starting from the evaporator producing non-potable water from sea water, and continuing to pumps, rudder, reloading equipment, refrigerators, air conditioners, gyrocompass, and navigation devices. Furthermore, the engine department had to manage both the big Diesel engine and the mechanics and electronics. Engaged in such tasks day after day, facing different conditions and the vagaries of the weather, the machine crew as well as the deck crew highly appreciated good meals prepared in the ship's kitchen.

8.1.3 Seafarers working in the kitchen and in services

Cooks and stewards[433] could become seafarers without any specific qualification. These men did the same work on the ship as on land with the only difference that on the ship they dealt with more difficult conditions because of tilting.

---

[433] The COS did not employ women as seafarers, even in occupations such as cook or steward because employment of women in continuous ship operation would be in contradiction to the Labour Code from 1965, mainly §149 and 150 (related internal COS directives on the issue are not available). It can be assumed that woman's work was not allowed from a practical point of view—leaving women to maternity with the stereotype that mothers are most important for child care, this assumption disqualified women from another embarkation after childbirth.

It's harder, when swinging, when you're bumping along for fourteen or fifteen days without stopping, all the time, bang, bum, sides, here and there. [...] It never happened, in all that time when cruising, and I'd spent there twenty-two years net time, that I wouldn't have cooked a meal. I was cooking in whatever weather. Not even a single time did I serve a t n. Never. I always did my best to prepare fresh and hot meals.[434]

The scope of the work that particular cooks and stewards did developed on the position. The chief cook prepared the meat, cooked the sauces, managed the stocks and fulfilled the role of a purser deputy; the 2nd chef took care of breakfasts, prepared the soups, side dishes, desserts, baked rolls and bread; the 3rd cook (if the position was occupied) took care of the supplementary jobs and dishwashing. As for two stewards—they served meals in the dining rooms (there were separate dining rooms for the crew and for officers) and took care of the housekeeping of the captain's and top officers' cabins. When the 3rd steward position was occupied, this man was dedicated to housekeeping, cleaning, and doing the laundry during long voyages; the laundry was otherwise provided by laundries in the ports (seafarers changed towels once a week and bedding every two weeks).

The food served on the Czechoslovak ships was always of a high quality and in sufficient quantity (one of the narrators mentioned, for example, races in schnitzels eating[435]). Cooks prepared hearty breakfasts, three-course lunch and two-course dinner menus; they prepared ice cream and baked rolls and bread,[436] cakes, and even Christmas sweets. The ships were supplied with quality ingredients, sometimes even with those unavailable on the domestic market. For example, a man born in 1963 remembered that until his thirties he had not known how olives taste like. On the other hand, becoming a seafarer, a man would eat olives served with pâté...

---

434 J. K., * 1946, chief cook, 22 years in the COS.
435 Ibid.
436 "In the USA, my meeting: grandma and grandpa: 'We are former emigrants'. I don't know, they may have emigrated in 1948. And they said: 'We see a Czech flag. Do you need anything, young men?' They got some food and the biggest shock for them was: 'Wow, you've got bread'. [...] Next day they turned up with a gallon of Scotch. 'That's for the bread. And would you have more?' 'Well, of course'. The cooks baked more bread for them, and they were so happy, satisfied, perhaps homesick". /V. B., * 1944, storekeeper, 27 years in the COS./

The kitchen department was headed by a purser, a graduate from an economic university,[437] who led the department staff and managed the stock of foods. He ensured food quality, dealt with customs officers in ports, stored the seafarers' passports and other documents, paid the salaries in cash in foreign currencies, etc. The purser ranked among the supreme ship command responsible directly to the captain, along with the chief mate and chief engineer officer and two more professions described below.

8.1.4 Seafarers providing medical care and ensuring communication

Both the doctor and the radio officer needed highly professional education for their jobs on ships. Actually, some ships sailed without a doctor:

> There wasn't much interest. The salary wasn't a big deal and people would lose their career. Or thought they were losing it. [...] We were so-called 're-serve' for Ocean Shipping. But they had to keep you a place in a hospital. Still, there were bosses who wouldn't want to do this favour. But I had a fantastic senior consultant, who enjoyed doing that favour. Anyway, they were quite demanding in terms of qualification. Practice in hospital, surgery or medical ward.[438]

The shortage in doctors was addressed in, for example, 1974, when the COS management reported a substantial agreement reached with the Ministry of Health, which was supposed to ensure a sufficient number of doctors for ships[439] (ship doctors remained employees of the health sector, excluded from the enterprise's permanent staff). Despite this agreement, also in 1976 (and again in 1981 and 1983) the company failed to employ doctors for different reasons. Many of the doctors who embarked for ship service (based on orders from the Ministry of Health) had no interest in embarking or they were only interested in embarking for one or two voyages. Physicians who had already worked on ships were willing to work only temporarily or their employer did not allow them longer service on ships.[440]

---

437 Similarly to previous departments, cooks and stewards were apprenticed in their profession, and they could be promoted according to the number of years of service.
438 Interview with I. P., * 1950, doctor, 13 years in the COS.
439 NA_138: Material No. 25 for the management meeting held on 21 March 1975.
440 NA_139: Material No. 39 for the management meeting held on 7 March 1977.

Although some ships had to sail off without a doctor, such a practice was impossible in the case of the radio officer (both in terms of safety and international regulations). The radio officer was not only the person indispensable for the ship's navigation; he was also a man who held (to a great extent) an information monopoly on the ship.

> Only radio connection was possible then, radio guys sailed the ships, every day there was a certain hour assigned for sending messages to the company. Mostly it was monthly reports, namely fuel consumption, position and things like that. At the same time the ship was receiving instructions from the company with some delay. There was also unofficial messaging going on between the radio guys about what's up there. Postal service worked only in the ports, for example newspapers, magazines, and letters. And when you're on the ship for about a month, crossing the Pacific takes over a month, you learn the news pretty late.[441]

Among other responsibilities, the radio officer got information about the ports that the ship was approaching, when to unload the cargo in the port or the status of the cargo preparation, etc. When necessary, he ordered food, repairs, and spare parts via radio. Quite importantly, the radio officer obtained information required for the ship's voyage, e.g. weather reports and calls on safety of navigation (information about military manoeuvres, changes in lighthouse operation or malfunctions of navigation equipment; reports on glaciers, wrecks, dead whales, large floes, etc.). All the mentioned objects and other obstacles had to be reported within an international emergency frequency. At this frequency, listening to SOS signals is obligatory: every hour there are two three-minute periods designated for SOS calls and broadcasting is prohibited. Everything on the waves goes silent and everyone must listen if any vessel needs help. All ships are ready to help.

But SOS situations were exceptional (though some Czechoslovak ships also participated in rescue events); most of the time the seafarers performed their everyday duty. Regardless of their job or status in the ship's hierarchy, their work was to some extent influenced by the activities of the Communist Party.

---

441 J. T., * 1951, 2nd engineer, 19 years in the COS.

8.2 "One had to decide"[442] (the impacts of the communist regime[443] on ocean shipping)

Today, when you speak with people about former Czechoslovak seafarers, the first misconception about seafarer's work is that this was an amazingly adventurous profession. The second (sometimes even the first) misconception is the belief that the seafarers had to be loyal to the communist regime or (and) cooperate with the State Security (the strength of this conviction varies). Awareness of how the communist regime restricted the freedom of movement indeed makes one believe that seafarers got this privilege in exchange for showing their loyalty to the regime. In reality, however, the role of the communist regime in the operation of the company and ships is rather complicated. Basically, there were two forms of activities that the regime performed among seafarers: 1) those of the organizations supporting the communist regime, the Communist Party of Czechoslovakia in the first case; 2) the State Security's control of seafarers.

The ships were part of Czechoslovak territory, so they followed the same regime as "onshore". Firstly, it meant that there were representatives on the ships from both the Communist Party and social organizations, the trade union, and youth union, so-called "gear levers" of socialism.[444] This enterprise-wide Party organization operated in conformity

---

[442] Paraphrase from the interview with M. B., * 1949, chief engineer, 29 years in the COS.
[443] The Communist Party's leading role in the country was embedded in the Constitution "as late as" in 1960. However, the provisions (democratic to some extent) of the 1948 Constitution often proclaimed what the regime did not follow in practice; so they were circumvented, modified, and upgraded in order to promote the Communist Party's interests.
[444] The essence of the system lay in the fact that the organizations gathered citizens based on their interests, which the communist power used and abused for its own needs. Thus, by satisfying the citizens' interests, the social organizations, which formed the "democratic facade" of the regime, were supposed to demonstrate that the majority of citizens willingly consent to the Communist Party. It worked as a tool of enforcing political decisions and encouraged citizens in implementing communist intentions. The largest organizations in the system were the Revolutionary Trade Union Movement and the Socialist Union of Youth. /Karel Kaplan, *Kořeny československé reformy 1968, II* [Roots of the Czechoslovak Reform 1968] (Praha: Doplněk, 2002), 386./

with the state Communist Party's policy.⁴⁴⁵ The head of the enterprise Communist Party organization ranked among the senior management, thus participating in the company's strategic decisions; he also managed the ships' Party cells. However, the distance between these two parts of the Communist Party (in Prague vs. around the world) needs to be considered. In fact, life on the ships was largely isolated from that in Czechoslovakia, and information exchange was slow (see the next section about life on ships).

Another very important variable in crew organization was the ship's hierarchy: while on land the leading force influencing the political, social, economic, and cultural aspects was the Communist Party, on the ship the supreme responsibility for the ship's operation, cargo, and human lives belonged to the captain. The problem began when even in this hierarchical arrangement the Communist Party tried to enforce its leading position. This sometimes led to contradictions: on the one hand the captain's responsibilities were given by law and the ships operated in an international arena outside the "supreme power of the Communist Party"; on the other hand, there was the leading position of the Communist Party in Czechoslovak society on land, affecting life on board.

> Yes, the captain is in command. But there were times when the Party leader or trade unionists gave the captain a grilling at a Party meeting. Which is absurd. This cannot happen. And this is something that doesn't exist today or in Western companies. They have a hierarchy, the captain is a captain, and whatever he says is right, and needs to be respected. If you want to complain, write it up, or deal with it outside the ship. The ship isn't meant for tackling some problems. The ship is for working there.⁴⁴⁶

This testimony adds to the absurdity, further illustrated by the fact that the captain's function belonged to the category of so-called nomencla-

---

445 The Communist Party employed two forms of control—direct and indirect. Indirect control, and it was also the case of the COS, was executed through Communists working in enterprises; these Communists applied the Communist Party's decisions and directives in their work place. Direct control was present in those organizations where the highest communist management assigned tasks and participated in their functioning within the organization. /Kaplan, *Kořeny československé reformy 1968,* 154./

446 M. B., * 1949, chief engineer, 29 years in the COS. This narrator remembered not only the past practice but also his experience with ship management today, as he has been employed by a foreign ship owner.

ture functions, i.e. those controlled by the Communist Party from the Central Committee of the Communist Party of Czechoslovakia level to the company-wide committee level. It did not play a role if the inspected person was a member of the CPC or not.[447] Yet at the same time, one of the key conditions for reaching the top of the ship hierarchy was membership in the Communist Party.

> They forced you and didn't force you. It was up to everyone. In the end, I entered [the Communist Party] for a while. That was when I was a captain. Three times I managed to get by, but this time I thought, 'Well, who cares.' Cos' they were having their Party meetings, deciding things, and didn't inform me about anything. It wasn't enough to be a captain to get invited. They told me, 'If you're not in the party, it's none of your business.' So in the end I thought: 'What can you do, twit, you have to join to get informed'. But this happened just before the end of it [before 1989], so I'd been a member for two and a half years.[448]

As this testimony confirms, Communist Party members sometimes intervened in the ship hierarchy—especially when refusing to inform a captain about all their activities and decisions (although the final responsibility for the crew, ship, and cargo rested only with the captain). The captain's experience also shows that in some periods it was possible to perform this highest function as a non-member of the Party. It can be explained by the company's need for a good professional work force (accentuated in the chapter describing the 1970s and the period of so-called normalization).

The COS management actually had to decide to what extent the Party membership was a condition for holding the role. Of course, there was pressure on captains' membership in the Communist Party.

> If you weren't in the Party, you could have passed the exams for captain and have all the qualifications and still you wouldn't become a captain for years. You were not trustful. At most you could sail as the chief mate, the master's deputy.[449]

---

447 This system was supposed to ensure the absolute influence of the Communist Party on the structuring power elites. /Hradecká and Koudelka, *Kádrová politika a nomenklatura KSČ 1969–1974*, 86–93./
448 P. K., * 1944, ship master, 36 years in the COS.
449 V. S., * 1942, ship master, 26 years in the COS.

I entered the Party many years later when one had to [emphasis] decide whether to carry on or stay stuck in a low function.[450]

This insistence on political loyalty together with the high qualification demands on the master and (high) officer positions led to a frequent shortage of qualified seafarers, mainly high ranking officers, able to operate all the ships. The problem was solved by hiring officers from abroad; for example, captains from the Soviet Union exclusively were brought in even though it was rather costly.[451]

Generally speaking, the company (along with the general state/Party policy) strove to prefer Communist Party's members in the COS, especially for the higher functions in order to establish "loyal" crews. Here a loyal person could signify also an "obedient" person (a man who kept his job, did not consider emigration, a reliable employee). However, this "political loyalty" came into conflict with individual attitudes, needs and experience and at the same time "loyalty" (and the punishment of the "disloyal") varied in each decade of the communist regime in Czechoslovakia.

Regarding the influence of communist policy on ships, few materials are available. For instance, an illustrative document from the beginning of "normalization" deals with "manifestations of terror in the COS in 1968–1969". It states that the origins of the poor political activity on Czechoslovak vessels are "as old as the company itself". Apparently, during the formation of the COS, there were virtually no experts in the maritime shipping industry with a strong political background, so the ships' teams were formed from people working in the maritime field already during the First Republic.[452] Given the specificity of the job, these people became indispensable experts and "absolute rulers" in the field. Those recruited later from the Party were "assimilated" by the old experts, thus

---

450 M. B., * 1949, chief engineer, 29 years in the COS.
451 ABS_37: Problems with providing ships with crews, 26 May 1989.
Some of the available crew lists show that officer functions were also hired from other countries: the crew consisted from Soviet, and mainly Polish seafarers, and there was one Hungarian. At the beginning of the COS's operation, mixed Chinese–Czechoslovak crew included also Greeks or Bulgarians. /NA_141: Book of crew members, the Republika I./
452 Period from the new Czechoslovak state constitution in 1918 until the Munich Agreement in 1938.

accepting (appreciating) the former policy, which had origins in the First Republic.[453] Because the First Republic was based on the democratic principles, these old tendencies on the ship were not to be tolerated.

The quoted document depicts this conflict as the need for a crew that would be both politically "reliable" and at the same time able to operate the ship in a professional way. Career reasons were also stressed when getting recruited into the Communist Party. The prospect of promotion to a higher function was the biggest incentive.

8.2.1 State Security activities among seafarers

The seafarers were also the subject of the State Security's interests (see more in the chapter on the 1970s). Here I will reflect on these issues from the micro-perspective—as perceived by the former seafarers themselves. In addition to their own employees (officers or members), the State Security used secret collaborators recruited from the population. This secret network consisted of: 1) agents (the most capable collaborators acquired for cooperation based on compromising materials, patriotic motives, or material benefits); 2) informants (committed on the basis of patriotic or compromising materials; they provided information about enemy elements in their surroundings); 3) residents (secret collaborators who controlled the work of other secret agents; they were recruited from experienced agents or informants or from the former employees of the Ministry of the Interior); 4) owners of conspiratorial flats (the contract obliged the owner to conceal that his/her flat is used for the State Security's needs; therefore he/she was regarded as a secret collaborator); 5) confidantes (politically mature citizens with the opportunity, ability, and desire to inform about partial knowledge from their environment important with respect to the State Security's interests).[454]

The preserved materials indicate that COS employees-collaborators ranked among the agent and confident categories, mainly. Besides using a secret collaborators' network, the State Security collected information and reports prepared by high managers, whose job description included this obligation. As for "ordinary" people, the most common rea-

---

453 ABS_3: Manifestations of terror in the COS in the years 1968–1969, 27 May 1970.
454 Koudelka, *Státní bezpečnost 1954–1968*, 46–47.

sons for cooperation (except for gaining a personal benefit or at least expecting it) followed from the State Security's three wide extortionate strategies: 1) threatening that if one refuses to cooperate, someone from his/her family will be damaged; 2) threatening that a man would not be allowed to travel, therefore forcing a seafarer to abandon his beloved profession; 3) holding over the seafarers their "weakness" such as alcoholism, amorous relations, monetary machinations, smuggling, black marketeering, etc. These were the reasons why the State Security collected this type of personal information extensively.

Here I do not aim to judge or blame those former seafarers who, in some form, were forced (or they decided) to cooperate with the State Security (this task needs to be performed by other researchers and institutions). I mainly strive to depict the main features of the collaboration system in the COS context. Here I am interested in the State Security's collaborators, and not the repressive body itself (officers, decision-makers, etc.). Especially noteworthy is today's public discourse (in the media, film, television), which pays disproportionately greater attention (in the negative sense) to collaborators of the former State Security than to its actual members and perpetrators. This practice (taking into account the power of the media) has probably distorted the perception of co-operation, which is now perceived as almost as despicable as the repressive body itself. Even a suspicion of collaboration is (could be) a stigma that harms personal lives, private relationships, or friendly ties.

Due to this stigmatization, it is not surprising that no former collaborator appeared in my oral history project. Either those seafarers did not respond to my request for an interview, or they managed to conceal the fact during the interview (which is not very likely). Thus the State Security activities on the vessels among seafarers or their collaboration with the State Security will be disclosed through the eyes of non-collaborators.

Looking closely at collaboration with the State Security, the oral history interviews reveal the following facts: 1) former seafarers did not mention spontaneously the theme of collaboration with the State Security in their memories; some of them even completely omitted the issue; 2) when I directly asked them about this form of collaboration, they often downplayed the scope, importance, and seriousness of collaborative activities; 3) none of the narrators was significantly damaged by the State Security's activities. These outputs indicate that the narrators did not find the topic worth mentioning. This finding raises the question of why they took this passively-defensive attitude towards my questions about the State Security.

The answer is not simple. Firstly, there is the sense of nostalgia, and the narrators tended to idealise their life spent on the sea, thus chasing any troublesome memories away (collaboration with the State Security belongs to the most frightening memories). Secondly, the seafarers' evasive attitude can be grounded in their fear that information could be misused (although our relationship between narrator and interviewer was ruled by valid legislation and the necessary contractual arrangement).

Yet another aspect that should not be overlooked is the sense of shame. The former seafarers are still very proud of their work. They worked hard in difficult conditions and feel convinced that no one in communist Czechoslovakia worked as hard as they did. On the other hand, today they are confronted with the fact that some of their colleagues were collaborating with the State Security. Here they can feel a sense of shame for their passivity, for their passive attitude when someone was (or could be) harmed because of the State Security collaborators' work. I would even argue that they did not speak about this theme because they do not reflect on (or do not want to) this sense of shame on the intentional level of their consciousness. But still, this shame is traceable on the unintentional level.[455]

To conclude this complex issue, I would say that the COS employees on board or at the headquarters collaborated with the State Security to a similar extent as other firms or groups in Czechoslovakia. Still, the collaboration of crew members with the State Security had a specific feature—the quite complicated and lengthy communication, which caused practical complications, above all providing out-dated information. Because they often sailed for months all over the world, collaborators

---

[455] The analysis and interpretation of oral history interviews allows for the identification of the meanings of the "silent places" in narratives.

could hardly get caught. Still, the primary task of the ships and seafarers was to transfer goods. Some details about work on the ships as well as non-working and leisure time will reveal the next section, mainly through the seafarers' memories.

8.3 "Is the sea salty? I really wanted to know!"[456] (travelling and emigration)

From the very beginning of this book, I have been repeatedly saying that in the context of former Czechoslovakia, seafarers' jobs were very exceptional, because among other things, they offered an opportunity to travel abroad. Before the voyage, and that was a crucial moment, the Czechoslovak authorities had to issue the seafarer with his passport and the so-called permanent exit visa to all countries of the world.[457] With these documents the seafarer could go abroad and travel around there almost independently. In every port where the ship dropped anchor, the seafarer could go away from the ship in his free time after he received approval from the local authorities. Even if his passport was held by the purser, he always had his Seaman's Book,[458] thus possessing an important identity document abroad.

Considering this genuine freedom of movement, much to my surprise the narrators did not associate their decision to work as seafarers with travelling opportunities or with the chance to get beyond the Iron Curtain. If they ever talked about travelling, then only in the sense of being

---

456 Paraphrase from the interview with J. J., 1952–2014, A/B sailor, 18 years in the COS.
457 This exit visa entitled its holder to travel virtually anywhere in the world; it could be issued essentially only for business purposes. /Jan Rychlík, *Cestování do ci-ziny v habsburské monarchii a v Československu* [Traveling Abroad in the Habsburg Monarchy and Czechoslovakia] (Praha: Ústav pro soudobé dějiny AV ČR, 2007), 69./
458 The Seaman's Book is a common name for the Seafarer's Identity Document created under the provisions of the International Labour Organization's Convention No. 108 from 1958 (last revision 2003, No. 185) as an internationally recognized identity document for seafarers; however, it does not substitute the passport. /International Labour Organization, "C185 – Seafarers' Identity Documents Convention (Revised), 2003 (No. 185)," http://www.ilo.org/dyn/norml ex/en/f?p=NORMLEXPUB:12100:0::NO::P12100_INSTRUMENT_ID:312330 (as of 29 October, 2014)./

able to travel to foreign countries, especially to exotic ones. They almost did not reflect on the fact that the majority of people in Czechoslovakia did not have this opportunity before 1989.

When the narrators were talking about the first voyage, they had very vivid memories. Especially those who worked on Czechoslovak ocean ships from their school years until retirement.

> We endocked and next morning we were somewhere on the Red Sea. And the vessel started to pitch from side to side. [...] And I had never seen the sea before. I went out to watch the sea, well, I didn't see much because it was foggy. [...] I really wanted to know if the sea is salty, if it is salty at all, so I secretly casted the bucket, and I drew the bucket up with some salt water, I dipped my fingers into it, and I tasted it, 'Wow, it's salty indeed! So, the sea is salty'.[459]

On the contrary, the seafarers who studied at the maritime academy did not reflect upon the topic of their first sea voyage. Since they underwent maritime training on a merchant ship within their school curriculum, the first voyage on a Czechoslovak ship was just a continuation of school voyages. When remembering their beginnings, the most important moment was their education, or better, the living and working conditions in the place of their study—the former Soviet Union or Poland.

Generally speaking, the older narrators-seafarers recollected the moment of their first journey outside the borders of socialist Czechoslovakia more often than the younger ones. This probably reflects the development and changes of the communist regime: for example, it is almost impossible to compare the travel options in the 1950s (when the oldest narrators first went abroad) and in the 1980s (when the youngest narrators undertook their first voyage). What is closely related to the issue of the communist regime on the one hand, and travelling possibilities on the other, is emigration.

8.3.1 Emigration

To introduce the theme, I will offer some basic "hard" data on seafarers' emigration. Although the COS archive file does not provide a comprehensive list of emigrants, there is data on emigration in the years 1968–1969. Apart from 1948, these years are considered the most critical in

---
459 Interview with J. J., 1952–2014, A/B sailor, 18 years in the COS.

terms of emigration from socialist Czechoslovakia. Emigration came as a response to disillusionment, disappointment, and maybe a fear of the future after the Warsaw Pact invasion and the subsequent "normalization", which signalled a retreat from basically all the principles and ideas of the democratizing process of 1968. In the first month after the August invasion, 24 seafarers emigrated (more than half of them with their wives and children); three other men emigrated until the end of 1969.[460] These 27 COS employees represented about two per cent of the overall ship headcount in 1969.

Even though 27 seems to be a small number, it looks different when compared with the total emigration in Czechoslovakia. In the period 1968–1969 137,600 people emigrated, i.e. about one per cent of the population. Since 1970 the strict measures led to a decrease in emigration, so between 1970 and 1989 it is estimated that some 50,000 people emigrated).[461] Maybe these figures are influenced by the fact that for seafarers it was relatively easy to travel and emigrate, even with their whole families. Other important explanations include the slower "normalization" process in the COS, perhaps a greater desire for freedom, or fear of sanctions by the "normalizing" regime as a response to the events of 1968 on the ships. (I discussed this issue in more depth in the part dedicated to the year 1968 and in the chapter on the 1970s.)

Since I interviewed only men who did not emigrate, the following opinions and experiences are one-sided, witnessed by men who remained on ships and stayed in Czechoslovakia. Explaining their decision not to emigrate, these men mentioned similar reasons and rationalizing strategies as the majority of the population.[462]

---

460 NA_142: Material No. 43 for the management meeting, 16 May 1969; Meeting record No. 43 from the management meeting, 31 October 1969. In the next years, on average two seafarers per year emigrated (but this is probably an underestimation, stated based on known numbers); I calculate that there must have been at least 40 other emigrating men.
461 Průcha, *Hospodářské a sociální dějiny Československa II, 1945–1992*, 935.
462 More on the issue, see Miroslav Vaněk and Pavel Mücke, *Velvet Revolutions: An Oral History of Czech Society*, manuscript, the chapter "The ban on travel".

> This wasn't even possible. I had two more brothers, they all studied well, they were all well employed. My father was a teacher; he would have ended up in a sugar factory as a bag counter. You know, this would be impossible. If I had escaped, I would have devastated so many people. If I had been alone, it would have been a different story.[463]

> I considered that, of course, but I thought that if I emigrated, loads of people would be in a big shit. What was I missing? I wasn't missing anything, actually. I brought what I wanted, I always had a lot of money, I never lived in grinding poverty. And as a captain, I also had nice dollars, I had the least reason to do it.[464]

However, the seafarers often emphasized that they "could have stayed abroad"—thus implicitly drawing attention to their professional qualities, abilities and skills that would enable them to be employed anywhere abroad, including capitalist countries with a competitive labour market. The second narrator quoted above mentioned also some basic reasoning for staying: basically they did not lack anything because of being seafarers, which means they felt job self-satisfaction but also sufficient earnings.

At the same time, the narrators did not reflect on the problems or difficulties associated with the job—mainly separation from their family and difficult working conditions. They perceived these issues simply as a necessary and inevitable part of their profession, and they made up for this simply by being on the ship, at sea. Thus, once their basic needs were satisfied—they had their satisfactory earnings, and a relative freedom of movement—they began to entertain the importance of higher values such as one's home, family and friendship, relationships, a place where one belongs to and where one can return to.

> But I am the ordinary guy from that village, close to Frýdlant. So I would say, 'What I would do in Germany. I love Frýdlant and the Jizera Mountains, so I have no reason to emigrate'. I did not stay. I said, 'Don't be stupid, you better go home. Your mum is there and the brothers and that'.[465]

After this seafarer got married, his wife tried to persuade him to emigrate ("She was scared to return to that greyness. That made her keep

---

463 J. N., * 1943, boatswain, 30 years in the COS.
464 P. K., * 1944, ship master, 36 years in the COS.
465 M. B., * 1949, chief engineer, 29 years in the COS.

on persuading me to emigrate".[466]) Trying to convince her to stay at home, he worked out various strategies. He started with considering their parents. Then he argued that their children were about to attend the first class of primary school. Later he insisted that it would be difficult for him to start a new career abroad, which would have an impact on the family income.

However, almost in all interviews, the seafarer confessed or insinuated that they decided to stay to keep their own home. These memories and experiences thus imply a clear conclusion. If a person does not suffer materially, if he or she experiences job satisfaction and, especially, when he or she is not restricted in the fundamental right to freedom of movement, the certainty of home background and friends, family roots and ties to the home country have tremendous value for an individual.

8.4 "To make some extra money"[467] (salaries and black marketeering)

Besides the previously described possibility to travel, job satisfaction, and a certain element of addiction, I will now discuss the third important variable of the seafarer's professional life—remuneration. First, I will shortly describe the system of rewards in the sector, and then I will focus on the specificities in seafarers' remuneration, which—compared to "normal" Czechoslovak citizens—implied certain advantages.

As an illustrative example on seafarers' wages, I will present the data from 1972, when a new salary scale was introduced to increase seafarers' salaries. Since the archival resources are incomplete, I cannot convincingly argue that this arrangement was made because the current salaries had been inadequate with regard to their purchasing power, motivational value, and reward for hard work. Possibly, this measure was implemented in relation to the so-called normalization period to compensate to a certain extent for the citizens' disillusion after the year 1968 with some social benefits.[468]

---

466 Ibid.
467 Paraphrase from the interview with J. N., * 1943, boatswain, 30 years in COS.
468 Průcha, *Hospodářské a sociální dějiny Československa II, 1945–1992*, 901.

This change included mainly increasing the basic tariffs in the range from 2.8 per cent (2nd engine officer; motorman) to 11.6 per cent (boatswain), 13.5 (chief cook), or 14.9 (senior sailor). The average increase was 8.4 per cent.[469] The salary was composed of three parts: basic tariff, general extra pay,[470] additional pay for stays in the tropics. Beside this, overtime work was paid in a flat rate of 30 per cent (not for the captain and first officers), then there was a loyalty surcharge[471] and a 20 per cent surcharge for men who served as deputies of higher functions. Also repair and service work and other "dirty" work was rewarded in the form of additional payment, which was often much cheaper for the company than paying shipyard service. Finally, seafarers got (as other Czechoslovak employees) some bonuses according to the economic results of their enterprise,[472] and, moreover, they did not pay anything for food[473] and accommodation on the ship.

Although it was not a general rule, the salary arrangements also comprised of a surcharge for dangerous cargo (mainly explosive or dangerous chemicals) at the rate of 60 crowns ($2.2[474]) per every 10 commenced days of transport, including loading and unloading.[475] For ex-

---

469 NA_144: Material No. 67 for management meeting held on 20 August 1971, Proposal for salaries for Czechoslovak ship crews, 4, Salary inventory.
470 Extra pay for difficult conditions at work on ships—noise, vibration, climatic changes, health conditions in foreign countries, bad weather conditions, limitations of cultural activities, increased risks, etc. /Ibid., Proposal for salaries for Czechoslovak ship crews, 4, Decision of the Ministry of Transport, 2./
471 For category I it was approximately from 5 per cent (staying five years in the COS) to 19 per cent (27 years of service and more); in the lowest category this surcharge was 7 (five years) and 23 per cent (27 and more years). /Ibid., Proposal for salaries for Czechoslovak ship crews, 4, Salary inventory./
472 Ibid., Proposal for salaries for Czechoslovak ship crews, 4, Decision of the Ministry of Transport, 2–4, appendix 1.
473 Besides meals three-times per day, in a room called "the pantry", which was equipped with kitchen utensils, coffee, tea, bread, butter, jam, eggs were always available—everything necessary for a small snack during the day or night. In the evening, the cooks put other foodstuffs into the pantry for preparing cold snacks during the night, mainly for the seafarers on watch guard, but also: "When there was a binge in the cabin, some party, name date, birthday, it took its toll. [...] So I had to refill the pantry at twelve o'clock". /J. K., * 1946, chief cook, 22 years in the COS./
474 Here I use the exchange rate 27 crowns per $1 as it is stated in the document.
475 NA_144: Material No. 67 for management meeting held on 20 August 1971, Proposal for salaries for Czechoslovak ship crews, 3, Salary inventory.

ample, the seafarer received extra $4.40 (obviously paid in Czechoslovak crowns) for the voyage from Poland to Cuba, lasting 17 days plus one day loading and one unloading (transporting such strategic material was very fast).

When the seafarer was at home during his gap months, spending his holiday and overtime compensation, he received approximately 40–45 per cent of his salary, which was technically the basic salary tariff plus the loyalty surcharge.[476] This was a logical arrangement since the seafarer did not bring any benefits to the company when he was at home. However, this financial compensation could also be seen as implicitly following from the state economic policy to "reclaiming" a proportion of high incomes.[477] Thus seafarers tried to find temporary or part-time jobs while they were at home, either with their employer's permission or without it. This practice was generally prohibited by the company. We can again consider two reasons for this arrangement—it was either an effort to force a man to get a proper rest for the next months to be spent on board, or an effort not to allow him to increase his income (the official remuneration in a socialist society was characterized by an emphasis on income equality).

An important moment in seafarers' remuneration was the receipt of the "boarding bonus" (additional allowance) paid from the embarkation to the disembarkation day. The amount of bonuses is stated in the chart. The categories represent the seafarer's job position and the appropriate rate per day. The rows include all the years for which I found relevant information; the fee might have been modified in the meantime.

---

476 Ibid.
477 In comparison with other Czechoslovak employees, not all seafarers' salaries exceeded the average rate. For example, after the salary arrangements provided in 1972, the highest monthly salary (ship master) was assigned 7,790 Czechoslovak crowns and the lowest (junior sailor) was 1,650 crowns. /Ibid./ The average monthly salary in Czechoslovakia in 1972 was 2,091 crowns. /Statistická ročenka ČSSR 1973 [Statistical Yearbook of the Czechoslovak Socialist Republic 1973] (Praha: Státní nakladatelství technické literatury, 1973), 126./ Generally speaking, the lowest salary groups VI and VII were below the country's average.

	category I	category II	category III	category IV	category V	category VI	category VII[478]
1956	At this time the so-called deep sea allowance was divided into eight categories and each of them was sub-divided into five classes according to the area: 1) China; 2) India; 3) South America; 4) Mediterranean, Black Sea, Near East, North America; 5) remaining European lines. The highest rate (combination of category and area) was $2.95 per day and the lowest $0.48 per day.[479]						
1963	$2,20	$2,20	$1,80	$1,40	$1,40	$1,40	$0,70
1968[480]	$2.20	$1.80	$1.80	$1.40	$0.70	$0.70	$0.70
1970	$3.10	$2.80	$2.30	$2.30	$1.80	$1.80	$1.80
1973	$3.20	$2.90	$2.60	$2.30	$1.90	$1.80	$1.30
1977	$4.16	$3.77	$3.38	$2.99	$2.47	$2.34	$1.69
1980[481]	$5.75	$5.50	$4.75	$4.75	$3.75	$3.75	$3.75
1989	$6.61	$6.32	$5.46	$5.46	$4.31	$4.31	$4.31

Table 13: Overview of seafarers' additional allowances paid in $ 1956–1989[482]

Now I will offer an insight into the real value of this additional earning in foreign currency, for example, in 1973 for men assigned to the lowest

---

[478] Description of categories—I: ship master; II: chief mate, 1st engineer; III: other mates, purser, doctor; IV: boatswain, storekeeper, chief cook; V: 1st class sailors; VI: 2nd class motormen, cooks, senior stewards, sailors, cadets; VII: motormen assistants, junior stewards, junior sailors. /NA_144: Material No. 67 for management meeting held on 20 August 1971, Proposal for salaries for Czechoslovak ship crews, Decision of the Ministry of Transport, appendix 2./

[479] NA_145: Report on negotiations with the PRC, 10 October 1956.

[480] Námořní plavba, "Mzdy a platy," http://www.namorniplavba.cz/cnp/2433.html (as of 15 November 2014).

[481] In the salary arrangements of 1963, 1968, 1970 and 1980 the fee was calculated only for four groups; for better comparison I assigned fees to all seven groups based on job position descriptions.

[482] The data in the table is based on the following documents: 1963 – NA_87: Material for the counsel of the Ministry of Foreign Trade, Draft of salaries of Czechoslovak ship crews, 12 June 1963; 1970 – NA_146: Material No. 1 for management meeting held no 9 January 1970, Proposal for salaries reorganization; 1973 – NA_144: Material No. 67 for management meeting held on 20 August 1971, Proposal for salaries for Czechoslovak ship crews; 1977 – NA_147: Material No. 155 for management meeting held on 28 November 1977, Overview on the salaries in the COS; 1980 – NA_33: Material for the counsel of the Ministry of Foreign Trade, Draft of changes in salaries of Czechoslovak ship crews, 30 September 1980; 1989 – NA_148: Meeting record from the meeting related to the new salary arrangements given by the Federal Ministry of Transport, 19 April 1989.

category (VII). Each seafarer had to work on a ship from nine to twelve months.[483] Apart from these conditions, the seafarers were considered to have disembarked when the ship anchored in a European port, which was the company's strategy to decrease costs. This condition could further prolong the time of embarkation. For instance, a seafarer who spent nine months at sea earned $356 in total. From this amount, he had to send an obligatory one third to his account in the Živnostenská banka [Trade Bank]; he could then draw this money in Czechoslovakia in a form of "Tuzex vouchers".[484]

After this reduction, this seafarer still had $274. This amount, however, was paid in the currency of the state where the ship anchored.[485] The seafarer could draw this money after arriving at a port, and the amount was counted according to the number of days he had spent on the ship up to that moment. This way the valuable dollars could be "converted", for example, into invaluable Indian rupees or Soviet roubles.

Furthermore, the seafarer could exchange a part of his salary paid in crowns into a currency of another socialist country. At the beginning of the 1970s it was 600 crowns for categories I and II; 450 crowns for III and IV; and 350 crowns for categories V VI, and VII. These sums of money represented about eight per cent of the salary in the group with the highest salaries but about 18 per cent for the group with lowest sala-

---

483 The data is valid for the year 1976 /NA_139: Material No. 39 for the management meeting held on 7 March 1977/; in the 1980s the range was stated from six to ten months.

484 In the centralized bank system of socialist Czechoslovakia, the Živnostenská banka was the only one providing foreign exchange transactions. It administered all foreign accounts of Czechs and Slovaks working abroad, foreign companies operating in Czechoslovakia and some state institutions, such as those in the tourism field. All people working abroad were paid through this bank—in Tuzex vouchers. In Tuzex (TUZemský EXport = domestic export) shops people could then buy foreign, especially Western goods, but also some kinds of shortage and valuable home goods, e.g. Škoda cars in the 1980s. In Tuzex, people could pay with vouchers only (*bon*, *bony* in plural), which they got in Živnostenská banka in exchange for foreign currencies (the exchange of foreign currencies for *bony* represented also a chance of illicit trading); Czechoslovak crowns were not accepted in Tuzex. This way, foreign currency was siphoned from the population into the national economy.

485 NA_144: Material No. 67 for management meeting held on 20 August 1971, Proposal for salaries for Czechoslovak ship crews, 4, Decision of the Ministry of Transport, 4.

ries. This money was also used to purchase goods at the ship canteen, where the seafarers used to buy cigarettes, alcohol, chewing gum, and men's cosmetics. When the seafarer did not spend this amount, he could convert it to Tuzex vouchers in the rate 1 crown : 0.6 *bon*[486]. Considering that on the black market one *bon* was purchased for about three or four crowns in the 1970s, this was an extortionate rate. Eventually, this was yet another way of decreasing the seafarers' wage and equalizing their income. However, the seafarers could exchange the vouchers for crowns at the "black-market rate" and thus get extra money.

Best of all, as part of the salary was paid in $ and partially also in Tuzex vouchers, it enabled seafarers to purchase Western goods—a sign of luxury and higher living status, because these goods were hardly accessible for the rest of the population. Thus the seafarers devoted a great deal of effort to saving their money in other socialist countries, in order to have enough money to buy goods in capitalist states, especially electronics, clothing, cosmetics. Apart from saving the money, some of them were quite diligent and they also tried to "earn" some additional money in socialist or Third World countries, either to satisfy their immediate needs in a port or to simply enrich themselves by exchanging the money. ("It would do if you changed rouble into Finnish marks in Murmansk. [...] And in Hamburg you changed that for Western money. You definitely made some extra money".[487])

Thus it is not surprising that in countries such as the Soviet Union, Cuba, or India the seafarers were actively engaged on the black market. As one of them said, "a place in poverty was a good place for the seafarers".[488] Despite the fact that some narrators still perceive trading on the black market as something threatening because it was illegal at that time,[489] half of them shared these practices with me. However, no soon-

---

[486] NA_144: Material No. 67 for management meeting held on 20 August 1971, Proposal for salaries for Czechoslovak ship crews, 4, Decision of the Ministry of Transport, Appendix 3.
[487] J. N., * 1943, boatswain, 30 years in the COS.
[488] J. J., 1952–2014, A/B sailor, 18 years in the COS.
[489] "The impact of illegal activities of some of our workers on ships is wide; specifically, the General Prosecutor's Office inquiries into the ship Blaník". /NA_149:

er had they started to tell the story than they added that they had been forced by external circumstances, i.e. insufficient salary (mainly its dollar part) to fulfil their needs. Some of them circumspectly described these activities as those done by other seafarers; still, their personal experience is often evident in the narrative. They perceived that the most severe punishment for such professional misconduct was a loss of their beloved employment on ships.

> Hamburg–Murmansk. It was a 'business valley'. [...] This was a golden path. To Murmansk, we would take Montana Jeans, and some rubbish back. [...] Eh, caviar and this stuff. [...] But I wasn't of those who wanted to get rich. I just sold that for the indirect expenses. I was always very moderate. I was moderate in business. Always. I thought, 'I will be fired, and what next?' It wasn't worth it. [...] Busted and sacked. Jesus. Busted and sacked. This was unacceptable. The Blaník in Cuba. The scarves. The scarf affair. For, you know, the people were greedy. It is not as if he sold 10 scarves. He had to have a hundred. A hundred and more. [...] But I lived in such a, I could say, modesty, took it easy. I would flog one or two pairs of jeans, that wasn't that, everybody knew this. It wasn't an offence or something.[490]

Many black marketeering cases also confirm that this illegal trade and smuggling were inseparable. Interestingly enough, the Czechoslovak seafarers were rather inventive in this respect.

> I knew a trick, I can say that now. For example, in Sweden, they would pay quite a lot of money, there was the prohibition. And I had two secret caches in the kitchen, which nobody ever discovered. And why? Because I always stashed that into the machines—food processor and ice cream maker. And when the boys in blue [customs' officers] came, I turned on the two machines. You could stash twelve bottles into the big food processor. In the back by the drive belt. I knew exactly where to tuck the bottles.[491]

The first narrator quoted above referred also to the so-called "scarf affair". It is the most famous, and one of the largest, cases of smuggling and black marketeering which became a legendary already at the time. The incident occurred in the fall of 1975 on the ship Blaník. When passing through the Kiel Canal, the crew ordered from the ship supplier in Kiel, the company Zersen, more than ten thousand nylon scarves, 60

Management meeting record No. 3, 6 February 1976./
490 J. N., * 1943, boatswain, 30 years in the COS.
491 K. T., * 1943, chief cook, 38 years in the COS.

wigs, 64 metres of crimplene, a number of sweaters, perfumes, chewing gums, and razor blades. The purpose of this transaction was to sell these products in Cuba. The crew paid partly in cash and partly on credit. The passenger Ivone Scott Austin, who had a Cuban husband, was supposed to take the scarves in her luggage through the checks in the Cuban port of Mariel, pretending these were her personal belongings. However, she was detained by Cuban customs officers when she was putting the luggage into the car. The luggage with 3,128 scarves was confiscated. To the surprise of the crew members, she was not arrested by Cuban authorities, and because some seafarers met her later during their stay in Mariel, they believed that Scott was working for the Cuban security police.[492]

The detention of Scott was followed by the examination of the ship by Cuban border guards. During the examination, they found: chewing gums, wigs, razors, perfumes, and a small amount of scarves. The majority of the scarves were not found because 10,000 of them had been concealed in the steam boiler in the engine room, which could be electrically ignited from the machinery control room.[493]

This affair was reported not only to the COS director, but also to the Deputy Prime Minister of the Federal Government, the Minister of Foreign Trade and other governmental institutions. The company's director asked the General Prosecutor's Office to investigate the whole affair.[494] The director also decided to impose strict controls to stop black mar-

---

[492] Here I describe the case based on documents took by the Czechoslovak State Security's investigators approximately two months after the event. After 35 years, mentioning the same event, one of the former seafarers (not an eye witness) remembered, "There were always some greedy guts, who were smacking their lips in this abundance. So when one boaster had, by all means, in a Havana's marine club in front of everyone—I mean mainly in front of the Havana jacks and our snitches—lit up a Havana cigar with a ten peso banknote, everything was clear". /I. P., * 1950, doctor, 13 years in the COS./ This event may have occurred, but it is also possible that today the "legend" image fits better with the second episode rather than with the fact that the seafarers were revealed by a Cuban secret police collaborator, and by a woman on the top of that, a woman who sailed with them and planned the whole smuggling case with them.

[493] ABS_38: Record of the business trip to Poland, Investigation of black marketeering affair, 24 February 1976.

[494] NA_150: Management meeting record No. 5, 5 March 1976.

keteering and smuggling. An investigation throughout the company revealed overall breaches of discipline, in addition to other cases of smuggling, such as the sale of whiskey to traffickers in India with a net profit of $12,000.[495]

Most of these cases of illicit enrichment were considered as to "disturb moral-political status of some collectives".[496] Although I do not want to defend this behaviour of the seafarers and overlook the problems, I would like to offer one parallel. During the first voyage of the first Czechoslovak ship Republika, the crew complained about bad living conditions, which "some people" explained as poor political leadership (see the chapter on the 1950s). Twenty years later, the company used the same reasoning. Similarly, these problems were not exclusively of political or moral origin, but they arose from the wider context, be they poor working conditions and financial reward in the 1950s, the hollowness of communist ideology after the 1968 invasion, or disillusionment with the regime and loss of loyalty in the 1970s.

In the cases where this forbidden "business" was not revealed and punished, it undeniably had an impact on the increasing material standard of living of the seafarer and his family. Another advantage of the job was the possibility of taking one's wife and children on a voyage, providing the rare opportunity to travel abroad for one's closest family. Thus I come to the topic of the seafarer's family and personal life. I will first look on the bright side of it—family travelling.

8.5 "His wife sailed around the world with him"[497] (family travelling)

The oldest account of wives travelling along with their husbands comes from 1965. At that time, the company introduced this measure as a stabilizing factor because the seafarers mostly left the company for family reasons, in particular because of the difficulties associated with the long

---

495 ABS_38: Record of the business trip to Poland, Investigation of black marketeering affair, 24 February 1976.
496 NA_150: Management meeting record No. 5, 5 March 1976.
497 Paraphrase from the interview with J. J., 1952–2014, A/B sailor, 18 years in the COS.

separation of the man from his family. The company did not allow wives and from 1969 also children on ships just for the purpose of lessening the burden of months of separation; it was also a calculation on the part of the enterprise. Travelling on board for wives and children was allowed only to seafarers who had been in service for at least five years, including the gap months. This was actually the time during which many of the seafarers left the company after their first voyage experience; usually, they quit the job after the first three years. So this benefit could largely solve also the problem of employee turnover.[498]

No later than in 1969, the seafarers called for shortening the "waiting period" for the first voyage with their wives from five to three years. However, the company's management refused this request.[499] Unfortunately, there are no available supporting documents on the decision. I can only surmise that the company benefited from having the seafarers wait for five years before taking their wives on board. Taking into account the context of the year 1969, shortly after the Warsaw Treaty troops' invasion, this decision might have been motivated by the fear of misusing this benefit for emigration. Still, some changes occurred in 1969—contrary to the original directives, children up to 25 years of age were now allowed to participate in voyages.[500]

The benefit of having family on board was apparently intensively used; in 1971 the company's management adopted measures that banned boarding for children younger than one year, as there was a risk of complications during illness and additional costs because of emergency anchoring in urgent cases. This measure was imposed after a nine-month-old baby had been permitted on a voyage.[501] Soon afterwards the lowest age limit was raised from one to three years of age.

---

[498] NA_154: Material for management meeting, Draft of principles of wives' voyages, 21 January 1965.

[499] NA_151: Management meeting record No. 26, 4 July 1969.

[500] NA_152: Material No. 65 for management meeting, 19 September 1969.
Rates for children's voyages were set as high as for other passengers, while wives were offered discounted rates. Later the children's rates were levelled with those for wives. /NA_153: Management meeting record No. 43, 31 October 1969./

[501] NA_155: Material No. 6 for management meeting, 19 February 1971.

Later, in 1975, the company updated the rules for wives' stays on anchoring ships and voyages on ships. The most important change was that the seafarer could invite his wife to join him for a voyage after only three years of employment on ships (a wife could be invited earlier only when the ship was anchored, not for a voyage). But the rule stated three years of actual time spent working on a ship, not including the time spent at home. Thus this shortening of the "waiting period" before the first family voyage was not as substantial as it might seem. The 1975 updated rule allowed seven wives on a ship at any one moment, which was a considerable increase from four wives in 1965.[502] The next modification of the rules for family voyages was adopted in 1980—permitting only children from three to 15 years of age on a voyage; older children could be only on an anchored ship.[503] I can only speculate about the reasons for this change. One of them could be the overuse of this benefit; for example, in 1981, 75 women and 73 children were on various voyages, and 175 women and 85 children stayed on anchored ships.[504]

The families used this benefit for various reasons—from efforts to better cope with the negative effects of their separation, through grasping the opportunity to travel, to the relatively favourable financial conditions of these stays for family members. The price for staying on board was stated as follows: in the 1960s it was 18 Czechoslovak crowns per day for wives and later also for children. From the 1970s, the wife paid 24 and children 12 crowns per day (older children 24 crowns per day).[505] Just for illustration, I present a rough calculation of one return trip to Cuba for the wife and two children up to fifteen years of age. Including some delay time during loading/unloading, this could be a 70-day-long stay. At the rate 24 crowns/day for an adult and 12 crowns/day for a child it totals 3,360 crowns, basically the seafarer's monthly salary.

---

502 NA_156: Material No. 72 for management meeting, 19 September 1975.
503 NA_157: Material No. 6 for management meeting, 8 February 1980.
504 NA_158: Material No. 6 for management meeting, 6 February 1981.
505 NA_157: Material No. 6 for management meeting, 8 February 1980.
In the mid-1980s the rates were unified to 24 Czechoslovak crowns per day for the family member on a voyage; lower rate 12 crowns per day for children (3–15) on an anchoring ship. I have no other available materials on other possible changes.

All the seafarers actually liked to remember the moments they had spent with their family on ships—especially in the context of it being primarily a compensation for their preference of time on board over their family. Nowadays, they do not mention that more children on a ship could be disturbing, for example, when the seafarer needed to sleep and rest during the day after a night watch duty. Similarly, they did not think the voyage was rather boring for the wife, besides visiting some foreign countries. She was not employed on the ship, she did not take care of the household, and leisure opportunities were generally very limited. Perhaps this may have been the reason of some partnership problems during such voyages.

> The wife simply got a crush on another seafarer. It was such a huge crush that she [fumbling for words] that she moved to that colleague's cabin. They went so far that she did not live with her husband, she lived with the other one, and so did the kids. There would be some frictions, the seafarers had a punch-out. [...] And then I met him on another vessel and he was telling me this, 'See the bitch. She didn't pick up a lathe operator from some factory back home, who had little money and who would never take her for a voyage. Surely enough, she found a colleague so that she could keep going for voyages and keep having the bucks and be better off. [laughter] And she brought disgrace on me. But I do not want her. Screw her'.[506]

No matter how serious these problems were, they personally affected only the two partners, while others could feel amusement and scorn, pity or sympathy. In extreme cases, however, the wife on board could be a problem for the whole crew.

> The captain K. Z. was in similar situation. His wife is a USSR citizen and she used to meddle in his steering and commanding so badly that he was dismissed from his position five years ago, and they let him on the sea only after he promised that he would not take her on board. Z. is one of those women who are boasting in the society by the status of her husband.[507]

Besides all the pros and cons of having the family on board with the seafarer, and although it was not used by all seafarers,[508] this travelling

---

506 J. J., 1952–2014, A/B sailor, 18 years in the COS.
507 ABS_39: Personal characteristics of the captain Z., 22 September 1989.
508 "People would say that women should keep off the ship. And there were some seafarers who never took their wives on board. He said, 'No, keep women off the ship. They have no business there'. That's an old superstition; women on

offered mainly a chance to strengthen family relationships, mitigate the long separation of spouses and the father's separation from his children.

8.6 "She went never nuts, she always toughed it out"[509] (the family life of the seafarer)

Considering the seafarer's strong need for family ties and home as reflected in the emigration topic, I was rather surprised that the narrators barely mentioned family life; some of them even tried to avoid speaking about their forlorn family back home. Still, after a careful scrutiny of the interviews, one can clearly see they are somehow unconsciously aware of the problems their wife could face being married to a seafarer: separation from the husband; envious attitudes of her neighbours towards her good life with a seafarer, and everyday problems she had to cope with alone when her man was at the sea.

When the husband came home for a few months, then a lot of things in his family life changed, as both spouses could share duties and worries. At such times, however, not all was "rosy" all at once; on the contrary, new problems arose. Although the husband (father) was on holiday, his wife and children had to fulfil their everyday duties. Because of this, many seafarers tried to get some voluntary work to solve the problem, in spite of the fact that it was not supported by the employer. Thus many seafarers experienced two different types of loneliness—when cruising they missed their family; when staying at home they missed the sea, their work. One of them even confessed he had been afraid of people when returning home, feeling alienated while walking around the town. Therefore, some seafarers solved these emotional and mental pressures with the help of alcohol.

---

the ship are bad luck". /J. J., 1952–2014, A/B sailor, 18 years in the COS./
Reasons for the decision not to invite one's wife for a voyage varied: from saving money for the family's trip, through superstition or fears of possibilities of the wife's infidelity when on board, to some highly personal and sometime selfish reasons. Wives' reasons not to travel with their husbands are not reflected here since information on the topic (interviews with women) are not available. Generally speaking, women decided not to spend long time on ships especially because of their career or need to care for the family (grandparents, child care).

509 M. B., * 1949, chief engineer, 29 years in the COS.

As for the seafarer's wife, during her husband's holiday spent at home, she suddenly had to "switch over" from her independence to a certain degree of dependence, though she had been accustomed to handling all duties when at home alone. It was essential not only to keep peace in family life, but mainly to boost her husband's self-esteem and social status. The seafarer's profession is perceived as strongly masculine and an independent woman was often undesirable for this (self)-image. However, precisely such a woman was needed to preserve the family during the man's absence.[510]

This issue was not reflected upon in the interviews and neither were the problems the wife had to deal with during her husband's long absence from home. Yet, to some extent, the narrators admitted they had to largely give up family life in exchange for the profession. I think that mainly because they realize this fact today, they probably were not willing to talk about their family life, and they emphasize the role of woman as mother. Those who have grandchildren are now trying to be better grandparents to make up for their insufficient parenthood.

> She lived that out in pain, but we came through, last year we had our 31st wedding anniversary. She lived that out perfectly, she brought the boys up well, they are both university graduates, she took care of them.[511]

Speaking about the impacts of the profession on family life, the seafarers also offered two rationalizing strategies for their long term absence—the already mentioned possibility of travel and material compensation.

> That I brought the JVC telly from Singapore and the whole family was astonished, and the brother-in-law, and the sister, everyone was astonished. JVC, remote control, sharp image. So they were envious. Also of my wife. She has a seafarer, she is well-off. There is a cost to everything. She was well-off. Not mentioning the other things I could bring her. Gold in the Arab world. Cheap gold. I bought her some gold necklaces. A necklace, ring. Everyone was

---

510 More on seafarer's wives' independence in Hana Hagmark-Cooper, "Being an Icon: The Perception of the Seafarer's Wife as a National Character," in *IOHA Conference Collection The Many Voices of Oral History* (Barcelona: International Congress of Oral History, 2014), http://www.ub.edu/historiaoral.barcelona2014/pdf/comunicaciones.pdf, (as of 6 January 2015), 225–235.
511 M. B., * 1949, chief engineer, 29 years in the COS.

astonished at work, the women in her work said, 'She has got a gold necklace, from Turkey or somewhere. Gold ring'. [512]

Concerning all these issues, an obvious question arises: Why did these men get married and live in a steady partnership? I can propose several answers: the need for procreation; the high marriage rate in Czechoslovakia before 1989 as a result of economic and social interventions, mainly in the 1970s;[513] the family as a "refuge from social control";[514] and the already mentioned need to keep family ties and a place when one belongs to. Thus the seafarer who succumbed to his profession and performed it his whole professional life "oscillated" between two places where he belonged to: family and home (land) on the one hand and a ship on the other.

Speaking about the seafarer's personal life, I cannot omit the topic of lovers, the stereotype that "a seaman has a different woman in each port". However, this statement does not reflect reality. Yet at the same time, I cannot write that Czechoslovak seafarers remained faithful until the end and their wives kept waiting for them as faithfully as Penelope.

8.7 "She was my sweetheart in Canada"[515] (women, men and lovers)

The narrators hardly spoke about their mistresses; however, it was considerably different in various situations when they were talking "of record", especially during their regular socials. As I also participated in some of those meetings, I know that at least once they visited an erotic event (such as a cinema or striptease show) in Western countries—mostly because they could have an experience there that was not avail-

---

512 J. J., 1952–2014, A/B sailor, 18 years in the COS.
513 Průcha, *Hospodářské a sociální dějiny Československa II, 1945–1992*, 900–903.
514 Barbara Havelková, "Genderová rovnost v cbdobí socialismu," [Gender Equality in the Socialist Era] in Michal Bobek and Pavel Molek and Vojtěch Šimíček, eds., *Komunistické právo v Československu. Kapitoly z dějin bezpráví* [Communist Law in Czechoslovakia. Chapters from the History of Injustice] (Brno: Mezinárodní politologický ústav, Masarykova univerzita, 2009), 186.
515 Paraphrase from the interview with J. J., 1952–2014, A/B sailor, 18 years in the COS.

able in Czechoslovakia.[516] Still, they did not undertake these activities very often, mainly because of the lack of Western currency. They preferred the purchase of scarce goods for their own use and their families. The situation, however, changed in poor countries where it was possible to "get a woman" for a completely ridiculous amount of money.

> Mainly in those poor regions, in poor countries, in the Philippines or Brazil, or where they live in poverty. The dollar or five had a high value there. And when the seafarer had a good time for the whole evening and in the morning gave five dollars to the girl, it was a handsome sum of money for her. And she knew that she will get this money only from the seafarer.[517]

In addition to paid sexual services, the seafarer had an occasional love affair in a port, whether temporary or long-term. In Western countries, such relationship in a port, whether temporarily or "permanently", was out of question. Anchorage was usually very short in these countries because of modern technology and the good organization of work during loading and unloading. Thus anchoring in the West took usually hours or days, while in the so-called developing countries it was weeks or months. Moreover, Western women did not see East European seafarers as desirable partners since they offered neither material security nor social status. However, there were also exceptions.

> So this was my love in Canada, the Eskimo. She fell for me. And I fell for her. I was about to leave the country, to go to the Churchill, to work there. [...] We were corresponding for four years. [...] I never went there anymore. [...] And I remember that the five of us [who fell in love there], went down to the cabin, opened a whisky, had a few drinks, and felt sad. We all made our minds up to get back there, 'We will run away, altogether, we will go to Canada. We will go to the chicks. We will stay here. We have good money here, we will make big money here. Why should we leave?' We were planning to leave. But anyway. We were planning. But the ship sailed, sailed, and sailed elsewhere, to Brazil,

---

516 "Who puts into circulation or makes publicly available printed matter, movie, picture or other objects that threatens morality, shall be punished with imprisonment of up to six months, or corrective measures, or fine or forfeiture". /Criminal Code 140/1961 Coll., § 205, article 1, available from the House of Commons, http://www.psp.cz/sqw/sbirka.sqw?r=1961&cz=140 (as of 12 November 2015)./ Under this act even the possession of a magazine such as Playboy was punishable, although in this case with forfeiture. On the other hand, in the field of artistic female nudes, quality works were created in Czechoslovakia, especially during 1960s, as well as later.

517 J. J., 1952–2014, A/B sailor, 18 years in the COS.

and I had another chick there, I, sadly, I simply forgot about the Eskimo, ehm.[518]

The reverse side of the coin, the infidelity of seafarers' wives, was kept in silence. It only appeared in the descriptions of some of the voyages with the wives on board and in a form of "funny" stories based on real life. For example, one seaman returned home after some months of cruising; when he came home, he found out that his wife had not only ran away from him but had also moved out all the things from their household, including the light switches. So, when he wanted to turn on the light, he got another "blow".

Naturally, I cannot omit homosexuality, which almost suggests itself when speaking about a seagoing ship where men were living together in close quarters for long months in isolation. The available resources suggest the seafarers did not have sexual relations with other men on board. They rather waited for the girls in ports, which follows from the above quoted interviews. Thus, most likely, sexual relations between the men on ships occurred only between homosexuals, not heterosexuals.[519] In any case, homosexuality was essentially taboo in Czechoslovakia before 1989 and this was also true for vessels.

Having discussed family life and personal relationships, I will close this chapter with a reflection on the seafarer's everyday free time on the ship.

8.8 "Surrounded by creature comforts on the ship"[520] (life on the ship)

First of all, while on a voyage, the seafarer suffered from being isolated from information from back home. Two important facts have to be considered: 1) technologies were not so developed at those times and the socialist camp consistently lagged behind; 2) phone calls back home

---

518 Ibid.
519 "J. was generally considered a homosexual by the crew. He would mostly be in touch with people of the ilk—the Chef Ž and the ship's doctor Š. The source saw J. and Š. locking themselves in the cabin". /ABS_13: Record – suspicion from homosexuality, 12 January 1984./
520 Paraphrase from the interview with J. J., 1952–2014, A/B sailor, 18 years in the COS.

were rather expensive in the ports for Czechoslovak seafarers (besides, the phone coverage of the country was insufficient for a long time). Thus for the seafarers far away from home, the main way of getting information was by "classic post" (i.e. letters and deliveries of newspapers by the company).

All letters for seafarers were sent or personally delivered to the COS headquarters in Prague, and there the whole batch was sent via so-called captain mail to a port (to cooperating agency) where the ship was expected to arrive. Similarly, the seafarers could use this channel, the free captain mail; or they could use standard postal services in a given country. The second possibility was used especially for sending postcards—these represented not only visible evidence of the foreign country the seafarer had visited, but also a valuable collector's item.

Sending letters by regular mail was not very advantageous taking into account that letters from abroad were almost sure to be controlled.[521] On the contrary, control of the captain mail could oscillate between very strict or none—depending on who distributed the letters. Because of this, the State Security was interested in the captain mail—considering it a very poorly controllable channel through which seafarers could smuggle documents, information, but also drugs.[522]

The lack and delay in information exchange could very negatively impact both the seafarers' and their families' mental health. At the time when the seafarer received a letter from home, all the news and events their relatives had been writing about were already the past. Still, bad news hurt them for a long time, until the next letter would be delivered to the ship. In exceptional cases (e.g. childbirth) a telegraph message was

---

[521] All correspondence to and from foreign countries went through the post office Praha 120, where it was checked [in various periods with various intensity] by the State Security's bodies. /Karel Kaplan and Dušan Tomášek, O cenzuře v Československu v letech 1945–1956 [Censorship in Czechoslovakia in 1945–1956] (Praha: Ústav pro soudobé dějiny AV ČR, 1994.), 53./

[522] For example, in May 1976, during the management meeting the headquarters' members discussed suspicion of drugs smuggling into Czechoslovakia from the ship Radhošť and the measures which would have to be adopted concerning this case; unfortunately, the case is not specified in greater detail. /NA_143: Management meeting record No. 11, 7 May 1976./

sent from headquarters to the ship, but the headquarters decided if the telegraph request was appropriate or not.

> Of course, there was no such thing as calling home. There were not satellites, so you arrived somewhere, and you either got some delivery or not. [...] And you got mails three months old, you know. Outdated for a long time. So the crew would always suffer a breakdown then. Because he either got a bad one or got none.[523]

> He does not know what it means to take care of the home. He does not know about the broken down washing machine, does not know the problems I'm having, has no ideas. I will write him a letter, 'The children are ill, they have fevers, the washing machine is broken down.' But when he gets the letter, it's after two months, the kids are healthy, and the washing machine fixed. [...] This is what one wife of an electrician would say. [...] It's partly true. Unfortunately, she should have expected that. It's seafarer's job.[524]

Wise and rational women learned not to send their spouses bad news and deal with everyday problems themselves.

Now I will proceed from family relationships to the seafarers' life on the ship, "surrounded by creature comforts" as one of them remembered. I will scrutinize whether this corresponded with reality or whether it only reflected this seafarer's personal feelings and his love for the sea and ships. The seafarers, except for officers, lived in cabins for two persons with shared bathroom facilities, having a wash basin in their cabin. This type of lodging corresponds with the situation on older ships. The standard gradually improved, and they had en-suite cabins and ships equipped with sports venues.

These facilities were very important since the seafarers who did not serve the watch duty had quite a lot of free time after the day shift and they had to spend the time on not too large a space when they were out at sea. While away they could read a limited number of books, watch some thirty feature films (about half of them had to be "ideologically correct") and a similar number of short films (documentaries, cartoons, etc.), and they could play cards or some parlour games. Modern ships were equipped with a heated pool, gym, or sauna. On older ships, the seafarers' only option for sports often was to run around the vessel, play

---

523 I. P., * 1950, doctor, 13 years in the COS.
524 J. J., 1952–2014, A/B sailor, 18 years in the COS.

table tennis, or use a tiny pool made by handymen. They could also indulge in their hobbies, such as DIY. Other studied—especially foreign languages and text books for qualifying exams. A real blessing for the crew was if one of the members was a guitarist and a born entertainer.

The seafarers also made countless practical jokes on ships. Even today the former seafarers mention some of these jokes and remember them as their best memories. They say that although they worked for little money, they enjoyed a lot of fun. Those seafarers still working in the profession say that today they earn enough money but do not experience any fun.

8.8.1 Alcohol

On the one hand the seafarers had hard and demanding work in difficult, sometimes even extreme conditions; on the other hand they had relative a lot of free time, with only a few incentives or opportunities for spending it. Hence, alcohol comes into play here, affordable alcohol. ("It was none too expensive in those times. It was actually very cheap. Compared with the prices back home it was dirt cheap on the ship".[525]) In these circumstances a party disrupted the everyday monotony of relax and long boring days.

However, it would be a gross simplification if I explained alcohol consumption only by its affordability and boredom. Other possible reasons for drinking were well captured in the document written by the Czechoslovak Embassy in Poland reporting on maritime traffic:

> The man on the sea is completely different in his behaviour and reactions than the man on dry land. While the man on the land is chatty and outgoing, seeking entertainment, the man on longer voyages becomes quick-tempered, annoyed, avoids the company, and is longing for solitude where he could sit and think about his family, home, and friends. A tough guy becomes a man who time and time weeps for the people at home who had forgotten him, for the wife who does not write any letter, and he often happens to feel useless about

---

525 M. S., * 1939, chief engineer, 26 years in the COS.
The issue is that alcohol was not generally cheaper on ships than in Czechoslovakia; but seafarers got much better quality alcohol for their money and in comparison with other expenditures it was cheap.

his existence, for nobody needs him. No wonder that this man resorts to alcohol, or he is even at the risk of taking drugs.[526]

Although the author was not an expert in psychology and he probably did not work as a seafarer, he quite clearly pointed out that the specificities and high requirements on the sea were demanding not only for the physical but also the psychological state of an individual. But these problems would sometimes continue even after returning home, where the seafarer experienced a different form of loneliness. Thus it is not surprising that some men in these conditions became addicted not only to the sea but also to alcohol.

The narrators did not talk much about the problem of excessive drinking. If they mentioned the topic, they usually pointed to someone else who had drunk heavily. When describing the problem they focused mainly on those colleagues they had had a negative relationship with. Thus they labelled those fellow workers as "drunkards", for example, Soviet captains, men affiliated to the Communist Party, and other "hated" people on the ship. All these people may well have consumed alcohol to excess, but some of the narrator's friends, or perhaps the narrator himself did the same. Yet, since this behaviour is considered socially undesirable, it was overlooked during the interview. Generally speaking, alcoholism among the seafarers was a problem of individuals as well as in any group of people.[527]

The seafarers' free time was not unique because of alcohol consumption, but in two other important ways: in a certain freedom compared to the constrains put on individuals by the undemocratic regime and, above all, in the great love of the sea for which they were ready to sacrifice the rest of their lives. Women, the bringing up of children, and other life plans or priorities, were often forgotten, or side-lined, because of the

---

526 ABS_6: Letter from the Czechoslovak Consulate General to the Czechoslovak Federal Ministry of Foreign Affairs, 6 November 1972.
527 Alcohol consumption was a socially respected part of Czech and Slovak everyday culture. The spread of alcoholism was possible also due to a weak development of motorization and relatively weaker pressure on labour productivity in some institutions and enterprises. /Martin Franc and Jiří Knapík, *Průvodce kulturním děním a životním stylem v českých zemích 1948–1967* [Guide to Cultural Events and Lifestyle in Czech Countries 1948–1967] (Praha: Academia, 2011), 130–132./

sea and ships. And just it is to those 44 ships operated under the Czechoslovak and later the Czech flag that the last part of this book is dedicated.

9 Ship memoirs

A book about shipping and seafarers would not be complete without portraying the individual ships. In this chapter each ship will be presented from three perspectives: 1) a chart describing the ship's parameters; 2) an explanation of the meaning of the ship's name, revealing the symbolism of the name (the names were proposed by the company's headquarters and approved by the responsible ministry); 3) minor episodes from the "ship's life", which investigates a variety of miscellaneous moments that had occurred on the ships or events the seafarers experienced there. The scope of these texts about the life on the ship varies greatly. Not just because some ships experienced smoother voyages than others; it is also a result of the unbalanced range of archival documents and personal testimonies. Besides, the ships running in the last phase of the COS business were in operation only for a very short time, sometimes only several months, thus providing little time for any strong memories.

Before introducing the ships, several remarks have to be made about the presentation of the ship's parameters.[528]

Length: maximum ship length from the extreme forward end of the bow to the extreme aft of the stern.
Breadth: ship's extreme breadth, commonly called beam; measured from the most outboard point on one side to the most outboard point on the other.
Draft: the vertical distance between the waterline and the deepest part of the keel.[529]

---

[528] If another source is not stated, the definitions are based on: Global Security, "Shipboard Measurements," http://www.globalsecurity.org/military/systems/ship/measurement.htm (as of 4 December 2014).

[529] "SeaTalk Nautical Dictionary," http://www.seatalk.info/cgi-bin/nautical-marine-sailing-dictionary/db.cgi?db=db&view_records=1&uid=default&Term=draft&submit=Look+it+up%21 (as of 14 February 2014).

DWT: dead weight tonnage; the weight of the total load (cargo, fuel, stores, passengers, crew); some available documents state a different DWT for winter, summer, and tropics; in such cases the data below reflect the lowest tonnage.

GRT: gross register tonnage; the entire cubic content capacity determining a merchant ship's size; 1 GRT = 100 cubic feet to the ton = 2.83 m^3; some technical lists on the ship state different GRT for open seawaters, for Panama, and for Suez; in these cases the parameter for seawaters is stated.

NRT: net register tonnage; cargo carrying capability (it is counted as the GRT without the spaces that cannot be used to carry cargo).[530]

Knts: knot(s); unit of speed, one nautical mile (1,852 m) per hour.

If not stated otherwise, the ships' technical data is based on files from the National Archive;[531] the ships are chronologically ordered.

I chose the here presented moments from the "ships' memoirs" according to any single principle. Sometimes these are stories typical for the shipping sector in a given historical context; sometimes I choice entertaining stories and sometimes those giving an impetus for thought. I have to admit that in some cases the stories described are the only available stories within the sources preserved. Throughout the chapter, the "memories" are very closely tied to the individual vessel. In a broader sense, however, a substantial part of the stories could have occurred on any other ship. Actually, this chapter strives to add a "personal" dimension to remembering events on each of the ships which are otherwise throughout the book presented only in the form of their parameters, transport capacity, and performance. Let us now explore the ships sailing from 1952 to 1998, to see what set them apart, and to trace what happened on their voyages.

---

530 Ibid.
531 NA_117: Files of individual ships.

Republika I

TYPE:	GENERAL CARGO	DWT:	10,865.00 T
LENGTH:	130.15 M	GRT:	6,592.00 T
BREADTH:	16.90 M	NRT:	3,841.60 T
DRAFT:	10.00 M	SPEED:	9.5 KNTS

ORIGIN:	BUILT IN 1920 IN GREAT BRITAIN
OPERATION:	1952–1962; 10 YEARS, 5 MONTHS

STORY: All the details concerning the purchase and first years of the operation of the ship Republika [Republic] are described in detail in the chapter about the 1950s. The Republika was not only the first Czechoslovak post-WWII seagoing ship, she was also the only ship that had "her own" picture book. The author, Václav Švarc, a documentary filmmaker, originally intended to make an artistic document about the origins of the Czechoslovak fleet. Why he eventually did not accomplish the plan is unknown. The most probable reason was an effort of the responsible ministries to keep the shipping cooperation with the People's Republic of China (PRC) a secret, which could have been revealed if the film had been made. Later, the Foreign Trade Ministry and the Ministry of Culture enabled Václav Švarc to participate in one voyage of the Republika from Poland to the PRC. On the ship, the author took many photos; 235 of them were finally published. This set includes not only contemporary traveller snapshots from Algeria, India, or China, but also unique images of the ship herself and the men working there.[532] The Republika became a "literary hero" once more in 1963—in a story about seafarers' work and life and about the ship's journey from Gdynia to India, Indonesia, and the PRC.[533]

---

532 Švarc, Přes moře a oceány.
533 Černý, Na daleké plavbě.

Julius Fučík

TYPE:	GENERAL CARGO	DWT:	7,108.00 T
LENGTH:	125.05 M	GRT:	5,081.52 T
BREADTH:	18.01 M	NRT:	2,782.00 T
DRAFT:	7.25 M	SPEED:	13.5 KNTS
ORIGIN:	BUILT IN 1949 IN FRANCE		
OPERATION:	1954–1965; 11 YEARS, 6 MONTHS		

MEANING OF THE NAME: This vessel was named after the Czech communist journalist, literary and theatre reviewer, and translator. In the years 1941–1942 he was a member of the second illegal Communist Party Central Committee. On 24 April 1942 he was arrested by the Gestapo. The following year, he was sentenced to death and then hanged in the Berlin-Plötzensee prison. His famous book *Notes from the Gallows* was written during a few months when he was jailed by the Gestapo in Prague-Pankrác in the spring of 1943. The manuscript of the *Notes* written on dozens of cards was secretly smuggled out of the prison by the warden Kolínský. After the 1948 communist coup d'état, Julius Fučík became a legend which the communist regime utilized for its propaganda reasons. Fučík was an ideal candidate for a hero: a communist, engaged in the anti-Nazi resistance and dead man, the fact ensuring that he could not and would not malign the regime nor do any harm. In 1950, Fučík was posthumously awarded the first Honorary International Peace Prize by the World Peace Council. His *Notes from the Gallows* were translated into many languages. The uncensored version of the *Notes* was published even in the early 1990s.

STORY: The ship Julius Fučík was actually the first ship purchased by the Czechoslovaks on the PRC account and then run with the Czechoslovak flag. Seafarers on this ship, initially mainly Chinese, sometimes faced their small worries, one of which was recorded in the log book (the record is literally transcribed; the Chinese officer recorded it in English):

3. 7. 1961 10:30 to 11:00 after the 4th engineers cabin flooded by sea water found some of his personal effects was damaged by sea water as follows: 1. one woollen overcoat, 2. one wrist watch, 3. six pieces of shirts, 4. one lighter and one set of playing cards.[534]

Lidice

TYPE:	GENERAL CARGO	DWT:	8,500.00 T
LENGTH:	139.40 M	GRT:	5,690.00 T
BREADTH:	17.60 M	NRT:	2,732.22 T
DRAFT:	7.87 M	SPEED:	14.5 KNTS
ORIGIN:	BUILT IN 1954 IN THE TURKU SHIPYARD, FINLAND		
OPERATION:	1954–1967; 12 YEARS, 3 MONTHS		

MEANING OF THE NAME: Lidice is the name of the Central Bohemian village burned in 1942 by the Nazis after the assassination of the Deputy Reich Protector and the chief of the Reichssicherheitshauptamt (Reich Main Security Office) Reinhard Heydrich on 27 May 1942 in Prague-Libeň. The assassination was a diversionary operation of Czechoslovak paratroopers who were specially trained for this task in the United Kingdom. Heydrich fell into a coma and he died on 4 June 1942. After the betrayal of one of the paratroopers, the assassins were captured and killed during a fierce combat.

In response to Heydrich's assassination, the Nazis killed several thousands of Czechs and burned down the village of Lidice on 10 June 1942 and then the village of Ležáky on 24 June. The men from Lidice were shot; the women were taken to a concentration camp, where only 60 of them survived. 82 children were gassed at Chelmno extermination camp, 17 children survived, having been sent to a children's home in Germany for Germanization. Lidice became a symbol of the so-called martyr victims. Several years later it also became a part of communist propaganda.[535]

---

534 NA_112: Log book from the Julius Fučík No 25.
535 Gabriela Havlůjová, "Lidice jako místo paměti – paměť na Lidice," [Lidice as a Place of Memory – Memory of Lidice] in Miroslav Vaněk and Přemysl Houda and Pavel Mücke, eds., *Deset let na cestě: Orální historie na Sovinci* [Ten Years on the Road: Oral History in the Sovinec Castle] (Praha: Fakulta human-

STORY: It is a paradox that the ship carrying this name was transporting weapons for the Algerian National Liberation Front. The previous chapters confirm that such cargo was not exceptional on Czechoslovak ships. However, the transport on the Lidice in 1959 mentioned here was certainly the first that was leaked, leading to the arrest of the ship and confiscation of the cargo, causing serious diplomatic problems between Czechoslovakia and France, which were settled as late as the mid-1960s.

Dukla

TYPE:	GENERAL CARGO	DWT:	10,070.00 T
LENGTH:	157.60 M	GRT:	6,507.86 T
BREADTH:	20.00 M	NRT:	3,777.00 T
DRAFT:	8.43 M	SPEED:	16.0 KNTS
ORIGIN:	BUILT IN 1958 IN THE WARNOWWERFT SHIPYARD, WARNEMÜNDE, GERMAN DEMOCRATIC REPUBLIC		
OPERATION:	1958–1965; 7 YEARS, 4 MONTHS		

MEANING OF THE NAME: Dukla refers to the Dukla Pass where the Slovak–Poland border meets. This place is well known from the time of WWII, when the Battle of the Dukla Pass took place there. On 8 September 1944 the Red Army launched this operation originally planned as a quick assistance to the Slovak National Uprising. However, the poorly prepared operation in bad terrain lasted about two months; tens of thousands of soldiers died during the fights. It is estimated 85,000 Soviet and 6,500 Czechoslovak fighters were killed or injured. After WWII, the Dukla was paradoxically recognized as a major strategic battle and evidence of the perfection of Soviet army leadership. This interpretation of the Dukla battle became a part of communist propaganda.

The name of this ship closes the first period when Czechoslovak vessels were named according to the key symbols of communist propaganda. Later, propaganda re-emerged with the ships' names Jiskra and Pionýr. Of course, the names Julius Fučík, Lidice, and Dukla reflected the only recently ended WWII and the fact that the fear of a "real" war was an important propaganda tool on both sides of the conflict during the Cold War. Maybe this is the reason why the next ship was named Mír [Peace].

STORY: When the Sino–Czechoslovak cooperation in shipping terminated in the 1960s, the Dukla was the first ship which the Chinese party withdrew from the joint venture into Chinese possession and operation. The takeover process took place in a rather tense and sharpened atmosphere:

> On the orders given by the representative of the Czechoslovak authorities, the captain commanded to lower the Czechoslovak flag [...] and to raise the PRC flag. The crew did not salute, did not stand to attention; the ship did not salute either. Immediately after the lowering of the flag, the ship's name on the bow and on the stern was painted over as well as the company's emblem on the chimney.[536]

Mír I

TYPE:	GENERAL CARGO	DWT:	12,540.00 T
LENGTH:	148.43 M	GRT:	9,312.61 T
BREADTH:	18.89 M	NRT:	5,570.00 T
DRAFT:	8.99 M	SPEED:	15.0 KNTS
ORIGIN:	BUILT IN 1958 IN THE ULJANIK SHIPYARD, PULA, YUGOSLAVIA		
OPERATION:	1958–1967; 8 YEARS, 4 MONTHS		

MEANING OF THE NAME: This ship's name, meaning peace, can be added to the group of ships named with a stress on communist propaganda, on war experience in particular (with the exception of the Republika). In fact, "the world of socialism was richly decorated with the attributes of peace, presented as a world of peaceful work with the same unambiguity as directly as the West was presented as a world of war and war preparations".[537]

---

536 MZV_8: Report about the business trip to Canton, 9 August 1965. (Canton is the former official name of the city of Guangzhou.)
537 Vladimír Macura, Šťastný věk a jiné studie o socialistické kultuře [Happy Age and Other Studies of Socialist Culture] (Praha: Academia, 2008), 36.

STORY: However, the name did not prevent the ship from transporting "non-peace" cargos and dangerous cargos (chemicals). For example, the ship transported 1,200 tonnes of xylene at the turn of 1964 and 1965 during voyage No. 28;[538] and during voyage No. 29 it transported a cargo of 130 tonnes of trinitrotoluene, i.e. a very strong and dangerous explosive. The profit was substantial: the freight for xylene transport was £12,880, in comparison with a non-dangerous cargo the net profit was £7,930. In the case of the trinitrotoluene, the net profit was £1,695. The ship command together with the trade union deputies proposed to pay a one-time reward to the crew for these transports of dangerous cargos. The amount of approximately £10 per person was proposed (paid in Czechoslovak crowns), i.e. £500 for the crew in total.

The company's management perceived this proposal for rewards for the crew as a precedent for rewarding other similar transports.[539] After the management consulted the issue first with the Ministry of Foreign Trade, which was the COS's superior authority, and then with the Central Committee of Trade Unions, they decided not to pay the reward. The management agreed that only war materials would be worth additional remuneration. Finally, they stated that "in this case it was a normal (sic!) cargo requiring heightened caution".[540]

---

[538] Clear colourless, flammable liquid, mostly used as a solvent in the printing, lacquering, rubber, and leather industries. Like other solvents, xylene is abused as an inhalant drug.
[539] NA_118: Material No. 38 for the management meeting, 2 April 1965.
[540] NA_119: Management meeting record, 16 April 1965.

Ostrava

TYPE:	TANKER	DWT:	20,518.00 T
LENGTH:	170.68 M	GRT:	13,338.92 T
BREADTH:	21.94 M	NRT:	8,310.00 T
DRAFT:	8.99 M	SPEED:	15.5 KNTS
ORIGIN:	BUILT IN 1959 IN THE ULJANIK SHIPYARD, PULA, YUGOSLAVIA		
OPERATION:	1959–1965; 6 YEARS, 1 MONTH		

MEANING OF THE NAME: The name Ostrava opens a group of names celebrating the successes of the building of socialist Czechoslovakia. The Ostrava was given her name with the aim to pay tribute to rapid socialist industrialization. Ostrava is a city on the border of Silesia and Moravia, in the northeast of the Czech Republic. It was a well-known industrial centre called at that time "the city of coal and iron" or "the steel heart of the Republic". Thus although this name is seemingly non-political, it actually referred to politics through references to the socialist state's achievements. As well as other similar ship names stated below—Kladno, Vítkovice, Třinec, Košice.

STORY: The Ostrava was the only tanker ship cruising under the Czechoslovak flag, although being in the possession of the People's Republic of China. During the time of operation she transported 648,000 tonnes of oil and petroleum products in total, delivered mainly from Romanian Constanta, and eventually from other Black Sea ports. One of these voyages turned out to be fatal for the ship master. In 1961, during a trip from China to Europe, he did not spare his health despite suffering health problems throughout the journey. On 29 October, after lunch he suffered a final heart attack; this time it was fatal.

As it was necessary to perform an autopsy, the ship approached the nearest port—Aden. In Aden the responsible crew members—the chief officers and the ship master's deputy for political affairs—asked either for cremation or for transport to Czechoslovakia. The Yemeni authorities, however, answered there was no crematorium in Aden. Thus the authorities ordered to bury the ship master within 24 hours in conformity with local regulations. So the captain was buried in a local cemetery in Aden on 30 October 1961, 10:15 local time.[541]

The widow strove to transport his remains into the country, especially with regard to the deceased's wishes. The exhumation was rejected several times by the official Yemeni sites. Then, during one voyage the ship Mír I was bunkering in Aden, and the ship master Antonín Fojtů asked the ship agent in the area to arrange the exhumation. Fojtů raised it as a captain's request, without any other official confirmation. The exhumation was carried out. The coffin was transported by the Mír I to Constanta and from Romania sent by a tourist plane to Prague (the COS paid the costs).[542] Thus, after several years the ship master Ladislav Makový finally arrived home.

Orava I

TYPE:	GENERAL CARGO	DWT:	10,070.00 T
LENGTH:	144.48 M	GRT:	6,503.31 T
BREADTH:	20.05 M	NRT:	N/A
DRAFT:	8.35 M	SPEED:	15.0 KNTS
ORIGIN:	BUILT IN 1958 IN THE WARNOWWERFT SHIPYARD, WARNEMÜNDE, GERMAN DEMOCRATIC REPUBLIC		
OPERATION:	1959–1965; 6 YEARS, 3 MONTHS		

MEANING OF THE NAME: Orava is the name of a Slovak dam built on the upper Orava river, reaching as far as Poland. With the total area of 35.2 km^2 it is the second largest dam in Slovakia. Its construction was started during the Slovak State in 1941. After WWII, the works were interrupted and re-started in 1949, i.e. in the first year of the first communist Five Year Plan. The first turbine of the dam was launched in 1953; the construction works continued until 1954. Similarly as in the case of the ship Ostrava, naming the ship after the dam implicitly re-

---

541 NA_120: Report written by the ship master's deputy for political affairs, 30 October 1961.
542 Antonín Fojtů, *Moře milované, moře proklínané II* [Beloved Sea, Sea Cursed] (Praha: Mare-Czech, 2006), 31.

ferred to the successes of the development of post-WWII Czechoslovakia and the achievements of the communist leadership.

STORY: The Orava was part of a set of four identical general cargo vessels, which were named after Czechoslovak dams. Three of them were named according to places in the Czech Republic; the Orava was chosen to give at least one of them a Slovak name. Since she was operated within the joint venture with the People's Republic of China, the crew was mixed. This fact proved to be important, for example, in 1959 when a minor collision occurred between the Orava and a fishing cutter from Eastern Germany near the Polish port of Świnoujscie. The Germans accused the Orava of causing the collision and asked for a strange procedure, prosecution of the guilt party in the Orava's home port, in Prague. This was probably because it could not be determined whether the collision had occurred in Polish coastal waters or on the high seas. Thus it was doubtful whether the Polish authorities would be willing to initiate the investigation. According to Czechoslovak law, however, only Czechoslovak citizens could be prosecuted for offenses like these committed abroad. On the condition that during the collision the Chinese ship master was responsible for steering the boat, there was sufficient reason to stop the criminal proceedings. In connection with these findings the City Prosecutor's Office in Prague then investigated the matter, and it concluded on the basis of an expert opinion that "no one under the jurisdiction of the Czechoslovak court had committed a crime".[543] Thus the matter was settled.

---

543 NA_116: Two documents from the file about the collision between the Orava and the cutter SAS 237: 14 April 1961, 20 May 1961.

Kladno

TYPE:	GENERAL CARGO	DWT:	12,880.00 T
LENGTH:	149.24 M	GRT:	8,837.16 T
BREADTH:	18.80 M	NRT:	5,446.50 T
DRAFT:	9.09 M	SPEED:	14.5 KNTS
ORIGIN:	BUILT IN 1959 IN THE HITACHI SAKURAJIMA SHIPYARD, OSAKA, JAPAN		
OPERATION:	1959–1973; 13 YEARS, 5 MONTHS		

MEANING OF THE NAME: The Kladno was the first new ship, which the Czechoslovak Republic purchased on its own account, and the second Czechoslovak ship in general (the above mentioned were purchased on the PRC account; see the chapter on the 1950s). Her name belongs to the group of ships named in order to promote the economic achievements of the socialist state, especially towards its own citizens. Naturally, at those times only few if any people abroad had any awareness of what the name Kladno meant. Today, many people would link the name of this Central Bohemian town with the birthplace of the famous ice hockey player Jaromír Jágr. The ship Kladno, however, was not named in 1959 in tribute to Jaromír Jágr already for the fact that he was born only a year before the ship was discharged. At the end of the 1950s, the ship was given her name to promote the extensive steel plant Poldi. The Poldi Kladno ironworks was founded in 1889 by Karl Wittgenstein, the father of the philosopher Ludwig Wittgenstein. Karl named the ironworks in honour of his wife Leopoldina (shortened to Poldi). After 1945, the plant was nationalized, further expanded and in the 1970s modernized in accordance with the persisting notion of Czechoslovakia as the "blacksmith's shop" of the Eastern bloc.

STORY: Both the ironworks and the ship of the same name faced their everyday life and the problems. One of the most serious events on the ship occurred in 1972:

On 10 July 1972, when the ship was anchoring in the port of Szczecin, in the wharf Ewa, a rooting corpse was found that had been lying in storage No. 2 for approximately one week. Polish security authorities found out that the corpse was a stowaway who had jumped in the dark into the cargo hold and fell from the height of 7.20 meters right onto the cargo of iron, thinking that the ship had already been loaded.[544]

Orlík I

TYPE:	GENERAL CARGO	DWT:	10,316.00 T
LENGTH:	146.48 M	GRT:	6,785.20 T
BREADTH:	19.43 M	NRT:	N/A
DRAFT:	8.30 M	SPEED:	15.5 KNTS
ORIGIN:	BUILT IN 1958 IN THE STOCZNIA GDAŃSKA, GDANSK, POLAND		
OPERATION:	1960–1967; 7 YEARS		

MEANING OF THE NAME: This is the third ship named according to a dam. The names were assigned in the same sequence as the dams were put into operation: the Orava dam in 1953, the Orava ship in 1959; the Slapy dam in 1955, the Slapy ship in 1960 (the name was used for a short time when the Chinese ship transported Chinese re-emigrants from Indonesia to the PRC). The dam Orlík was built between the years 1954–1966, including the preparatory and cultivation works; the construction itself lasted from 1957 to 1962. Giving the ship the name even before the completion of the dam can be perceived as another example of emphasizing the socialist regime's construction achievements. The dams Slapy and Orlík built on the Vltava river form part of the Vltava Cascade, the system of water works based on the concept of building as large as possible water projects, which accumulated huge reserves of water for economic usage and the improvement of navigation conditions on the Vltava and lower Elbe rivers.

STORY: The Orlík was one of those vessels transferred to the Chinese side when cooperation in the field of maritime transport was finished

---

544 ABS_6: Letter from the Czechoslovak Consulate General to the Czechoslovak Federal Ministry of Foreign Affairs, 6 November 1972.

(see chapter about the 1960s). On the day of transfer, 16 February 1967, the ship master wrote these two last recordings in the log book:

> Today at 07:35 the electrical engineer J. H.[545] was accidentally strangled in the dining room. The ship doctor was immediately called; he provided first aid. At the time the chief mate, the 2nd engineer and the 3rd engineer were in the dining room. At 09:45 comrade J. H. was transferred into the boat and transported to hospital.
>
> Today at 12:00 the protocol was signed on handing over the ship Orlík to the Chinese ship owner. [...] The Czechoslovak flag was lowered and the Chinese flag was raised. The ship Orlík ended her activities in the Czechoslovak Ocean Shipping under the Czechoslovak flag.[546]

Pionýr

TYPE:	GENERAL CARGO	DWT:	3,025.00 T
LENGTH:	92.05 M	GRT:	1,960.00 T
BREADTH:	13.50 M	NRT:	844.08 T
DRAFT:	5.64 M	SPEED:	11.5 KNTS
ORIGIN:	BUILT IN 1960 IN THE GRIGOR DIMITROV SHIPYARD, VARNA, BULGARIA		
OPERATION:	1960–1969; 9 YEARS, 1 MONTH		

STORY: The Pionýr[547] was the only ship of the COS that wrecked and sank—it happened on 6 August 1969 at 7:10.[548] On that day the ship was sailing from the Cuban port of Moa to Rostock in East Germany loaded with 1,400 tonnes of copper ore in bulk and 1,330 tonnes of unspecified general cargo. On the same day at 20:52, the ship collided with a coral reef near the lighthouse N. W. Point near Mayaguana Island (the Bahamas), geographical position 22°29'0N, 73°08'2W. Based on the available materials, the main cause of stranding was not a fatal error but rather the coincidence of various circumstances, mainly technical

---

545 The name of the electrician is kept in anonymity and other names are omitted to maintain private data.
546 NA_56: Log book from the Orlík I No. 25.
547 For more information about the name see the ship Jiskra.
548 The information on the Pionýr wrecking is based on the documents NA_121: Report for the insurance company, 16 September 1969; Ship master's report about the accident, 2 September 1969.

problems: at the time of the accident the ship could use neither the radar because of its failure nor its echo-sound because of malfunction. Thus the distances were given according to the number of the propeller's rotations, and the courses were held according to the gyrocompass[549] and the main magnetic compass.

Getting stuck ashore, almost the entire bottom of the ship was destroyed, and water leaked into all three cargo holds as well as into the engine room. The cargo in lower parts was flooded and partially discarded. No life loss or serious injuries occurred. During the night, the crew slept rough on deck in order to be able to abandon the ship in case the ship broke or overturned. Four days after the accident (10 August), the danger increased when the helpless vessel was exposed to several strikes of the Atlantic swell. Because of this, the ship master evacuated 20 crew members to the rescue ship Cable. Five people were sent home on 28 August, and the rest of the crew, the ship master plus five seafarers, continued to stay on the ship. The rest of the crew abandoned the ship approximately within a month after the accident, on 9 September in the morning.

The rescue operation was performed as follows: The day after the accident, 7 August, 11:30, the US border guard vessel Courageous came to the Pionýr and US specialists executed a preliminary ship examination for the next two days. On 10 August, another ship joined the operation—the rescue boat Cable (Murphy Pacific Salvage) and the salvage master came to the Pionýr. This special vessel from the Merit New York—Murphy Pacific Salvage Co. cooperated on the ship's rescue from that point onwards.

The experts from Murphy Salvage concluded their inspections and observations with the following results: 80 per cent of the ship's bottom was destroyed, there was about a seven meter transverse fissure in the third cargo hold, so the ship was in danger of breaking. The repair costs were estimated as not less than $500,000. Moreover, the COS would have to pay approximately $100,000 for ship salvage. Thus, proclaiming her a total loss, the COS decided to give up further work on the ship's rescue, demanding payment of insurance value.

---

549 Compass used in maritime navigation to determine true North of the Earth.

Two other Czechoslovak ships that were in the area cooperated with the rescue teams: from 21 August, the ship Blaník was on the site; the seafarers rescued some of the cargo with the help of a special watercraft as well as some valuable material and the inventory from the Pionýr according to the instructions from the headquarters. The Blaník sailed off on 30 August, two days later (1 September), the ship Jiskra arrived at the scene to re-load eight barrels of nickel-cobalt from the Pionýr; she sailed off the same day. At the end of the operations, the Pionýr's ship master stated:

> After almost a month in danger and insecurity, extraordinary physical and nervous strain, the small group of seafarers who stayed on the ship until the operation finishes, were all very tired. However, their discipline and extraordinary devotion should be highly valued.

Jiskra

TYPE:	GENERAL CARGO	DWT:	3,047.00 T
LENGTH:	92.85 M	GRT:	1,702.53 T
BREADTH:	13.53 M	NRT:	764.74 T
DRAFT:	5.62 M	SPEED:	11.7 KNTS
ORIGIN:	BUILT IN 1963 IN THE GRIGOR DIMITROV SHIPYARD, VARNA, BULGARIA		
OPERATION:	1963–1980; 17 YEARS, 3 MONTHS		

MEANING OF THE NAME: Although it is not obvious at first glance, the name of the ship Jiskra could be included in the group of names related to communist ideology, similarly to the ship Pionýr mentioned above. Pionýr means pioneer in English; however, this word was not used in its primary meaning during the communist period. Almost everyone connoted the word with the organization for children that provided "education" according to the principles of Marxism-Leninism. Even though it was not explicitly declared, membership in the Pionýr organization was mandatory; children who did not join could be disadvantaged in various ways or even ostracized.

The system of ideological education of children and young people had three stages. The Jiskra was a children's mass organization to which virtually all children were signed up when entering primary school. The main objective was to prepare children for entry into the next stage, the Pionýr [Pioneer] organization of the Socialist Youth Union at the age of nine or ten. After turning 15, young people could enter the Youth Union itself. This was another mass organization, in a sense a pre-step for entering the Communist Party.

STORY: The Jiskra, the Pionýr's sister ship, was one of the ships often assigned with the task of military transports. This is also the reason why she achieved very good performance results, in certain aspects the highest in the fleet. Its cargo was often destined for Libya. As military items were always "hot" goods, the ship was unloaded immediately after approaching the port. However, when the ship did not carry "special goods", the ship's unloading could be significantly prolonged. The long stay at the roadstead and in the port could subsequently cause problems with supplies. Here is one such story.

During one trip in 1979, the ship was probably not carrying goods eagerly awaited by the Libyan side. Thus, when arriving at the port of Benghazi, she was directed to the roadstead where she anchored from 6 October to 7 November; meanwhile, the seafarers started to face problems with decreasing water supplies. The shipmaster decided that water would be rationed:

> 3. 11. 1979, Benghazi – roadstead, 19:00, water allocation was introduced, a bucket per crew member per day. 7. 11. 1979, Benghazi – roadstead, 13:00, the crew was informed about the situation of the ship's water supply. Water allocation was further reduced to one bucket per man per two days.[550]

From 8 November the problem began to be resolved since the ship arrived in the port for unloading and here the water supply was replenished.

---

550 NA_113: Log book from the Jiskra No. 61.

Košice I

TYPE:	BULK CARRIER	DWT:	26,974.00 T
LENGTH:	181.20 M	GRT:	16,759.87 T
BREADTH:	24.88 M	NRT:	12,553.51 T
DRAFT:	9.91 M	SPEED:	14.8 KNTS
ORIGIN:	BUILT IN 1963 IN THE INOSHIMA SHIPYARD, JAPAN		
OPERATION:	1963–1986; 22 YEARS, 6 MONTHS		

MEANING OF THE NAME: The ship bore a name of the second largest city in Slovakia and the metropolis of Eastern Slovakia—Košice. As the contemporary records evidences, the ship was named mainly after the new centre of metallurgic industry called Košice, located in the city of Košice. It is the largest Slovak company for steel production and processing (today U.S. Steel Košice). The construction of this industrial complex on an area of 800 hectares began in January 1960. The ship was named after this plant in 1963 when the construction was in progress—the first blast furnace was lit in 1965. The link between the metallurgical company and the ship's name includes some symbolism—the Košice I was the first vessel specialized in iron ore transports. At the beginnings of her operation, she transported mainly ore from Brazil to Czechoslovakia. After being re-built in 1967 in Hamburg, she was used to carry also other bulk substrates.

STORY: The Košice was the first ever Czechoslovak ship to circumnavigate the globe. On 28 October 1965 she set off from Szczecin in Poland to Vitória, Brazil; then she sailed around Africa to Nagoya. From Japan the Košice went to the Port of Chanaral in Peru and then back through the Panama Canal to Yugoslav Rijeka, where she arrived on 2 February 1966, i.e. less than four months after her departure from Europe. This might be the reason why the Košice I also had "her" own novel *Pilgrim on oceans*.[551] In 1974, the National museum in Prague asked via the Federal Ministry of Foreign Trade for a model of the ship, which they wanted to add to their collection. The COS board of managers approved

---

551 Jakeš, *Poutník oceány.*

the request on 23 December; maybe as a Christmas present for the museum.[552]

Republika II

TYPE:	GENERAL CARGO	DWT:	13,928.00 T
LENGTH:	156.39 M	GRT:	10,896.70 T
BREADTH:	20.40 M	NRT:	6,284.44 T
DRAFT:	8.92 M	SPEED:	14.2 KNTS
ORIGIN:	BUILT IN 1964 IN THE STOCZNIA ADOLFA WARSKIEGO, SZCZECIN, POLAND		
OPERATION:	1964–1973; 9 YEARS, 1 MONTH		

MEANING OF THE NAME: The Republika I aroused and still arouses the memories of the founding of the Czechoslovak fleet. The Republika II was the first ship in the fleet carrying the name of her discharged predecessor. After the sale of the Republika II, however, the name was not given to any other ship. It was an unwritten rule not to give one name more than twice.

STORY: During nine years of operation, she transported various types of cargo; until 1968 she run mainly on the Cuban line for transports of sugar. One of these voyages was very unhappy: a group of seafarers went for an excursion in the Cuban sugar factory Tunas de Zaza. During the tour in the mill, they were standing on a platform when it suddenly tumbled down. One seafarer died during the transport to hospital, four were seriously injured, and three others slightly injured.[553]

---

552 NA_123: Management meeting record, 23 December 1974.
553 NA_124: Log book from the Republika II No. 7, 23 January 1966.

Brno

TYPE:	GENERAL CARGO	DWT:	15,250.00 T
LENGTH:	156.55 M	GRT:	10,842.59 T
BREADTH:	20.44 M	NRT:	5,997.56 T
DRAFT:	9.49 M	SPEED:	14.2 KNTS
ORIGIN:	BUILT IN 1965 IN THE STOCZNIA ADOLFA WARSKIEGO, SZCZECIN, POLAND		
OPERATION:	1965–1981; 16 YEARS, 2 MONTHS		

MEANING OF THE NAME: The Brno was the first ship named after the capital of an individual part of Czechoslovakia—Brno is the capital of Moravia.

STORY: Former seafarers often mentioned the Brno as the ship from which the highest number of seafarers emigrated in 1968. One of the narrators, however, had also some other memories from the ship Brno—the extremely long ship's waiting at the Basra roadstead in Iraq at the turn of 1979/1980:[554]

> The ship Brno went for a voyage to Iraq. And she was at the roadstead anchoring in Basra, she was anchoring for 120 days there. One month on the way there and one month on the way back, 120 days of anchorage. Plus the port, they did one voyage for six months. They went bonkers during the anchorage. Heat, the tropics, they ran out of cigarettes, run out of alcohol, there was nothing. They were running out of food, vegetables, milk, everything was running out. The ship has supplies for six months, but the basic foodstuff and the vegetables have to be replenished. Cigarettes for the crew. The seafarers had nothing to smoke. And suddenly they were there almost five months. So the crew was a nervous wreck. They said they did not talk to each other, they were worn-out anchoring all that time. They went even so far as to swap wives.[555]

---

[554] NA_125: Log books from the Brno No. 54, 55. The ship was staying in the Basra roadstead from 8 November 1979 to 4 February 1980.
[555] J. J., 1952–2014, A/B sailor, 18 years in the COS.

Vítkovice I

TYPE:	BULK CARRIER	**DWT:**	41,207.00 T
LENGTH:	209.60 M	**GRT:**	24,326.45 T
BREADTH:	27.50 M	**NRT:**	15,320.37 T
DRAFT:	11.56 M	**SPEED:**	15.2 KNTS
ORIGIN:	BUILT IN 1966 IN THE BARCLAY & CURLE, CO. LTD., GLYDEHOLM, GLASGOW, GREAT BRITAIN		
OPERATION:	1966–1987; 20 YEARS, 4 MONTHS		

MEANING OF THE NAME: The ship Vítkovice I belongs to the group of ships named in honour of important industrial places in Czechoslovakia. Vítkovice ironworks is a heavy engineering company unique for its location directly in the urban area in Ostrava-Vítkovice, in the North-West of Moravia. In the past, it was a combine with a full metallurgical production, i.e. from the production of pig iron and related products, through the production of steel, to processing of steel products. Currently the ironworks does not include metallurgical primary production, i.e. high furnaces.

STORY: The Vítkovice I was exceptional with her dimensions; from 1966 until 1990 she was the largest ship of the fleet. The Vítkovice I was a bulk carrier, often carrying out long voyages: Japan, Greenland, the United States, South America. For many seafarers the ship had a certain indefinable magic. Thus they made an amateur film to preserve her in their memories. Inspired by these seafarers, Czech Television, the public broadcaster, made a documentary film in 2005 about the ship's circumnavigation of the globe. The film was made based on excerpts from the seafarers' amateur film and recollections of former seafarers. Here are three different excerpts:

> I went through many storms, the biggest one was probably on the Vítkovice in Greenland, where I saw the waves some 70 meters long and about 12 metres high. And I know we got turned somehow, going to the David Straight, and we got blown back a bit to the Atlantic, and we turned in the morning at eight and we were going two and a half day back, to get to the place where we got turned. We got there, each of us having some troubles, double vision, terrible bellyache.

The voyage took 40 days. So we decided to pass the time, so we were running around the ship. And there was this competition, 10 of us have signed up, 10 seafarers, to do 100 kilometres. So 10 laps every day. But one lap is 250 metres. Wasn't that easy when the weather was bad. The ship was tilting, but we would run. Once there were waves coming from one side, so we were running on the other. And we succeeded before arriving in Japan, those 100 kilometres.

We as a crew were against it, against selling the ship. We were feeling down. Many of us. We arrived in Taiwan, tied up the ship, and about 10 of us stayed down in the corridors and the chief went to shut down the engine. But shutting down auxiliary engines, the light is turned off, all the energy on the boat is turned off. It's like he went to shut down the heart. The ship simply dies. [...] The sudden silence, the lights turned off, darkness in the corridors. We were left alone there, it was very sad for us. We left the ship, we had to leave the ship that was our home.[556]

Blaník

TYPE:	GENERAL CARGO	**DWT:**	6,000.00 T
LENGTH:	126.95 M	**GRT:**	5,516.84 T
BREADTH:	17.01 M	**NRT:**	3,036.80 T
DRAFT:	6.86 M	**SPEED:**	14.7 KNTS
ORIGIN:	BUILT IN 1967 IN THE STOCZNIA ADOLFA WARSKIEGO, SZCZECIN, POLAND		
OPERATION:	1967–1990; 22 YEARS, 3 MONTHS		

MEANING OF THE NAME: The Blaník is the first vessel from the series of four ships named after two Czech and two Slovak mountains, among which the Blaník is the most well-known in the Czech Republic. Blaník is a 638 metres high hill in Central Bohemia. In difficult moments of Czech history it has been a symbol of hope for gaining freedom and independence for the Czech nation. The legend says that inside the hill troops are resting, waiting for the worst moment of the Czech nation to come. The commander of the troop is Saint Václav [Wenceslas], the patron of the Czech lands. At the moment when the country will be in the greatest

---

556 Česká televize, "Vítkovice kolem světa," [Vítkovice on Her Trip Around the World] http://www.ceskatelevize.cz/porady/1181662874-zapomenute-vypravy/405235100221028-vitkovice-kolem-sveta/ (as of 10 February 2015), time sequences 5:58, 10:05, 18:55.

need, the dry oak on Blaník will turn green, the spring under it will give so much water that the fountain will overflow, and the water will flow down the slope. Then the mountain will open, the knights inside awake from their deep sleep, and under the Czech patron's leadership set off against the enemies, defeat them, and Bohemia will regain peace.

STORY: This series of ships was equipped with six double passenger cabins arranged in a separate part of the ship superstructure for regular passenger transport. The service flourished at the end of the 1960s; in 1976 it was abolished, mainly for restrictions on travelling in the "normalization" period. The Blaník was intended (as well as the three other ships of the series) to ensure transport of cargo following from the developed goods exchange between Czechoslovakia and Cuba in the 1960s. Three ships (the Blaník, the Sitno, the Radhošť) were deployed on the Cuban line, while the fourth of the set (the Kriváň) was time chartered to other destinations. These four ships were very helpful in terms of size, location of storage areas, economy of operation, and their universal use for various cargos. They were also well-liked by seafarers.

One ship of this series became a famous "movie star" carrying the name Morava [Moravia].[557] She acted in the series The Thirty Cases of Major Zeman. The series was based on 30 criminal cases, many of them based on true stories, properly "adjusted" to be in the conformity with contemporary historical interpretations. The 30 episodes are set in the period from 1945 to 1973, on the basis of one year—one episode; two episodes are set in 1947. The main character is Zeman, a member of the National Security Corps (Police) gradually promoted from civilian to the chief of the Prague criminal police. The episode where the ship appeared is from 1970, titled The Bella Vista Hostage. The State Security reveals a sabotage of Czechoslovak locomotives transported to Chile. Major Hradec, who is assigned to investigate in the field, sails on the Czechoslovak ship and follows the crewman Barkl to find out who is behind this sabotage.

---

[557] Comparing film shots with photographs clearly confirms that in the film played one of the Blaník series. Unfortunately, according to available materials (meeting records, log books, some crew lists) I cannot determine which one played in the film. Unofficial resources (Facebook) speak that it was the ship Radhošť.

Sitno

TYPE:	GENERAL CARGO	DWT:	5,945.00 T
LENGTH:	123.91 M	GRT:	5,310.21 T
BREADTH:	17.04 M	NRT:	2,939.69 T
DRAFT:	6.89 M	SPEED:	14.7 KNTS
ORIGIN:	BUILT IN 1969 IN THE STOCZNIA ADOLFA WARSKIEGO, SZCZECIN, POLAND		
OPERATION:	1969–1990; 20 YEARS, 2 MONTHS		

MEANING OF THE NAME: The ship was given the name of a similar origin as the Blaník. Sitno is the highest peak (1,009 metres) of the Štiavnické Mountains, part of the Slovak Central Range. The ruins of the 13th century castle Sitno are located at the top of the hill. Also this mountain is rumoured to be the dwelling of powerful knights who will wake up when the Slovak nation is in dire straits and the knights will fight for the Slovaks. Every seven years they wake up to ask the old knight who guards the entrance if they are needed. The old Knight ascends the top of the Sitno and calls in all directions: Is this the time? Now? If there is no answer, he closes the iron gate and the knights rest for the next seven years.

STORY: Everyday life on the ship Sitno, however, was far removed from the legend that lent the ship its name. Let us look at one record written in 1984 by the ship master Alexander Golub (a Soviet national) about the "political-moral condition of the crew": During the voyage the crew performed the planned tasks in very difficult conditions, mainly because of the dangerous situation in the ports of embarking, namely Luanda (Angola), Maputo (Mozambique),[558] and Tema (Albania). It is no surprise that the ship transported military cargo to these destinations. Concerning that some families of the seafarers were on the ship, the ship master recommended the headquarters consider in the future "if it is appropriate that family members are present on ships carrying cargo of

---

558 In 1984 the civil war continued in Mozambique. In Angola, the Movement Popular for Liberation of Angola supporting by Cuba and the Soviet Union fought against the National Union for the Total Independence of Angola (UNITA) supported by the South Africa and the United States.

the 1st class to the areas with an unclear situation". The risks following from dangerous stays in some ports caused also problems among the crew:

> Demanding stays in ports and impacts of international situation on the planned route increased nervousness among some crew members; this concerned mainly the chief mate and the 3rd mate. Both of them also abnormally abused alcohol.[559]

Radhošť

TYPE:	GENERAL CARGO	DWT:	5,961.00 T
LENGTH:	124.00 M	GRT:	5,310.21 T
BREADTH:	17.03 M	NRT:	2,939.81 T
DRAFT:	6.88 M	SPEED:	14.7 KNTS
ORIGIN:	BUILT IN 1970 IN THE STOCZNIA ADOLFA WARSKIEGO, SZCZECIN, POLAND		
OPERATION:	1970–1990; 19 YEARS, 9 MONTHS		

MEANING OF THE NAME: Radhošť is a mountain in the Beskydy Mountains in the easternmost part of the Czech Republic, near the Slovak border. According to legend, Radhošť is the seat of the Slavic god Radegast, the god of sun, war, and victory.

STORY: In 1973, three years after the ship had left the Szczecin shipyard, it was also in Szczecin that the chief mate ran into trouble when speaking with local journalists. Without the headquarters' permission he provided the Polish newspaper Głos Szczeciński with information about the cargo—new containers with donations sent from the Czechoslovak people to Cuba. The chief mate revealed the precise number of containers on board the Radhošť "which should have been confidential information". The COS delegate in Szczecin reported the issue to the State Security body. Having verified the matter, the headquarters informed the State Security that the chief mate had not disclosed any secret data. The COS admonished the chief mate and downplayed the af-

---

559 ABS_32: Ship master's report about the Sitno voyage No. 116 out, 27 October 1984.

fair, stating that the chief mate did not have any experience in how to communicate with journalist.[560]

Kriváň

TYPE:	GENERAL CARGO	DWT:	5,923.00 T
LENGTH:	124.05 M	GRT:	5,313.00 T
BREADTH:	17.04 M	NRT:	2,942.00 T
DRAFT:	6.88 M	SPEED:	14.7 KNTS
ORIGIN:	BUILT IN 1970 IN THE STOCZNIA ADOLFA WARSKIEGO, SZCZECIN, POLAND		
OPERATION:	1967–1987; 16 YEARS, 8 MONTHS		

MEANING OF THE NAME: Mount Kriváň with its height of 2,494 metres, located in the High Tatras, is one of the highest peaks in Slovakia. This mountain was represented, together with a bonfire, on the Slovak State Emblem of the Czechoslovak (Socialist) Republic between 1960 and 1990.

STORY: A different problem to the one experienced by the chief mate mentioned above was experienced by a seafarer on the ship Kriváň. It was in 1981 in the Libyan port of Tripoli. One Panamanian ship flying the Taiwanese flag anchoring next to the Kriváň brought military jeeps to Libya. Her ship master asked the ship master from the Kriváň to assist them during the jeeps' unloading, to pull out the jeeps when they were being unloaded. The Kriváň ship master assigned three seafarers to the task. One of them hit the ship's side and damaged the one of the jeep, thus causing damage of approximately $150–200. The seafarer was detained by the Libyan police who asked the ship master to pay a $20,000 bail, otherwise the seafarer would be prosecuted and the ship arrested. The ship master refused the bail, arguing the total price of the jeep was about $5,000. The Czechoslovak consul in Libya protested against the detention of the seafarer. Based on these steps the seafarer was released from custody the same day and returned to the ship. Ob-

---

560 ABS_20: Report about the meeting of a State Security's officer and the chief mate on the ship Radhošť, 2 September 1973.

taining this information, the Czechoslovak State Security was concerned mainly with two issues: 1) why the ship master provided three seafarers for the job; 2) if he or the seafarers received any payment for the work.[561] The State Security controlled two areas with top priority: free movement and one's income. This case proves it very well.

Praha

TYPE:	BULK CARRIER	DWT:	32,357.00 T
LENGTH:	198.43 M	GRT:	20,318.00 T
BREADTH:	24.47 M	NRT:	15,454.00 T
DRAFT:	10.70 M	SPEED:	14.3 KNTS
ORIGIN:	BUILT IN 1972 IN THE STOCZNIA ADOLFA WARSKIEGO, SZCZECIN, POLAND		
OPERATION:	1972–1994; 21 YEARS, 8 MONTHS		

MEANING OF THE NAME: Praha [Prague] is the capital of former Czechoslovakia as well as the capital of the Czech Republic. Prague was also the registry port of Czechoslovak and later Czech vessels. Former seafarers, however, did not attach great importance to this name evoking the capital of their homeland.

STORY: All the witnesses and fans of the Czechoslovak/Czech shipping, nevertheless, could follow via youtube.com documentary footage presenting pictures from life on the ship and her last voyage from Barcelona to Belfast.[562] The footage captures the moments when the ship anchored in Barcelona from 3 to 11 January 1994 and her subsequent journey to Finland. She reached the Finnish port of Vaasa after a complicated voyage through many ice floes. The Praha could not manage entering Vaasa nor leaving the port without the help of Finnish icebreakers. On 2 February 1994 she set off from Vaasa for the United States loaded with grain and then to Belfast. In this Irish port the Praha ended her life's journey.

---

561 ABS_21: Record on detention of the seafarer in Libya, 4 August 1981.
562 On the youtube.com search: *Poslední plavba lodi Praha* [Last Voyage of the Ship Praha].

Mír II

TYPE:	GENERAL CARGO	DWT:	13,870.00
LENGTH:	152.75 M	GRT:	9,651.43 T
BREADTH:	20.30 M	NRT:	5,249.67 T
DRAFT:	9.32 M	SPEED:	14.5 KNTS
ORIGIN:	BUILT IN 1972 IN THE WARNOWWERFT SHIPYARD, WARNEMÜNDE, GERMAN DEMOCRATIC REPUBLIC		
OPERATION:	1973–1993; 21 YEARS, 1 MONTH		

MEANING OF THE NAME: The last ships named in conformity with communist propaganda were the Pionýr (1960) and the Jiskra (1963). Thus naming the ship Mír II [peace] could be a response to an implicit need to assign again a name with an ideological connotation, especially considering this was at the beginning of "normalization" period. However, no other ship during the time of "normalization" was named after ideological symbols. The meaning of the concept of peace within the propaganda is explained above in the text dedicated to the Mír I.

STORY: During the twenty years of operation, the Mír II tackled various critical situations, including helping others at sea:

> 8. 4. 1986: A message received about salvage action radioed from the French ship Ville de Bordeaux located at the position 27°00'0 N, 34°30'0 E. They were searching for nine missing persons from the Greek ship Araska Two, which had exploded in the morning. [...] The Mír's ship master informed the Ville de Bordeaux that they would join the rescue operation. 15:20 Raised a Man Overboard alarm. 15.21 Half Ahead. On the right, an empty lifejacket was spotted near the ship. 15.25 The Mír crew was lined-up at the rescue boat No. 1; the boat was prepared to be launched. Four observers at the bridge. [...] 15:35 The ship Maritsa announced seeing two survivors. 15.56 The ship Shumaru picked up two survivors. Message from the Ville de Bordeaux: seven shipwreck survivors salvaged, four are still missing. From 16:00 to 05:00 the ship master on the bridge, the Mír continues to search for four missing people. 16:25 in agreement with the Ville de Bordeaux the Mír agreed to cease assisting in the operation.[563]

---

563 NA_122: Log book from the Mír II No. 48.

Bratislava

TYPE:	BULK CARRIER	DWT:	32,780.00 T
LENGTH:	199.01 M	GRT:	20,589.00 T
BREADTH:	24.45 M	NRT:	12,716.80 T
DRAFT:	10.70 M	SPEED:	14.8 KNTS
ORIGIN:	BUILT IN 1974 IN THE STOCZNIA ADOLFA WARSKIEGO, SZCZECIN, POLAND		
OPERATION:	1974–1994; 20 YEARS, 3 MONTHS		

MEANING OF THE NAME: To keep the individual regions of the Republic equally represented, the COS run three ships named after the country's major cities: Brno, the capital of Moravia (purchased in 1962); Praha, the capital of Bohemia and of the whole federation (purchased in 1972); and Bratislava, the capital of Slovakia, put in operation in 1974.

STORY: The Bratislava was a ship of a similar type to the Praha, but with a high degree of automation and remote control enabling a 16-hour unattended operation of the engine room. The ship offered also a high standard of accommodation—each crew member had their own cabin, and she was equipped with facilities such as a gym or sauna. Later, similar equipment and standards were provided in most newly built ships. But the Bratislava was the first of its kind offering this standard.

Maybe the high standard of accommodation was one of the reasons why the director of human resources combined a business trip on this ship with a family vacation. She prolonged her planned stay on the ship from 30 to 70 days at the expense of the COS, which was approved by the general director.[564] One interpretation of this episode could be that of disorder and bad management in the company. However, it could also be evidence of the power of the HR department at that time. The department was fairly powerful because they made decisions about personnel policy and individual careers, and moreover they were connected with the State Security, etc.

---

564 ABS_14: Report about the investigation of anonymous complaints to the COS management, 22 March 1977.

Třinec

TYPE:	BULK CARRIER	DWT:	33,230.00 T
LENGTH:	199.10 M	GRT:	20,596.00 T
BREADTH:	24.40 M	NRT:	12,726.86 T
DRAFT:	11.00 M	SPEED:	15.0 KNTS
ORIGIN:	BUILT IN 1975 IN THE STOCZNIA ADOLFA WARSKIEGO, SZCZECIN, POLAND		
OPERATION:	1975–1998; 23 YEARS		

MEANING OF THE NAME: Leaving aside the names that were given twice, the Třinec is the last ship named in connection with the Czechoslovak heavy industry. The Třinec represented ironworks located in the town of Třinec in the North-East of the Czech Republic. The link between the ship and the ironworks is indisputable, as the ship's godmother was an employee from the ironworks.

STORY: The State Security searched, among other things, for evidence of religious literature "on board". It was an indispensable part of its control of the crew and everything what happened on the ship. Considering those materials subversive, the Czechoslovak communist regime watched their movement very vigilantly. Thus religious texts were controlled in a similar way as erotic magazines or the National Geographic (these examples are mentioned in the chapter about the 1980s).

This type of printed materials appeared on the voyage of the Třinec to Montreal. Christian missionaries in Canada came to the ship and offered to deliver various religious magazines and books free of charge the next day. An "informant" of the State Security took advantage of this offer and asked for the New Testament. The next day, he received the book with a dedication, but as the informant later stressed, there was no signature. He probably ordered the religious book to demonstrate to the State Security how easy it was to obtain this type of material abroad. He concluded the report with the statement that nobody from the ship command had objected to these visits, all of them, including the ship master, had just stood by.[565]

---

565 ABS_31: Visit of missionaries in the ship Třinec in Montreal, 20 February 1984.

Orlík II

TYPE:	GENERAL CARGO	DWT:	15,870.00 T
LENGTH:	145.50 M	GRT:	10,416.00 T
BREADTH:	21.60 M	NRT:	6,718.00 T
DRAFT:	9.40 M	SPEED:	14.8 KNTS
ORIGIN:	BUILT IN 1980 IN THE 3. MAJ SHIPYARD, RIJEKA, YUGOSLAVIA		
OPERATION:	1980–1996; 15 YEARS, 2 MONTHS		

MEANING OF THE NAME: Giving the name Orlík for the second time, the COS returned to naming its ships after Czechoslovak dams. Apart from the Orlík II (built in 1980), the COS named two other ships after the dams of the so-called Vltava Cascade—Slapy and Lipno, and one ship after the Slovak dam Orava, all three purchased in 1981.

STORY: The ship was probably one of the first to experience some pirate activity. On 8 June 1989 at 21:10, near the Anambas Islands, Indonesia, robbers approached the ship from the stern. They went via the outdoor decks to the captain's deck and entered his cabin. They tied the ship master and his wife and held them for ransom. The captain was convinced that the robbers had mistaken the vessel for an American or Japanese one. They stole a video camera, some jewellery, all valuable money (the captain's $300 and 200 Western German marks) and a set of kitchen knives. Secret documents and the crew's passports had not been stolen. The captain added that they could not have been professional pirates since they acted very nervously and chaotically. After looting the cabin they disappeared, probably satisfied with the loot.[566]

---

566 NA_126: The ship master's statement about the ship assault case, 10 June 1989.

Slapy

TYPE:	GENERAL CARGO	DWT:	15,916.00 T
LENGTH:	145.66 M	GRT:	10,416.00 T
BREADTH:	21.60 M	NRT:	6,716.00 T
DRAFT:	9.38 M	SPEED:	14.07 KNTS
ORIGIN:	BUILT IN 1981 IN THE 3. MAJ SHIPYARD, RIJEKA, YUGOSLAVIA		
OPERATION:	1981–1999; 17 YEARS, 7 MONTHS		

MEANING OF THE NAME: The ship was named after the dam on the river Vltava; see the previous descriptions of the ships Orlík I and Orlík II. As described in the chapter about the 1960s, one ship had already sailed under the name Slapy before. It was only for several days when the People's Republic of China needed to transport its Indonesian immigrants; thus the Slapy from the 1960s is not included in the list of ships run by the COS, neither in the official documents nor in the memoirs.

STORY: The Slapy crew as well as the crew members of all other ships convinced themselves many times that we do not live in an ideal world. In 1985, they had to face this reality on the Slapy. On 14 May 1985, when the ship was in Veracruz, two motormen reported to the ship master the theft of 24,000 Mexican pesos and $546. The ship master held a hearing with both aggrieved men, wrote a report about the theft, and took into safekeeping the wallet and the diary where the men kept the money. Finally, he took fingerprints of all crew members, including himself. Then the captain sent all the materials to the COS headquarters and they proceeded the matter to the police investigation. Since no usable fingerprints were found on the objects, the matter was closed unsolved.[567]

---

567 ABS_33: Information about the crime, 25 July 1985.

Lipno

TYPE:	GENERAL CARGO	DWT:	15,916.00 T
LENGTH:	145.66 M	GRT:	10,416.00 T
BREADTH:	21.60 M	NRT:	6,716.00 T
DRAFT:	9.38 M	SPEED:	14.8 KNTS
ORIGIN:	BUILT IN 1981 IN THE 3. MAJ SHIPYARD, RIJEKA, YUGOSLAVIA		
OPERATION:	1981–1998; 17 YEARS, 5 MONTHS		

MEANING OF THE NAME: The Lipno represents the Lipno dam, the hydroelectric plant built on the Vltava river between 1952 and 1959. With an area of 48.7 km^2 it is the dam with the largest surface as well as with the largest water volume in the Czech Republic. Because of this, Lipno is sometimes referred to as the Czech or South Bohemian Sea.

STORY: During one of the Lipno's voyage to Cuba, the ship's doctor was suspected of the crime of espionage. The whole affair started when he was walking around the Cuban military port of Mariel (where Czechoslovak ships embarked, too). He came close to a "dead drop", where he allegedly "checked whether he was being followed". The next day he was detained by the Cuban police for violation of the customs zone, where he had made photographs, took samples of soil and collected intersect. The Czechoslovak State Security did not prove any espionage activities. Their investigation ascertained that the man had been engaged in his hobby—taking photographs and entomology.[568]

---

568 ABS_34: Proposal for archiving the file, 13 June 1985.

Orava II

TYPE:	GENERAL CARGO	DWT:	15,916.00 T
LENGTH:	145.66 M	GRT:	10,416.00 T
BREADTH:	21.60 M	NRT:	6,716.00 T
DRAFT:	9.38 M	SPEED:	14.8 KNTS
ORIGIN:	BUILT IN 1981 IN THE 3. MAJ SHIPYARD, RIJEKA, YUGOSLAVIA		
OPERATION:	1981–1997; 15 YEARS, 8 MONTHS		

MEANING OF THE NAME: The symbolism of giving the name Orava for the second time is obvious. The Orava I was the last ship purchased on the PRC account for the Sino–Czechoslovak joint venture at the end of the 1950s, and the Orava II was the only ship the Czechoslovak party invested into the "revival" of the joint venture with the People's Republic of China at the end of the 1980s. The joint venture was called COSSHIP (more on the topic in the chapter about the 1980s).

Karlovy Vary

TYPE:	BULK CARRIER	DWT:	22,623.00 T
LENGTH:	164.30 M	GRT:	13,569.00 T
BREADTH:	22.86 M	NRT:	8,576.00 T
DRAFT:	9.87 M	SPEED:	13.0 KNTS
ORIGIN:	BUILT IN 1974 IN THE IHI, TOKIO, JAPAN		
OPERATION:	1986–1996; 9 YEARS, 6 MONTHS		

MEANING OF THE NAME: Looking at all the names of the Czechoslovak ships indicates they could be roughly sorted into four groups: 1) symbolic names associated with national pride, represented mainly by symbol of the republic (the ships Republika I and II) and by the protagonists of the Hussite movement of the late Middle Ages discussed below in more detail in the presentation of the last four ships; 2) historically conditioned names associated with contemporary communist propaganda; 3) names associated with the construction of heavy industry in Czechoslovakia; 4) all other names which fall into the geographic category, such as the capitals of the individual regions of the country, mountains, rivers, or dams (the dams also partially refer to the socialist state's achievements). On the one hand, the names included in the fourth group do not carry such significant ideological baggage; on the other hand, they have a certain implicit imaginary connection with the mother country.

The city of Karlovy Vary does not fit in any of these four groups. After the names of the capitals were exhausted, the responsible authorities may have decided to name the ship after some other city. And the Karlovy Vary (t the spa, the city) is perceived as a sort of "mark" towards the foreigners. The other possible explanation for this name might be the location of the company holiday home fifteen kilometres from Karlovy Vary. The home was used occasionally for training courses for employees; most often, however, it served for winter ski trips for children and for summer family holidays.

STORY: After the late 1950s, the ship Karlovy Vary was the first and the last used ship that was purchased. The sh p became a nightmare mainly for the engine department and everyone avoided working there. One chief engineer, however, managed a daring feat: during his two long stays on the ship, he carefully repaired the engine and performed maintenance of related devices, so the Karlovy Vary ceased to be a nightmare and became popular to some extent. This chief engineer described the rigmarole he went through maintaining the Karlovy Vary and other COS ships in the memoir book *Odyssey of a Socialist Seafarer.*[569]

Vltava

TYPE:	DRY/GENERAL CARGO	DWT:	7,939.00 T
LENGTH:	119.01 M	GRT:	6,425.00 T
BREADTH:	18.64 M	NRT:	3,320.00 T
DRAFT:	7.71 M	SPEED:	13.5 KNTS
ORIGIN:	BUILT IN 1988 IN THE XINGANG SHIPYARD, TIANJIN, THE PEOPLE'S REPUBLIC OF CHINA		
OPERATION:	1988–1995; 7 YEARS, 1 MONTH		

---

569 Michal Svoreň, *Slaný chléb. Odyssea socialistického námořníka* [Salty Bread. Odyssey of a Socialist Seafarer] (Praha: Ma˙e Czech, 2013).

Otava

TYPE:	DRY/GENERAL CARGO	DWT:	7,947.00 T
LENGTH:	119.01 M	GRT:	6,425.00 T
BREADTH:	18.64 M	NRT:	3,320.00 T
DRAFT:	7.71 M	SPEED:	13.5 KNTS
ORIGIN:	BUILT IN 1988 IN THE XINGANG SHIPYARD, TIANJIN, THE PEOPLE'S REPUBLIC OF CHINA		
OPERATION:	1988–1994; 5 YEARS, 5 MONTHS		

Berounka

TYPE:	DRY/GENERAL CARGO	DWT:	7,920.00 T
LENGTH:	119.01 M	GRT:	6,425.00 T
BREADTH:	18.59 M	NRT:	3,067.00 T
DRAFT:	7.71 M	SPEED:	13.5 KNTS
ORIGIN:	BUILT IN 1988 IN THE XINGANG SHIPYARD, TIANJIN, THE PEOPLE'S REPUBLIC OF CHINA		
OPERATION:	1988–1995; 6 YEARS, 4 MONTHS		

Sázava

TYPE:	GENERAL CARGO	DWT:	7,405.00 T
LENGTH:	118.93 M	GRT:	6,425.00 T
BREADTH:	18.61 M	NRT:	3,067.00 T
DRAFT:	7.49 M	SPEED:	13.5 KNTS
ORIGIN:	BUILT IN 1988 IN THE XINGANG SHIPYARD, TIANJIN, THE PEOPLE'S REPUBLIC OF CHINA		
OPERATION:	1989–1995; 5 YEARS, 6 MONTHS		

MEANING OF THE NAME: **Vltava**, **Otava**, **Berounka**, and **Sázava** are rivers in the Czech Republic. The Vltava is a more than 400 kilometres long stream which forms a natural axis of the country, crossing the capital city of Prague. The river has frequently been portrayed by various artists. The most famous work in this respect is the symphonic poem Vltava by Bedřich Smetana. The rivers Berounka and Otava are Vltava's left tributaries, Sázava the right one. All the rivers are surrounded by scenic landscapes and they are also very popular with the canoers.

STORY: The purchase of the four ships, however, was not as charming as the rivers themselves. Within the framework of the cooperation with the People's Republic of China (PRC) in the 1980s, a contract was signed in August 1985 for the delivery of equipment and services for a thermal power plant station in the PRC. This was a strategic contract for Czechoslovak industry worth a total of 525 million of Swiss francs. This "deal", however, was "redeemed" by the Czechoslovak commitment to an increased purchase of Chinese goods.[570]

In the case of the merchant fleet, this meant purchasing ships for higher prices, which can be documented by the following State Security records: The deputy of the general manager of China National Machinery "pointed out in a friendly manner that the contract was only a goodwill gesture of the Chinese side to demonstrate its interest to further developing relations with Czechoslovakia". He continued that it had been only a political concession because China had received a much better and cheaper offer for the power plant at a higher technical level. Finally, the deputy of the general manager added that if they had been willing to sign the contract with Czechoslovakia for the power plant, the Czechoslovaks should be more indulgent and accept the contract for the supply of four ships by the PRC.[571]

The ships were delivered as follows: the **Vltava** – April 1988; the **Otava** – November 1988; the Dunaj delivered in February 1989 from Poland; the **Berounka** – June 1989; the Labe delivery from Poland in August 1989; the Vítkovice II from a Yugoslav shipyard in October 1989; **Sázava** – November 1989. From this time on, even less information about the vessels is available; either because they were in operation only for a short time, or due the fact that the documents about the period after 1989 are not available as they were not submitted to the archives.

---

570 Skřivan, Československý vývoz do Číny 1918–1992, 266–267.
571 ABS_22: Record of the PRC opinions about the Czechoslovak sale of the power plant to the PRC, 12 September 1985.

Dunaj

TYPE:	BULK CARRIER	DWT:	33,230.00 T
LENGTH:	195.11 M	GRT:	21,339.00 T
BREADTH:	25.30 M	NRT:	12,516.00 T
DRAFT:	10.69 M	SPEED:	14.5 KNTS
ORIGIN:	BUILT IN 1989 IN THE STOCZNIA ADOLFA WARSKIEGO, SZCZECIN, POLAND		
OPERATION:	1989–1997; 8 YEARS, 9 MONTHS		

Labe

TYPE:	BULK CARRIER	DWT:	33,230.00 T
LENGTH:	195.30 M	GRT:	21,339.00 T
BREADTH:	25.30 M	NRT:	12,516.00 T
DRAFT:	10.69 M	SPEED:	14.5 KNTS
ORIGIN:	BUILT IN 1989 IN THE STOCZNIA ADOLFA WARSKIEGO, SZCZECIN, POLAND		
OPERATION:	1989–1997; 8 YEARS, 4 MONTHS		

MEANING OF THE NAME: Contrary to the previously mentioned four "local" Czech rivers, the significance of the Dunaj (Danube) and the Labe (Elbe) exceeds the borders of the country. The Danube is after the Volga Europe's second longest river, flowing through 10 states. For Slovakia, Hungary, Serbia, and Moldova the river represents some compensation for their landlocked economies. The Labe, one of the major waterways in Europe originates in the mountains of Northern Bohemia; it connects the Czech Republic with the North Sea.

The purchase of all ships named after rivers takes us to 1989 and the following period of transition toward democracy and the market economy. Unfortunately, there is very little documentation, and even less reliable sources, about the development of the Czechoslovak/Czech fleet after this year. The information about the ships purchased since 1989 is fragmentary, thus I am often limited to explaining the origin of their names only. All these ships were sold between 1997 and 1998. Basic information on fleet development in the post-1989 years is provided in the "Epilogue".

Vítkovice II

TYPE:	BULK CARRIER	DWT:	40,908.00 T
LENGTH:	196.31 M	GRT:	26,128.00 T
BREADTH:	28.00 M	NRT:	12,843.00 T
DRAFT:	11.21 M	SPEED:	13.5 KNTS
ORIGIN:	BUILT IN 1989 IN THE 3. MAJ SHIPYARD, RIJEKA, YUGOSLAVIA		
OPERATION:	1989–1997; 8 YEARS, 1 MONTH		

STORY: The ship Vítkovice I was sold in 1987. Two years later, the ship Vítkovice II was put into operation, only about three weeks before the Velvet Revolution of 1989. Seafarers did not have time enough to become attached to this second ship as strongly as to the Vítkovice I. Still, I am convinced that they desperately needed some "Vítkovice" on the sea to have their "home", at least the men who had been on the Vítkovice I for a year and a half without interruption. The man who held the record in the longest stay on the Vítkovice I would work on the ship, then went home for a fortnight, and back to the Vítkovice I. He was there thirteen years altogether: "For me, Pepa Konečný is the father [emphasis] of the Vítkovice. I see Pepa, I see his cabin with the doorplate 'Pepa Konečný—father of the Vítkovice' and then 'adieu'."[572]

---

572 Remembering the legend of the ship Vítkovice I in the interview with J. J., 1952–2014, A/B sailor, 18 years in the COS; interview with J. V., * 1964, A/B sailor, 6 years in the COS. The memories relate to the ship Vítkovice I; here they are quoted to illustrate how strongly a seafarer could become attached to one specific ship.

Košice II

TYPE:	BULK CARRIER	DWT:	40,908.00 T
LENGTH:	196.30 M	GRT:	26,128.00 T
BREADTH:	28.00 M	NRT:	12,849.00 T
DRAFT:	11.21 M	SPEED:	13.5 KNTS
ORIGIN:	BUILT IN 1989 IN THE 3. MAJ SHIPYARD, RIJEKA, YUGOSLAVIA		
OPERATION:	1989–1997; 7 YEARS, 9 MONTHS		

MEANING OF THE NAME: The Košice II, similarly as the Vítkovice II, was assigned the same name for the second time probably because of: 1) its symbolic meaning—the Vítkovice I as the biggest ship in the Soviet bloc, the Košice I as the first Czechoslovak ship circumnavigating the globe; 2) the similar purpose of the two ships, i.e. time charters, ore and other bulk cargo transport, etc.

Tatry

TYPE:	BULK CARRIER	DWT:	66,088.00 T
LENGTH:	225.00 M	GRT:	35,350.00 T
BREADTH:	32.20 M	NRT:	21,472.00 T
DRAFT:	12.92 M	SPEED:	13.5 KNTS
ORIGIN:	BUILT IN 1990 IN THE DAEWOO SHIPBUILDING AND HEAVY MACHINERY LTD., OKPO, REPUBLIC OF KOREA		
OPERATION:	1990–1998; 8 YEARS, 7 MONTHS		

Beskydy

TYPE:	BULK CARRIER	DWT:	70,456.00 T
LENGTH:	225.00 M	GRT:	37,550.00 T
BREADTH:	32.20 M	NRT:	23,072.00 T
DRAFT:	13.32 M	SPEED:	13.5 KNTS
ORIGIN:	BUILT IN 1990 IN THE DAEWOO SHIPBUILDING AND HEAVY MACHINERY LTD., OKPO, REPUBLIC OF KOREA		
OPERATION:	1993–1998; 4 YEARS, 8 MONTHS		

Šumava

TYPE:	BULK CARRIER	DWT:	70,120.00 T
LENGTH:	225.00 M	GRT:	37,550.00 T
BREADTH:	32.20 M	NRT:	23,072.00 T
DRAFT:	13.30 M	SPEED:	13.5 KNTS
ORIGIN:	BUILT IN 1990 IN THE DAEWOO SHIPBUILDING AND HEAVY MACHINERY LTD., OKPO, REPUBLIC OF KOREA		
OPERATION:	1996–1998; 2 YEARS, 4 MONTHS		

MEANING OF THE NAME: At the turn of the 1960s/1970s, the COS contracted a delivery of four ships named after four mountain ranges. Just before November 1989, Czechoslovak Ocean Shipping contracted the delivery of three other ships with names assigned according to mountain ranges. The first one was the ship **Tatry** [High Tatras], Slovakia's highest mountain range. The second ship was the **Beskydy**, named after the mountains in North-Eastern Moravia and the third was the **Šumava**, a reminder of the extensive mountain range on the border of the Czech Republic, Austria, and Bavaria in Germany.

STORY: The financing of these ships offers a nice illustrative example of the malfunction of the foreign trade monopoly in the Czechoslovak socialist economy. The rewarding of directors of enterprises producing goods for export, together with the rewarding of managers from Czechoslovak foreign trade companies, used to be dependent on meeting export tasks. In order to meet the export plan, the foreign trade organizations did not check whether the recipients met their obligations, or fulfilled their deliveries to Czechoslovakia. Even when problems with deliveries arose, these Czechoslovak monopoly organizations granted the foreign recipients with exceptions. This approach, for example, caused the enormous debts of Libya and Syria to Czechoslovakia. These countries were willing to fulfil their obligations by supplying raw materials. However, they offered such materials which the Czechoslovak industry could not process. Therefore Czechoslovakia was forced to resell these raw materials without any profit.

In the case of the Libyan debt, South Korea was interested in its takeover to receive Libyan oil. Both parties then negotiated that South Korea would pay this debt to Czechoslovakia by delivering three ships, and about 3,000 cars, electronics, etc. For South Korea it was more profitable to barter than pay the debt in money. The transaction brought Czechoslovakia two advantages: 1) payment of the Libyan debts; 2) saving foreign currency when purchasing new ships. The option of selling the ships if it did not find employment for them was also considered.[573]

A problem occurred when the Korean side failed to get the oil supplies from Libya. As a consequence, Korea stopped their deliveries and asked for payment for the ship Tatry that had already been delivered (1990). South Korea also wanted to cancel the re-assignment of Libyan debts. Their main argument was that the re-assignment was not executed properly since it had not been approved by the Libyan side. The disputes escalated when Daewoo Shipbuilding initiated arbitration proceedings to get payment for the Tatry on 20 April 1994. In addition, Daewoo started a direct trial in London. On 12 June 1995, the Supreme Court in London issued a court order to detain the ship Tatry. This order was applied immediately after the ship's arrival at the port of Immingham, 15 June 1995.[574] In the end, the matter had to be settled since the Tatry was in operation in the COS until 1998. But the relevant documents are not available. As for the other two ships covered by this deal, after the disputes in 1993, the COS pulled out of the contract and the ships were bought by the National Navigation Co Cairo.[575] Based on new orders, two vessels were purchased by the COS and put into operation as the Beskydy and the Šumava.

---

573 ABS_35: Situation in the field of unblocking of receivables in Libya and Syria, 16 August 1989.
574 NA_127: Materials for the Czech Government meeting, 12 July 1995.
575 Trond Lillestolen, "National Navigation Takes Up Bulker Option," *TradeWinds*, 15 June 1995.

Svitava

TYPE:	BULK CARRIER	DWT:	29,043.70 T
LENGTH:	180.82 M	GRT:	17,630.00 T
BREADTH:	24.85 M	NRT:	10,220.00 T
DRAFT:	10.43 M	SPEED:	13.5 KNTS
ORIGIN:	BUILT IN 1995 IN THE 2 MAI SHIPYARD, MANGALIA, ROMANIA		
OPERATION:	1995–1998; 3 YEARS, 4 MONTHS		

MEANING OF THE NAME: The ship Svitava was named according to the 97 kilometre long river in Moravia. Maybe she was given the name with the aim to fill the gap between the ships named according to the rivers in Bohemia and the Danube in Slovakia.

Jan Hus

TYPE:	BULK CARRIER	DWT:	26,045.30 T
LENGTH:	171.97 M	GRT:	16,405.00 T
BREADTH:	25.00 M	NRT:	9,211.00 T
DRAFT:	10.00 M	SPEED:	14.0 KNTS
ORIGIN:	BUILT IN 1997 IN THE GSI, GUANGZHOU, THE PEOPLE'S REPUBLIC OF CHINA		
OPERATION:	1997–1998; 1 YEAR, 5 MONTHS		

Jan Žižka

TYPE:	BULK CARRIER	DWT:	26,068.80 T
LENGTH:	171.96 M	GRT:	16,405.00 T
BREADTH:	25.07 M	NRT:	9,211.00 T
DRAFT:	10.00 M	SPEED:	14.0 KNTS
ORIGIN:	BUILT IN 1997 IN THE GSI, GUANGZHOU, THE PEOPLE'S REPUBLIC OF CHINA		
OPERATION:	1997–1998; 1 YEAR, 2 MONTHS		

Prokop Holý

TYPE:	BULK CARRIER	DWT:	26,096.40 T
LENGTH:	171.92 M	GRT:	16,405.00 T
BREADTH:	25.07 M	NRT:	9,211.00 T
DRAFT:	10.00 M	SPEED:	14.0 KNTS
ORIGIN:	BUILT IN 1997 IN THE GSI, GUANGZHOU, THE PEOPLE'S REPUBLIC OF CHINA		
OPERATION:	1997–1998; 1 YEAR		

Jan Želivský

TYPE:	BULK CARRIER	DWT:	26,096.40 T
LENGTH:	171.94 M	GRT:	16,405.00 T
BREADTH:	25.06 M	NRT:	9,211.00 T
DRAFT:	10.00 M	SPEED:	14.0 KNTS
ORIGIN:	BUILT IN 1997 IN THE GSI, GUANGZHOU, THE PEOPLE'S REPUBLIC OF CHINA		
OPERATION:	1998; 7 MONTHS		

MEANING OF THE NAMES: Between June 1997 and April 1998, the Chinese shipyard delivered four bulk carriers. They were registered under the Czech flag, not Czechoslovak, since Czechoslovakia divided on 1 January 1993. Thus these ships' names were probably intended to be somehow connected with supremely Czech phenomena. What is surprising is that the names chosen only a few years after the Velvet Revolution had their origin in the Hussite movement (the Middle Ages), which communist ideology presented as its ideological predecessor and often ideologically misused for its own propaganda. Perhaps this naming was caused by someone's passion for the given historical period (and for the Hussites especially). Perhaps a lack of creativity was to blame. On the other hand, it is indisputable that the Hussite movement is one of the most important parts of Czech history and identity.

Foreign commentators explained this naming with an effort of the COS management to demonstrate that it is a Czech company, despite the fact that shareholders resided outside the country.[576] Putting into operation these four ships, the company also wanted to present the Hussites to their business partners in abroad. With this aim they published a brief colour leaflet with the picture of the characters and description of their involvement in the Hussite movement. Here are brief excerpts from these promotional texts:

> Jan Hus is an integral part of the Czech national identity. For Czechs, he is a symbol of a moral leader, a person who is reacy to die for his beliefs. [...] He is also seen as the father of the first mass reformist movement inside the Catholic Church. [I only add that in 1415 Jan Hus was denounced by the Council of Constance as a heretic and thus he was hanJed to the secular power to be burned at the stake when he refused to take back his teaching. The date of his burning became a Czech national holiday.]
>
> Prokop Holý was both a great general and a skilful diplomat who overcame differences of various factions within the Hussite movement after Jan Žižka's death in 1425. Moreover, he made several successful attacks abroad which gained peace, money and moral support for Hussite ideas.
>
> Jan Žižka is a Czech national hero. The legendary undefeated one eyed general made his enemies fear his name, successfully defending the Czech kingdom against foreign invasions. Žižka was a military genius and changed profoundly 15th century military strategy and tactics.
>
> Jan Želivský was a charismatic Hussite preacher who encouraged the masses to revolt not only against the Catholic Church but the whole social system.

Jan Želivský was the 44th ship which cruised around the seas and oceans, at least for a short time, under the Czechoslovak or Czech flag. This ship is often used as a synonym for the vessels "lost" during the transition period. When seafarers speak about the Czech shipping transformation, sometimes they use in one sentence both the name of the charismatic priest Jan Želivský (of course they mean the ship) and the name of unscrupulous businessman Viktor Kožený. The history of Czechoslovak Ocean Shipping, however, is not only full of paradoxes, or "peculiar" moments. It is also the history full of work hard and shipping services providing. The most important milestones of this history are summarised in the conclusion of this book.

---

576 Trond Lillestolen, "Czech Ocean Keeps the Handysize Faith," *TradeWinds*, 24 April 1997.

10 Conclusion: Four decades of Czechoslovak shipping in a nutshell

So far, this book has told the story on HOW Czechoslovakia ran maritime business during the Cold War. Still, there is one more crucial question at a stake, namely that of WHY a small landlocked country ran a maritime business. Who benefited from it? Was the shipping trade established and developed as a matter of business or politics? Although answers to these questions have been implied in the previous chapters, they need to be discussed here to draw final conclusions about the key motivations behind the Czechoslovak ocean shipping experience.

The creation of the Czechoslovak shipping business was accompanied by several dark historical events. Firstly, the establishment of the Iron Curtain and the communist coup d'état in Czechoslovakia in 1948 interrupted the on-going democratic development and cast Czechoslovakia into the area controlled by the Soviet Union. Whatever bizarre it may sound, another two important historical events in the Far East influenced the shipping industry in Czechoslovakia: 1) communist victory in the Chinese civil war and the proclamation of the People's Republic of China (PRC) in 1949 under the rule of Mao Zedong; 2) the involvement of the PRC in the Korean War, supporting North Korea. These events led to a greater dependence of the PRC on the Soviet Union and to significant economic problems following from the Western and the UN economic embargo and the naval blockade of the PRC. The US countermeasures (supported by other capitalist states) aimed to isolate communist China both economically and politically and represented a significant negative impact on the viability of the communist regime in China due to the country's large dependence on maritime transport.

To overcome the obstacles in purchasing vessels and running merchant shipping, the PRC would "cover" its ships by flags of other Soviet bloc countries including Czechoslovakia. Although Czechoslovakia was a landlocked country, it acquired the right to register and run its own shipping vessels within the Versailles Treaty (1919) and Barcelona Convention (1921). Still the shipping business did not start immediately after the war because it required considerable initial funds, which were scarce in the post-war period of rebuilding the country.

Several years later, however, after the communist coup d'état, the maritime business in Czechoslovakia came into existence. It was not cheaper than in the post-war years, but still easily implementable in the 1950s when the development of this transport field was triggered mainly by political reasons—by an effort to help communist China to overcome the embargo and naval blockade. The heart of this support consisted in the coverage of Chinese ships under the Czechoslovak flag while maintaining the highest secrecy about the matter. Disclosure would have meant serious problems for Czechoslovakia, both economic and political.

Helping communist China in evading the naval blockade during the Korean War would have been interpreted as Czechoslovak involvement in the conflict on the side of North Korea, the consequence being international isolation. In the economic area, despite the proclaimed autarky, the Eastern bloc socialist countries were still dependent on imports from Western countries, with varying degrees of intensity and disclosure of the deal would have had severe impacts on Czechoslovak economic cooperation with Western partners.

To maintain absolute secrecy, Czechoslovak leaders needed to take more precautions than merely raising the Czechoslovak flag on a Chinese ship full of Chinese sailors and goods. The ship had to be officially run as Czechoslovak and subordinated to both international maritime law and Czechoslovak legislation. The owner of the ship in the nationalized economy was the Czechoslovak state, which had responsibility for the ship, crew, and cargo. To disguise the deal and comply with legislation, it was desirable that the captain or at least the highest mate of the "covered" ship was a Czechoslovak citizen and that more Czechoslovaks worked on the ship. The presence of Chinese seafarers could then be explained as the PRC's help to a landlocked socialist country in the maritime sector, referring to China's long maritime tradition. Even though this reasoning may have never been used in the international context, the idea of "sharing maritime skills and experience" appears both in non-fiction books about the Czechoslovak shipping and in popular narratives.

To cloak the cooperation in complete secrecy, Czechoslovakia had to demonstrate its intention to manage its own shipping business by running at least one naval ship. So, in 1952, the ship Republika I was purchased from the Greek owner as a basis for future Czechoslovak fleet development. Her first voyage from Europe to the PRC was a political act, giving priority to transporting goods for communist China. But because necessary repairs to the ship were carried out hastily, on the way back to Europe, the Republika I was severely damaged by a typhoon, and then it underwent lengthy repairs from August 1952 until June 1954. The first years of the shipping sector thus brought significant losses, which burdened the economy: Czechoslovakia invested money into the ship's purchase and then in her rather costly repairs. Still, at least the process of covering the PRC shipping was accomplished by this unfortunate voyage. The cooperation in the shipping sector was confirmed in June 1953 by signing the top secret Protocol on the Development of Maritime Transport between Czechoslovakia and the People's Republic of China.

In 1954, the first two ships in Chinese ownership began to be operated under the Czechoslovak flag. Despite the optimistic plans about the future development of shipping between the two partners, there was a time gap and the PRC invested another two ships into the joint venture as late as in 1958. It could have been caused by problems in the PRC's home economic policy but also by the fact that China developed a shipping cooperation with other partners, mainly with Poland, which, of course, could offer more skilled seafarers and much more experience in the industry. In 1959, the PRC invested other two ships into the joint venture and Czechoslovakia purchased its second ship on its account. Moreover, in 1959 the legal form of cooperation was changed and a specialized shipping enterprise was established, Czechoslovak Ocean Shipping (COS). In 1960, the PRC invested the last (the seventh) ship into the joint venture and Czechoslovakia purchased its third ship.

At this moment it did not seem to be probable that the Czechoslovak party considered increasing its fleet significantly. And during the first half of the 1960s, the Chinese side rather began to lose interest in the joint venture, whether it was because of more favourable international conditions for its independent shipping or because of the Great Leap Forward policy which had started in 1958 and ultimately brought great losses for the PRC's economy. Czechoslovakia, on the contrary, executed some investments and in 1966 it operated seven ships on its account. In the same year, the cooperation with the PRC disintegrated.

This rupture was not only a logical outcome of the declining cooperation in shipping. The political interests of both countries played a role, mainly their interpretation of the "struggle against imperialism", which at this moment manifested particularly in the support of North Vietnam in the Vietnam War. When transporting goods to Vietnam ("material help for the Vietnamese people" as stated in the documents), the ships moving in Vietnamese coastal waters could be subjected to checks by US guards. For the PRC it was definitely unacceptable to let the ships be not only stopped, let alone checked. They argued that the Chinese seafarers would rather die than let the ship to be inspected by Americans. The Czechoslovak side was not so clear-cut and uncompromising. After all, it was responsible for the ship cruising under its flag. The dispute finally escalated to the aforementioned disintegration of the joint shipping venture and a transfer of the ships owned by the PRC back to China.

The mid-1960s was a time when Czechoslovakia had to decide on its own future shipping operation. Growing profits during the first half of the decade showed that this business could bring much needed foreign currency, in particular in convertible currencies, both indirectly and directly: 1) indirectly when Czechoslovak exporters saved money for transport fees that they would otherwise pay to capitalist ship owners in convertible currency; 2) directly when operating Czechoslovak ships in time charters for capitalist partners. In addition, more than 10 years of the shipping operation under the Czechoslovak flag proved that vessels owned by Czechoslovakia could bring great advantages, such as the transport of various "special" cargoes for very good pay (whether these were weapons, explosives, dangerous chemicals or, for example, money printed in Czechoslovakia for Cuba).

Beside the services provided for Czechoslovak foreign trade enterprises, time charters, and the delivery of "special cargoes", in the 1960s and mainly in the 1970s Czechoslovak ships started cooperation with the Third World. Using its own fleet, Czechoslovakia also reduced potential losses caused by the fact that economic relationships were often conditioned by the political interests of the socialist bloc, mainly those of the Soviet Union. Because the "fight" for spheres of interest in the Cold War, the focus shifted to developing countries, Third World countries, and other countries not firmly tied to the US sphere of influence, such as India. It is precisely these political circumstances that provide a substantial part of the answer to the WHY question mentioned at the beginning of this chapter: Why did a landlocked country ran a shipping business? The answer is: Because it was politically advantageous and economically profitable at that time.

Nevertheless, national Czechoslovak shipping would not have yielded profit had it not been for other favourable circumstances. Indisputably, political reasons rank among the most important. Political affairs and decisions were essential mainly in the first years of the fleet development. Later the company's results proved that the maritime business could be economically advantageous, too. An important variable in the evaluation of shipping profitability, however, was the fact that the COS ran the business within one-sector (state) economy, centrally planned and directed. The effects of this economic model on shipping performance was twofold: 1) the company paid a substantial part of its profit to the state budget which limited its business activities; 2) when the company did not achieve profit, the loss was covered by the state budget, too.

During a substantial part of its pre-1989 history, the company was profitable. The mechanism of covering the losses by state budget proved to be important mainly in those years where the world oil crisis negatively affected the world economy, and subsequently the shipping market (decreasing time charter rates, fewer goods available for transport, and increasing of recurrent costs). Losses needed to be covered slightly in the second half of the 1970s and then significantly in 1983. The second half of the 1980s then was the period marked by an effort to run the fleet effectively and profitably. This business endeavour was associated with gradual changes in the economy and policy following from the changes triggered by Gorbachev in the Soviet Union.

Like many other companies and enterprises, the COS entered the period after 1989 with optimism, mainly because the new period put an end to rigid state control and encouraged independence in business activities. It was the period when all the professionals in the shipping sector in Czechoslovakia believed the future would be favourable for them. But these expectations did not come true. Leaving aside for the moment the privatization process that led to selling the fleet, a question arises as to the newly appointed COS management (after removing the Party officials and people fiercely loyal to the former regime). Were the new company leaders experienced enough to realistically estimate the business impacts of all the changes occurred after the 1989?

The managers were professionals in the shipping field accustomed to trade on the maritime market. However, it is possible that they underestimated what the disintegration of the foreign trade monopoly would mean for running the business. Now privatized companies decided independently how they would transport goods abroad. That was a substantial change compared to the past when Čechofracht was cooperating with the COS, which had the monopoly on transport services, or when the COS negotiated the use of its fleet directly with monopoly foreign trade organizations. Moreover, the arms market disintegrated, thus causing a significant drop in the fleet's profitability.

It was probably desirable to make some changes in the portfolio of services provided, reconsider carefully investments and fleet renewal, and especially find a stronger partner for a joint venture. None of this happened. It is a task for future research, provided that the archive sources become available, to find out what actually happened with the fleet in the period of newly acquired freedom until the sale of the last ship.

In hindsight, the "big" business history of the COS developed in a direction that significantly disrupted the "small" history, that of the lives and destinies of seafarers. After selling off the fleet, some men switched their professional career while others, those more addicted to the sea, found work in foreign ship companies. Even with the conclusion that the shipping trade in Czechoslovakia would hardly have thrived without the circumstances of the Cold War, one thing is undeniable: Czechoslovaks, Czechs and Slovaks, although born in a landlocked country, proved they could be good seafarers.

List of archival resources and interviews

Throughout the text I state the English translation of the quoted documents for easier understanding. Each reference is marked by an abbreviation of the source archive and number. Within the list of archival resources below, I provide the index number with a full reference in Czech which serves as a guide to the document quoted in the relevant archive.

Archiv bezpečnostních složek

Security Services Archive, www.abscr.cz; all the documents are stored in the object file [objektový svazek] 4147, Československá námořní plavba.

- ABS_1: 4147, část 3, Dopis bývalého zástupce pro věci politické na lodi Kladno, 13. 4. 1970.
- ABS_2: 4147, část 4, Informace o hospodářsko-politické situaci na úseku ČNP, 2. 6. 1976.
- ABS_3: 4147, část 2, Projevy teroru na ČNP v roce 1968–1969, 27. 5. 1970.
- ABS_4: 4147, část 2, Analýza o kádrové práci a jejích důsledcích v ČNP v období 1968–1969, 12. 5. 1970.
- ABS_5: 4147, část 2, Nedostatky v politické a personální praxi u ČNP, 10. 11. 1971.
- ABS_6: 4147, část 1, Dopis od generálního konzulátu ČSSR pro FMZV a velvyslanectví ve Varšavě, 6. 11. 1972.
- ABS_7: 4147, část 8, Záznam – situace v polském přístavu Gdaňsk, 18. 1. 1982.
- ABS_8: 4147, část 13, Příloha k plánu kontrarozvědné ochrany na II. pololetí 1986, 7. 7. 1986.
- ABS_9: 4147, část 4, Záznam – služební cesta do přístavu Štětín, 4. 3. 1976.
- ABS_10: 4147, část 13, Plán hlavních úkolů kontrarozvědné ochrany ČNP na rok 1986, 6. 2. 1986.
- ABS_11: 4147, část 12, Návrh na uložení do archivu spisu Geograf, 22. 10. 1985.

- ABS_12: 4147, část 2, Služební záznam, 28. 9. 1970.
- ABS_13: 4147, část 10, Záznam – podezření z homosexuality, 12. 1. 1984.
- ABS_14: 4147, část 5, Zpráva o výsledku prošetření nové anonymní stížnosti na pracovníky ČNP, 22. 3. 1977.
- ABS_15: 4147, část 9, Potíže Československé námořní plavby na námořním trhu v kapitalistických státech, 5. 1. 1983.
- ABS_16: 4147, část 9, Diskriminační opatření americké pobřežní stráže, 2. 3. 1983.
- ABS_17: 4147, část 10, Problematika tzv. vyloučených oblastí při zaměstnávání čs. tonáže na cizí účet, 31. 5. 1983.
- ABS_18: 4147, část 11, Předpoklady ekonomické výslednosti Československé námořní plavby v roce 1984, 30. 7. 1984.
- ABS_19: 4147, část 13, Stav opatření pro velení čs. lodím za bojové pohotovosti státu, nedatováno (podle obsahu cca začátek roku 1986).
- ABS_20: 4147, část 2, Záznam o oficiálním styku s 1. palubním důstojníkem, schůzka 2. 9. 1973 na lodi Radhošť.
- ABS_21: 4147, část 8, Záznam o zadržení námořníka v Libyi, 4. 8. 1981.
- ABS_22: 4147, část 25, Záznam – názor čínských představitelů na prodej tepelné elektrárny Československem do ČLR, 12. 9. 1985.
- ABS_23: 4147, část 19, Záznam – operativní situace na Čsl. námořní plavbě Praha k 19. 9. 1989, došetření věci nepoužitelných rublových přebytků, 20. 9. 1989.
- ABS_24: 4147, část 25, Materiál Federálního ministerstva zahraničního obchodu pro poradu vedení – Upravený návrh na založení společného československo-čínského podniku pro námořní dopravu, 13. 3. 1987.
- ABS_25: 4147, část 25, Čsl.-čínské námořní sdružení COSSHIP v Praze, poznatky, 19. 2. 1988.
- ABS_26: 4147, část 25, Čsl.-čínské námořní sdružení v COSSHIP v problematice námořní plavby, poznatky, 23. 3. 1988.
- ABS_27: 4147, část 25, Memorandum k ČSSR–ČLR sdružení COSSHIP v problematice námořní plavby, 30. 3. 1988.

- ABS_28: 4147, část 25, Československo-čínská akciová společnost COSSHIP v problematice námořní plavby – výskyt vážných problémů v ekonomické oblasti, 4. 7. 1988.
- ABS_29: 4147, část 25, Čs.-čínská námořní společnost COSSHIP – zkušenosti z prvního roku činnosti, 19. 1. 1989.
- ABS_30: 4147, část 19, Vyhodnocení operativní situace na m.a.s. Čsl. námořní plavba k 31. 8. 1989, 22. 9. 1989.
- ABS_31: 4147, část 10, Záznam – návštěva misionářů na lodi Třinec v Montrealu, nabízení náboženské literatury, 20. 2. 1984.
- ABS_32: 4147, část 11, Hlášení velitele lodi Sitno o politicko-morálním stavu posádky za cestu 116 out, 27. 10. 1984.
- ABS_33: 4147, část 17, Informace o trestném činu, 25. 7. 1985.
- ABS_34: 4147, část 11, Návrh na uložení svazku do archívu, 13. 6. 1985.
- ABS_35: 4147, část 19, Zhodnocení situace na úseku deblokací čsl. pohledávek v Libyi a Sýrii, 16. 8. 1989.
- ABS_36: 4147, část 19, Vyhodnocení operativní situace na ČNP k 31. 8. 1989.
- ABS_37: 4147, část 18, Problémy v zajišťování posádek lodí, 26. 5. 1989.
- ABS_38: 4147, část 4, Záznam o služební cestě do PLR, vyšetřování, 24. 2. 1976.
- ABS_39: 4147, část 19, Záznam – charakteristika kapitán Z., 22. 9. 1989.

Archiv České národní banky

Archive of the Czech National bank; www.cnb.cz/cs/o_cnb/archiv_cnb/.
- CNB_1: fond Banka Československých legií, sg. BČL/4/5, 12. 7. 1920, Koupě lodi.
- CNB_2: fond Banka Československých legií, sg. BČL/13/10, 14. 3. 1928, Lodní oddělení.
- CNB_3: fond Banka Československých legií, sg. BČL/10/7, 6. 2. 1929, Lodní oddělení.
- CNB_4: fond Banka Československých legií, sg. BČL/4/41, 11. 10. 1933, Prodej lodi.

Archiv Ministerstva zahraničních věcí

Archive of the Ministry of Foreign Affairs; http://www.mzv.cz/jnp/cz/o_ministerstvu/organizacni_struktura/utvary_mzv/specializovany_archiv_mzv/archiv_ministerstva_zahranicnich_veci.html.
- MZV_1: fond **Teritoriální odbor – tajný (TO–T)**, 1965–1969, karton Čína 4, Telegram z Pekingu (text diplomatické nóty), 29. 7. 1965.
- MZV_2: fond TO–T, 1965–1969, karton Čína 4, Záznam z návštěvy chargé d'affaires s. Chu Čchen-fanga u s. náměstka ministra zahraničních věcí dr. L. Šimoviče, 12. 7. 1965.
- MZV_3: fond TO–T, 1965–1969, karton Čína 4, Telegram z Pekingu pro MZV, 31. 7. 1965.
- MZV_4: fond TO–T, 1965–1969, karton Čína 4, Telegram z MZV pro Peking, 5. 8. 1965.
- MZV_5: fond TO–T, 1965–1969, karton Čína 4, Návrh nóty pro čínský zastupitelský úřad v Praze, 28. 1. 1967.
- MZV_6: fond TO–T, 1965–1969, karton Čína 4, Informace pro velvyslanectví v Pekingu – text diplomatické nóty, 25. 1. 1967.
- MZV_7: fond TO–T, 1965–1969, karton Čína 4, Záznam z přijetí chargé d'affaires Čínské lidové republiky v Praze, 27. 1. 1967.
- MZV_8: fond TO–T, 1965–1969, karton Čína 4, Zpráva o služební cestě do Kantonu, 9. 8. 1965.

Národní archiv

The National Archive; www.nacr.cz.

- NA_1: fond MZO 1945–1968, SM, T a PT registratura, ka 1354, Tajná zpráva z velvyslanectví v Pekingu pro MZV, 11. 9. 1951.
- NA_2: fond MZO 1945–1968, SM, T a PT registratura, ka 1354, Report 26 z velvyslanectví v Pekingu pro Metrans, 25. 9. 1951.
- NA_3: fond Úřad předsednictva vlády 1945–1959, tajná spisovna, sg. 35/2/1, ka 44, Dopis Jaroslava Tomandla, 15. 5. 1950.
- NA_4: fond Úřad předsednictva vlády 1945–1959, tajná spisovna, sg. 35/2/1, ka 44, Dopis ministerstva zahraničního obchodu, 4. 1. 1951.
- NA_5: fond FMZO, karton 1608, MZO 124, tajná spisovna, zřízení Čechofrachtu, Návrh na zprávu pro s. náměstka předsedy vlády s. Slánského, 17. 11. 1951.
- NA_6: fond FMZO, karton 1608, MZO 124, tajná spisovna, Materiál pro politický sekretariát – zpráva o koupi lodi, listopad 1951.
- NA_7: fond Úřad předsednictva vlády, 1945–1959, tajná spisovna, sg. 35/2/1, ka 44, Zpráva o průběhu generálních a klasifikačních oprav lodi Republika, 7. 7. 1953.
- NA_8: fond FMZO, karton 1608, MZO 124, tajná spisovna, Návrh dopisu o křtu lodi Republika pro s. ministra Širokého, 1951.
- NA_9: fond FMZO, karton 1608, MZO 124, tajná spisovna, Dopis z velvyslanectví v Pekingu pro MZO, s. Gregor, 27. 9. 1952.
- NA_10: fond FMZO, karton 1608, MZO 124, tajná spisovna, První cesta do Číny, 22. 7. 1952.
- NA_11: fond FMZO, karton 1608, MZO 124, tajná spisovna, Zpráva o koupi lodi, listopad 1951.
- NA_12: fond FMZO, karton 1608, MZO 124, tajná spisovna, Situace na lodi Republika, 28. 7. 1952.
- NA_13: fond FMZO, karton 1608, MZO 124, tajná spisovna, Zpráva o havárii lodi Republika, 26. 8. 1952.
- NA_14: fond MD, inv. č. HS 05, sg. 05131, tajné, 1954, karton 721, Dopis z generálního konzulátu v Šanghaji pro MZV, 19. 6. 1954.

- NA_15: fond FMZO, karton 1396, tajná spisovna, svazek 5, Zpráva o výsledku jednání československé delegace odborníků s delegací Čínské lidové republiky o převedení obchodních lodí Čínské lidové republiky do československého námořního rejstříku pod československou vlajku, 26. 2. 1953.
- NA_16: fond FMZO, karton 1395, MZO 86, tajná spisovna, Protokol mezi Československou republikou a Čínskou lidovou republikou o rozvoji námořní dopravy, 11. 6. 1953.
- NA_17: fond FMZO, karton 1396, tajná spisovna, šanon 1, svazek 3, Dopis od Richarda Dvořáka, ministra zahr. obchodu pro ČLR ministra komunikací Chang-Po-Cun, 24. 3. 1958.
- NA_26: fond FMZO, karton 1396, tajná spisovna, šanon 1, svazek 1, Zápis z prvého jednání Spojovací komise v Praze, 2. 8. 1955.
- NA_18: fond FMZO karton 1397, MZO 88, tajná spisovna, svazek 1, Informace pro velvyslanectví v Pekingu, 6. 11. 1953.
- NA_19: fond FMZO, karton 1397, MZO 88, tajná spisovna, svazek 3, Dopis od vedoucího dopravního odboru MZO s. Böhnelovi, velvyslanectví ČSR v Pekingu, 19. 1. 1954.
- NA_20: fond FMZO, karton 1395, MZO 86, tajná spisovna, Protokol o provozu námořní lodě Julius Fučík, 9. 7. 1955.
- NA_21: fond FMZO, karton 1397, MZO 88, tajná spisovna, svazek 3, Dopis od vedoucího dopravního odboru MZO s. Böhnelovi, velvyslanectví ČSR v Pekingu, 14. 4. 1954.
- NA_22: fond FMZO, karton 1354, MZO 1945–1968, tajná spisovna, Šifra z velvyslanectví v Pekingu pro MZO, 21. 1. 1952.
- NA_23: fond FMZO karton 1397, MZO 88, svazek 2, Dopis pro předsedu vlády Viliama Širokého, 12. 10. 1954.
- NA_24: fond FMZO, karton 1397, MZO 88, tajná spisovna, svazek 3, Dopis vedoucího dopravního odboru pro s. ministra zahraničního obchodu, 23. 11. 1954.
- NA_25: fond FMZO, karton 1397, MZO 88, tajná spisovna, svazek 4, Příprava jednání s. vm. Schmelze s asistentem čínského ministra komunikací o provozu lodí Fučík a Lidice, 1. 7. 1955.
- NA_26: fond FMZO, karton 1396, tajná spisovna, šanon 1, svazek 1, Zápis z prvého jednání Spojovací komise v Praze, 2. 8. 1955.

- NA_27: fond FMZO, karton 1396, tajná spisovna, svazek 4, Dopis od ředitele Čechofrachtu pro ministra zahr. obchodu, 4. 1. 1959.
- NA_28: fond FMZO, karton 1396, tajná spisovna, šanon 1, svazek 1, Dopis pro náměstkyni předsedy vlády s. Jankovcovou, 11. 11. 1955.
- NA_29: fond FMZO, karton 1396, tajná spisovna, svazek 1, Dopis od vedoucího dopravního odboru min. zahr. věcí pro redakci Rudého práva, 20. 3. 1958.
- NA_30: fond FMZO, karton 1396, tajná spisovna, šanon 1, svazek 2, Zpráva MZO pro Politbyro ÚV KSČ, Zpráva o převodu čínské námořní lodi pod československou vlajku, 19. 6. 1958.
- NA_31: fond FMZO, karton 1396, tajná spisovna, šanon 1, svazek 3, Dopis z MZO pro ředitele ČNP, 7. 5. 1959.
- NA_32: fond FMZO, karton 1394, MZO 85, tajná spisovna, Protokol o společném provozování podniku ČNP na základě předchozí dohody z 9. 3. 1959.
- NA_33: fond FMZO kolegia 1980, karton 17–23, Materiál pro kolegium ministra zahraničního obchodu – Návrh na změnu odměňování členů posádek čs. námořních lodí, 30. 9. 1980.
- NA_34: fond ÚV KSČ Sekretariát, 1954–1962, arch. j. 188, bod 3, sv. 143, Materiál pro Politbyro ÚV KSČ, 13. 6. 1957.
- NA_35: fond ÚV KSČ Sekretariát, 1954–1962, arch. j. 194, bod 19, sv. 147–149, Materiál pro Politbyro ÚV KSČ, 3. 8. 1957.
- NA_36: fond FMZO karton 1369, tajná spisovna, svazek 4, Dopis pro presidenta a prvního tajemníka ÚV KSČ Antonína Novotného, 23. 1. 1959.
- NA_37: fond FMZO, karton 1396, tajná spisovna, šanon 1, svazek 3, Technický stav lodí Dukla a Orava (materiál MZO), 8. 4. 1960.
- NA_38: fond FMZO, karton 1394, MZO 84, tajná spisovna, Zápis o první schůzi představenstva ČNP, konané od 2. do 16. 4. 1959.
- NA_39: FMZO, karton 1394, MZO 85, tajná spisovna, Zápis o jednáních mezi zástupci MZO ČSR a ministerstva komunikací ČLR, 11. 12. 1958.
- NA_40: fond Československá námořní plavba, nezpracovaný, **(dále uváděno/following f. ČNP)**, VII-A-16-6-1, parametry lodí.

- NA_41: fond FMZO, karton 1396, tajná spisovna, šanon 1, svazek 1, 17th meeting of the Liaison Committee held on 30th July 1958.
- NA_42: f. ČNP, VII-A-16-5, základní informace o lodích v meziválečném období.
- NA_43: f. ČNP, karton 1, ředitelské porady 1963 (12. 4. 1963, 7. 6. 1963, 9. 8. 1963, 15. 11. 1963).
- NA_44: fond FMZO, karton 1394, MZO 85, tajná spisovna, Protokol z druhého zasedání představenstva „Československé námořní plavby, mezinárodní akciové společnosti", které se konalo v Pekingu v době od 31. 3. do 13. 4. 1960.
- NA_45: fond FMZO, karton 1396, tajná spisovna, svazek 1, Dopis z Ministerstva zahraničního obchodu pro I. tajemníka ÚV KSČ a prezidenta republiky Antonína Novotného (Předání lodi Ostrava), 1. 6. 1965.
- NA_46: fond FMZO, karton 1393, MZO 83, tajná spisovna, Protokol ze IV. zasedání Představenstva Československé námořní plavby, mezinárodní akciové společnosti, které se konalo v Pekingu ve dnech od 2. do 5. dubna 1962.
- NA_47: f. ČNP, VII-A-16-5-4, parametry lodí.
- NA_48: fond FMZO, karton 1396, tajná spisovna, svazek 5, Převzetí nové čs. námořní lodi, dopis od MZO pro I. tajemníka ÚV KSČ a prezidenta Antonína Novotného a pro Viliama Širokého, předsedu vlády, 25. 3. 1960.
- NA_49: fond FMZO, karton 1396, tajná spisovna, svazek 6, Telegram pro MZO od velvyslance s. Šedivého – pomoc Čínské lidové republice při dopravě pšenice z Austrálie a Kanady, 15. 3. 1961.
- NA_50: fond FMZO, karton 1396, tajná spisovna, svazek 6, Dopis od MZO pro I. tajemníka ÚV KSČ a prezidenta Antonína Novotného a pro Viliama Širokého, předsedu vlády, 3. 11. 1960.
- NA_51: fond FMZO, karton 1396, tajná spisovna, svazek 5, Informace MZO o vyúčtování nákupu osobní lodi Slapy pro ČLR, 14. 1. 1961.

- NA_52: fond FMZO, karton 1396, tajná spisovna, svazek 6, Dopis od ředitele Československé námořní plavby pro náměstka ministra zahraničního obchodu, 5. 10. 1960.
- NA_53: fond FMZO, karton 1396, tajná spisovna, svazek 6, Dopis od ředitele Československé námořní plavby pro náměstka ministra zahraničního obchodu, 6. 2. 1961.
- NA_54: fond FMZO, karton 1396, tajná spisovna, svazek 4, Dopis ministerstva zahraničního obchodu pro I. tajemníka ÚV KSČ a prezidenta Antonína Novotného – předání tankové lodi Ostrava čínské straně, 27. 3. 1965.
- NA_55: f. ČNP, lodní deníky Lidice, Mír I, Orlík I.
- NA_56: f. ČNP, lodní deníky Lidice č. 44, Orlík I č. 25, Mír I č. 27.
- NA_57: fond FMZO, karton 1393, MZO 83, tajná spisovna, Protokol z VI. zasedání Představenstva Československé námořní plavby, mezinárodní akciové společnosti, které se konalo v Pekingu ve dnech 4. dubna až 18. dubna 1964.
- NA_58: fond FMZO, karton 1397, MZO 88, svazek 7, Dopis předsedovi vlády Viliamu Širokému z MZO – Uzavření dohody o provozu námořních lodí pod čs. vlajkou, 27. 7. 1955.
- NA_59: f. ČNP, VII-A-16-7-4, parametry lodí, Vítkovice, časopis Maják 38/1982.
- NA_60: f. ČNP, lodní deník Košice I č. 18.
- NA_61: f. ČNP, karton 4, Porady generálního ředitele, Zápis z mimořádné porady konané 23. 8. 1968.
- NA_62: f. ČNP, lodní deník Pionýr č. 30.
- NA_63: f. ČNP, lodní deník Republika I č. 17.
- NA_64: f. ČNP, lodní deníky Brno č. 12, 13.
- NA_65: f. ČNP, karton 5, Porady generálního ředitele:
    - Zápis č. 2 z ředitelské porady konané 5. 1. 1969.
    - Zápis č. 13 z ředitelské porady konané 1. 4. 1969.
    - Materiál č. 28 pro ředitelskou poradu konanou 4. 4. 1969.
    - Zápis č. 21 z ředitelské porady konané 5. 6. 1969.
- NA_66: fond ÚV KSČ Sekretariát, 1962–1966, arch. j. 13, bod 5, sv. 3, Směrnice pro zástupce kapitána pro věci politické na čs. námořních lodích, 24. 5. 1963.

- NA_67: f. ČNP, karton 6, Porady generálního ředitele:
  - Zápis č. 8 z ředitelské porady konané 6. 3. 1970.
  - Zápis č. 33 z ředitelské porady konané 18. 9. 1970.
- NA_68: f. ČNP, karton 1, Operativní porady:
  - Zápis z mimořádné porady, 27. 2. 1969.
  - Zápis č. 2 z operativní porady konané 19. 4. 1968.
- NA_69: f. ČNP, kartony Komplexní rozbory, Komplexní rozbor 1971, Materiál č. 30 pro ředitelskou poradu konanou 3. března 1972, Zpráva o zhodnocení výsledků hospodaření za rok 1971.
- NA_70: f. ČNP, lodní deník Brno č. 10.
- NA_71: f. ČNP, lodní deník Kladno č. 15.
- NA_72: f. ČNP, VII-A-16, parametry lodí, všechny lodě.
- NA_73: f. ČNP, kartony X – roční rozbory, Komplexní rozbor 1961 (ČNP-X-A-5-1-5), Zápis č. 8 z ředitelské porady konané 22. 2. 1962.
- NA_74: f. ČNP, kartony X – roční rozbory, Komplexní rozbor 1962 (ČNP-X-A-5-2-2).
- NA_75: f. ČNP, kartony X – roční rozbory, Komplexní rozbor 1964 (ČNP-X-A-5-4), Plnění provozního plánu za rok 1964.
- NA_76: f. ČNP, kartony X – roční rozbory, Komplexní rozbor 1965, Výkaz o námořní plavbě československými loděmi.
- NA_77: f. ČNP, kartony X – roční rozbory, Komplexní rozbor 1965, Plnění celoročních plánovaných úkolů a chozrasčotních úkolů za II. pololetí 1965.
- NA_78: f. ČNP, kartony X – roční rozbory, Komplexní rozbor 1966, Provozní výsledky ukončených cest v roce 1966.
- NA_79: f. ČNP, kartony X – roční rozbory, Komplexní rozbor 1966, Výkaz o námořní plavbě československými loděmi za rok 1966 pro MZO.
- NA_80: f. ČNP, kartony X – roční rozbory, Komplexní rozbor 1967, Zpráva o zhodnocení výsledků za rok 1967, 15. 2. 1968.
- NA_81: f. ČNP, kartony X – roční rozbory, Komplexní rozbor 1968, Zpráva o zhodnocení výsledků hospodaření za rok 1968, 24. 2. 1969.

LIST OF ARCHIVAL RESOURCES AND INTERVIEWS 261

- NA_82: f. ČNP, kartony X – roční rozbory, Komplexní rozbor 1969 (ČNP-X-A-5-3-1), Zpráva o zhodnocení výsledků hospodaření za rok 1969, 25. 2. 1970.
- NA_83: f. ČNP, kartony X – roční rozbory, Komplexní rozbor 1970 (ČNP-X-A-5-3-6), Zpráva o zhodnocení výsledků hospodaření za rok 1970.
- NA_84: f. ČNP, kartony X – roční rozbory, Komplexní rozbor 1970 Interní (ČNP-X-A-5-3-6), Zhodnocení činnosti obchodně provozního střediska za rok 1970, 17. 2. 1971.
- NA_85: f. ČNP, kartony X – roční rozbory, Komplexní rozbor 1968, Statistický výkaz o námořní plavbě československými loděmi za rok 1968.
- NA_86: f. ČNP, kartony X – roční rozbory, Komplexní rozbor 1966, Stanovisko ministra zahraničního obchodu k Rozboru činnosti a návrhu finančního vypořádání roku 1966 Československé námořní plavby.
- NA_87: fond MZO kolegia 1963, MZO 3130, karton 3, Materiál pro kolegium ministra zahraničního obchodu – Návrh zásad nové platové úpravy členů posádek čs. námořních lodí, 12. 6. 1963.
- NA_88: f. ČNP, kartony X – roční rozbory, Komplexní rozbor 1971 (ČNP-X-A-5-4), Zápis č. 15 z mimořádné ředitelské porady konané dne 6. dubna 1972, Hodnocení hospodářských výsledků podniku za rok 1971.
- NA_89: f. ČNP, kartony X – roční rozbory, Komplexní rozbor 1972 (ČNP-X-A-5-4), Materiál č. 21 pro ředitelskou poradu konanou 5. března 1973, Zpráva o zhodnocení výsledků hospodaření za rok 1972.
- NA_90: f. ČNP, ředitelské porady 1974, karton 10, Zápis z mimořádné ředitelské porady konané 9 dubna 1974.
- NA_91: f. ČNP, kartony X – roční rozbory, Komplexní rozbor 1974 (ČNP-X-A-5-4), Zpráva o plnění rámcové kolektivní smlouvy za rok 1974, 26. 3. 1975.

- NA_92: f. ČNP, kartony X – roční rozbory, Komplexní rozbor 1975 (ČNP-X-A-5-4), Zápis č. 7 z mimořádné ředitelské porady konané 23. března 1976, Závěrečné komplexní hodnocení činnosti Československé námořní plavby za rok 1975.
- NA_93: f. ČNP, kartony X – roční rozbory, Komplexní rozbor 1972 (ČNP-X-A-5-4), Zápis č. 15 z mimořádné ředitelské porady konané 19. 4. 1973, Hodnocení hospodářských výsledků podniku za rok 1972.
- NA_94: f. ČNP, kartony X – roční rozbory, karton 5 roční rozbory a výsledky 1975–1977, Zápis č. 8 z mimořádné ředitelské porady konané 4. dubna 1977, Závěrečné komplexní hodnocení činnosti Československé námořní plavby za rok 1976.
- NA_95: f. ČNP, kartony X – roční rozbory, karton 6 roční rozbory a výsledky 1977–1978, Komplexní rozbor 1978 (ČNP-X-A-5-11-1), Zpráva o výsledcích ročního rozboru hospodářské činnosti za rok 1978, 5. 3. 1979.
- NA_96: f. ČNP, kartony X – roční rozbory, karton 7 roční rozbory a výsledky 1978–1980, Čtvrtletní výkaz o odvodech do státního rozpočtu k 31. 12. 1979, Výkaz o námořní plavbě československými loděmi za rok 1979.
- NA_97: f. ČNP, kartony X – roční rozbory, karton 7 roční rozbory a výsledky 1978–1980, Komplexní rozbor 1980 (ČNP-X-A-5-13-7), Zpráva o výsledcích ročního rozboru hospodářské činnosti za rok 1980, 5. 3. 1981.
- NA_98: f. ČNP, kartony X – roční rozbory, karton 5 roční rozbory a výsledky 1975–1977, Materiál č. 34 pro ředitelskou poradu konanou 7. 3. 1977, Zpráva o zhodnocení výsledků hospodaření za rok 1976.
- NA_99: f. ČNP, kartony X – roční rozbory, Komplexní rozbor 1973 (ČNP-X-A-5-4), Situace na námořním trhu v roce 1973, Hodnocení činnosti obchodně provozního úseku za rok 1973, 25. 2. 1974
- NA_100: f. ČNP, kartony X – roční rozbory, Komplexní rozbor 1970 Interní (ČNP-X-A-5-3-6), Statistický výkaz o námořní plavbě československými loděmi za rok 1970.

- NA_101: f. ČNP, kartony X – roční rozbory, karton 7 roční rozbory a výsledky 1978–1980, Komplexní rozbor 1979, Dopis ekonomického náměstka Federálnímu statistickému úřadu, 21. 1. 1980.
- NA_102: f. ČNP, kartony X – roční rozbory, karton 7 roční rozbory a výsledky 1978–1980, Komplexní rozbor 1979, Přihláška k vyhodnocení výsledků socialistické soutěže organizací zahraničního obchodu za rok 1979.
- NA_103: f. ČNP, ředitelské porady 1978, karton 17, Materiál č. 36 pro ředitelskou poradu konanou 10. 3. 1978, Závěry k plnění hospodářských úkolů v roce 1977.
- NA_104: f. ČNP, operativní porady, karton 2, Materiál č. 5 pro operativní poradu konanou 5. 2. 1982, Plnění plánovaných úkolů za leden – prosinec 1981.
- NA_105: f. ČNP, ředitelské porady, karton 19, Materiál č. 8 pro ředitelskou poradu konanou 25. 2. 1983, Zpráva o výsledcích ročního rozboru za rok 1982.
- NA_106: f. ČNP, ředitelské porady, karton 20, Materiál č. 5 pro ředitelskou poradu konanou 2. 2. 1984, Plnění hospodářských výsledků podniku za leden–prosinec 1983.
- NA_107: f. ČNP, ředitelské porady, karton 20, Materiál č. 3 pro ředitelskou poradu konanou 30. 1. 1985, Plnění hospodářských výsledků ČNP za leden–prosinec 1984.
- NA_108: f. ČNP, ředitelské porady, karton 20, Materiál č. 3 pro ředitelskou poradu konanou 27. 1. 1986, Kontrola plnění plánu k 31. 12. 1985.
- NA_109: f. ČNP, ředitelské porady, karton 20, Materiál č. 3 pro ředitelskou poradu konanou 29. 1. 1987, Kontrola plnění plánu k 31. 12. 1986.
- NA_110: f. ČNP, ředitelské porady, karton 21, Materiál č. 3 pro ředitelskou poradu konanou 28. 1. 1988, Kontrola plnění plánu k 31. 12. 1987.
- NA_111: f. ČNP, ředitelské porady, karton 21, Materiál č. 3 pro ředitelskou poradu konanou 26. 1. 1989, Kontrola plnění plánu k 31. 12. 1988.
- NA_112: f. ČNP, lodní deník Julius Fučík č. 25.

- NA_113: f. ČNP, lodní deník Jiskra č. 61.
- NA_114: fond MZO kolegia 1978, 26–29, MZO 3208, karton 59, Materiál pro kolegium ministra zahraničního obchodu – Návrh koncepce rozvoje čs. námořní floty do roku 1985 a výhled do roku 1990, 20. 10. 1978.
- NA_115: f. ČNP, operativní porady, karton 8, Zápis č. 9 z mimořádné operativní porady konané 5. 7. 1989.
- NA_116: f. ČNP, V-A-2-2-1, složka o srážce Orava a kutr SAS 237, 14. 4. 1961, 20. 5. 1961.
- NA_117: f. ČNP, VII-A-16-6, složky jednotlivých lodí.
- NA_118: f. ČNP, karton 1, Porady generálního ředitele, Materiál č. 38 pro ředitelskou poradu konanou 2. 4. 1965.
- NA_119: f. ČNP, karton 1, Porady generálního ředitele, Zápis č. 8 z ředitelské porady konané 16. 4. 1965.
- NA_120: f. ČNP, V-A-2-2-2, Zpráva zástupce pro věci politické, 30. 10. 1961.
- NA_121: f. ČNP, V-A-16-6-7, Zpráva pro Českou státní pojišťovnu, 16. 9. 1969; Hlášení velitele o nehodě, 2. 9. 1969.
- NA_122: f. ČNP, lodní deník Mír II č. 48.
- NA_123: f. ČNP, karton 11, Porady generálního ředitele, Zápis č. 38 z ředitelské porady konané 23. 12. 1974.
- NA_124: f. ČNP, lodní deník Republika II č. 7, záznam 23. 1. 1966.
- NA_125: f. ČNP, lodní deníky Brno č. 54, 55.
- NA_126: f. ČNP, V-A-2-50-3, Prohlášení velitele o případu napadení lodi, 10. 6. 1989.
- NA_127: f. ČNP, V-A-2-59-4, Materiál pro schůzi vlády České republiky, 12. 7. 1995.
- NA_128: fond FMZO, karton 1393, MZO 83, tajná spisovna, Protokol z V. zasedání Představenstva Československé námořní plavby, mezinárodní akciové společnosti, které se konalo v Praze ve dnech 29. dubna–12. května 1963.
- NA_129: fond FMZO, karton 1393, MZO 83, tajná spisovna, Protokol ze VII. zasedání Představenstva Československé námořní plavby, mezinárodní akciové společnosti, které se konalo v Praze ve dnech 17. května až 4. června 1965.

- NA_130: fond FMZO, karton 1393, MZO 83, tajná spisovna, Protokol z VIII. zasedání Představenstva Československé námořní plavby, mezinárodní akciové společnosti, které se konalo v Pekingu ve dnech 11.–23. dubna 1966.
- NA_131: f. ČNP, karton 13, Porady generálního ředitele, Zápis č. 10 z ředitelské porady konané 23. 4. 1976.
- NA_132: fond FMZO, karton 1393, MZO 83, tajná spisovna, Protokol z III. zasedání Představenstva Československé námořní plavby, mezinárodní akciové společnosti, které se konalo v Pekingu od 27. dubna do 10. května 1961.
- NA_133: fond Čechofracht, nezpracovaný, Protokol o schválení ročního výkazu za rok 1955 podniku zahraničního obchodu Čechofracht, 16. 3 1956.
- NA_134: fond Čechofracht, nezpracovaný, Rozhodnutí o schválení ročního výkazu za rok 1953 Čechofrachtu, podniku zahraničního obchodu, 15. 3. 1954.
- NA_135: f. ČNP, kartony X – roční rozbory, Komplexní rozbor činnosti ČNP za rok 1959 (ČNP-X-A-5-1-3).
- NA_136: fond Čechofracht, nezpracovaný, Roční výkaz 1958, X-A-R-1-1.
- NA_137: fond Čechofracht, nezpracovaný, šanon Rozbor k 1. lednu, Zpráva k ročnímu výkazu za rok 1956.
- NA_138: f. ČNP, karton 11, Porady generálního ředitele, Materiál č. 25 pro ředitelskou poradu konanou 21. 3. 1975.
- NA_139: f. ČNP, karton 15, Porady generálního ředitele, Materiál č. 39 pro ředitelskou poradu konanou 7. 3. 1977.
- NA_140: f. ČNP, V-A-2-7-3, složka o kolizi lodi Bratislava, seznam posádky, 1981.
- NA_141: f. ČNP, Kniha Seznam posádky, Republika I.
- NA_142: f. ČNP, karton 4, Porady generálního ředitele, Materiál č. 43 pro ředitelskou poradu konanou 16. 5. 1969, Zápis č. 43 pro ředitelskou poradu konanou 31. 10. 1969.
- NA_143: f. ČNP, karton 13, Porady generálního ředitele, Zápis č. 11 z ředitelské porady konané 7. 5. 1976.

- NA_144: f. ČNP, karton 7, Porady generálního ředitele, Materiál č. 67 pro ředitelskou poradu konanou 20. 8. 1971, Návrh platového výnosu členů posádek čs. námořních lodí.
- NA_145: fond FMZO, karton 1396, tajná spisovna, svazek 1, Zápis z jednání s ČLR, 10. 10. 1956.
- NA_146: f. ČNP, karton 6, Porady generálního ředitele, Materiál č. 1 pro ředitelskou poradu konanou 9. 1. 1970, Návrh zásad přestavby mezd posádek čs. námořních lodí.
- NA_147: f. ČNP, karton 16, Porady generálního ředitele, Materiál č. 155 pro ředitelskou poradu konanou 28. 11. 1977, Přehled o výdělkové úrovni pracovníků ČNP.
- NA_148: f. ČNP, karton 21, Zápis ze schůze komise pro realizaci nového výnosu FMDS o odměňování námořníků, která se konala dne 19. 4. 1989.
- NA_149: f. ČNP, karton 13, Porady generálního ředitele, Zápis č. 3 z ředitelské porady konané 6. 2. 1976.
- NA_150: f. ČNP, karton 13, Porady generálního ředitele, Zápis č. 5 z ředitelské porady konané 5. 3. 1976.
- NA_151: f. ČNP, karton 5, Porady generálního ředitele, Zápis č. 26 z ředitelské porady konané 4. 7. 1969.
- NA_152: f. ČNP, karton 5, Porady generálního ředitele, Materiál č. 65 pro ředitelskou poradu konanou 19. 9. 1969.
- NA_153: f. ČNP, karton 5, Porady generálního ředitele, Zápis č. 43 z ředitelské porady konané 31. 10. 1969.
- NA_154: f. ČNP, karton 1, Porady generálního ředitele, Návrh zásad na spolujízdy manželek členů lodních posádek, 21. 1. 1965.
- NA_155: f. ČNP, karton 6, Porady generálního ředitele, Materiál č. 6 pro ředitelskou poradu konanou 19. 2. 1971.
- NA_156: f. ČNP, karton 12, Porady generálního ředitele, Materiál č. 72 pro ředitelskou poradu konanou 19. 9. 1975.
- NA_157: f. ČNP, karton 18, Porady generálního ředitele, Materiál č. 6 pro ředitelskou poradu konanou 8. 2. 1980.
- NA_158: f. ČNP, karton 18, Porady generálního ředitele, Materiál č. 6 pro ředitelskou poradu konanou 6. 2. 1981.

Oral history interviews

All the oral history interviews were recorded and transcribed by the author; they are stored at the Lenka Kratka's personal archive.

- I. P., * 1950, doctor, 13 years in the COS; interview recorded on 6 May, 2010.
- J. J., 1952–2014, A/B sailor, 18 years in the COS; interview recorded on 3 March (1st interview) and 13 April (2nd interview) 2010.
- J. K., * 1946, chief cook, 22 years in the COS; interview recorded on 12 November 2010.
- J. N., * 1943, boatswain, 30 years in the COS; interview recorded on 15 April 2010.
- J. T., * 1951, 2nd engineer, 19 years in the COS; interview recorded on 5 May 2010.
- J. V., * 1964, A/B sailor, 6 years in the COS; interview recorded on 6 April 2010.
- K. T., * 1943, chief cook, 38 years in the COS; interview recorded on 12 February 2010.
- M. B., * 1949, chief engineer, 29 years in the COS; interview recorded on 26 May 2010.
- M. R., * 1930, captain, 40 years in the COS; interview recorded on 22 November 2010.
- M. S., * 1939, chief engineer, 26 years in the COS; interview recorded on 23 May 2010.
- P. K., * 1944, captain, 36 years in the COS; interview recorded on 9 May 2010.
- V. B., * 1944, storekeeper, 27 years in the COS; interview recorded on 3 June 2010.
- V. S., * 1942, captain, 26 years in the COS; interview recorded on 8 May 2010.

Summary in Czech

Československá námořní plavba (1948–1989)

Kniha přináší komplexní pohled na problematiku založení a rozvoje námořní plavby v bývalém Československu a na fungování samostatného podniku Československá námořní plavba. Zpracování tématu je ohraničeno roky 1948 a 1989. Rok 1948, respektive únorový komunistický převrat, změnil vlastnické vztahy i podmínky podnikání v Česko-slovensku. Pro rozvoj námořního podnikání byly nejvýznamnější změnou nacionalizace majetku a vytvoření státních monopolních organizací zahraničního obchodu. Rokem 1989 pak zpracování historie námořního podnikání v poválečném Československu končí, další vývoj floty je pouze stručně nastíněn. Související politické, ekonomické a sociální změny polistopadového vývoje ovlivnily oblast námořní plavby tak zásadním způsobem, že by vyžadovaly samostatnou studii.

Velká pozornost je v knize věnována rozvoji námořního podnikání na začátku padesátých let 20. století. Autorka představuje okolnosti nákupu první československé námořní lodi Republika v roce 1952 a především mechanismus spolupráce v oblasti námořní přepravy s Čínskou lidovou republikou (ČLR). Pro komunistickou Čínu bylo v prvních letech její existence v podstatě nemožné provozovat vlastní námořní plavbu. Souviselo to jednak s vítězstvím komunistů v občanské válce a vyhlášením Čínské lidové republiky (1949), jednak se zapojením ČLR do války v Koreji na straně Severní Koreje. ČLR embargo na nákup lodí a námořní blokádu obcházela především tím, že své námořní lodě nakupovala a následně provozovala pod vlajkou jiného státu socialistického bloku. Tímto způsobem ČLR provozovala několik svých lodí i pod československou vlajkou (Julius Fučík, Lidice, Dukla, Mír, Ostrava, Orava, Orlík), formálně v československém vlastnictví. V roce 1959 byl založen společný podnik Československá námořní plavba. Participace ČLR v tomto podniku byla tajena, stejně jako existence protokolu o spolupráci v oblasti námořní přepravy z roku 1953.

V souvislosti s měnícím se mezinárodním postavením ČLR (zmírňování mezinárodní izolace, roztržky se Sovětským svazem), byla spolupráce s ČLR v oblasti námořní přepravy v polovině šedesátých let ukončena. Československo se tehdy rozhodlo v provozování námořních lodí pokračovat. Postupně rozvíjelo svou flotu, v polovině sedmdesátých let vlastnilo dvanáct lodí, v osmdesátých letech čtrnáct lodí a na přelomu let osmdesátých a devadesátých dokonce osmnáct námořních lodí.

Autorka sleduje rozvoj samostatné československé námořní floty na pozadí některých důležitých mezinárodních událostí: reflektuje především dva ropné šoky (1973–1974; 1979), Karibskou krizi, období détente, nástup Michaila Gorbačova do vedení Sovětského svazu atd. Analýza finančních výsledků hospodaření podniku, která je nedílnou součástí každé kapitoly, prokázala vysoký ekonomický přínos podniku v letech šedesátých a především v první polovině let sedmdesátých. Ziskovost byla dosažena vzájemnou souhrou několika faktorů: efektivní pronájmy lodí zahraničním rejdařům, levná pracovní síla, monopol zahraničního obchodu v Československu, který kontinuálně zajišťoval zaměstnání pro část floty, a realizace velmi ziskových přeprav tzv. speciálních nákladů (zbraně, munice, výbušniny, nebezpečné chemikálie atd.). V osmdesátých letech (především v první polovině) již dosahované výsledky nebyly tak uspokojivé, v některých letech podnik dokonce vykázal celkovou ztrátu. Příčin bylo několik: útlum produkce a vývozu zbraní; stále horší konkurenceschopnost československého zboží na zahraničních trzích, tedy menší potřeba přepravních kapacit, a dopady druhého ropného šoku. Rozpad monopolu zahraničního obchodu po roce 1989, určité chyby v koncepci rozvoje floty v tržním prostředí a některé privatizační kroky pak vedly k postupnému úpadku v oblasti námořní přepravy.

Vedle ziskovosti a provozních výkonů se v jednotlivých kapitolách autorka věnuje problematice spolupráce s ČLR, událostem roku 1968 na námořních lodích, období tzv. normalizace v prostředí námořní plavby i aktivitám Státní bezpečnosti v podniku i mezi námořníky. Tento „makro" pohled doplňuje vzpomínkami bývalých československých námořníků. Prostřednictvím životních příběhů i dalších pramenů autorka představuje lodní hierarchii, činnosti jednotlivých oddělení, příjmy námořníků, každodennost na námořní lodi atd. Věnuje se také tématu emigrací či působení vládnoucí ideologie na námořních lodích. V závěru knihy jsou představeny jednotlivé námořní lodě (44 plavidel), které pod československou (po rozpadu federace českou) vlajkou pluly od roku 1952, kdy byla zakoupena první loď, do roku 1998, kdy byla prodána loď poslední. Vedle technických parametrů jsou u každé lodi uvedena určitá specifika či zajímavosti z jejich provozu.

Všechna témata jsou zpracována s využitím velkého množství archivních materiálů, z nichž většina dosud nebyla publikována. Dílčím způsobem jsou využita orálně historická interview s bývalými námořníky. V tomto ohledu se jedná o první publikaci svého druhu v české historiografii.

SOVIET AND POST-SOVIET POLITICS AND SOCIETY

Edited by Dr. Andreas Umland

ISSN 1614-3515

1 *Андреас Умланд (ред.)*
Воплощение Европейской
конвенции по правам человека в
России
Философские, юридические и
эмпирические исследования
ISBN 3-89821-387-0

2 *Christian Wipperfürth*
Russland – ein vertrauenswürdiger
Partner?
Grundlagen, Hintergründe und Praxis
gegenwärtiger russischer Außenpolitik
Mit einem Vorwort von Heinz Timmermann
ISBN 3-89821-401-X

3 *Manja Hussner*
Die Übernahme internationalen Rechts
in die russische und deutsche
Rechtsordnung
Eine vergleichende Analyse zur
Völkerrechtsfreundlichkeit der Verfassungen
der Russländischen Föderation und der
Bundesrepublik Deutschland
Mit einem Vorwort von Rainer Arnold
ISBN 3-89821-438-9

4 *Matthew Tejada*
Bulgaria's Democratic Consolidation
and the Kozloduy Nuclear Power Plant
(KNPP)
The Unattainability of Closure
With a foreword by Richard J. Crampton
ISBN 3-89821-439-7

5 *Марк Григорьевич Меерович*
Квадратные метры, определяющие
сознание
Государственная жилищная политика в
СССР. 1921 – 1941 гг
ISBN 3-89821-474-5

6 *Andrei P. Tsygankov, Pavel
A.Tsygankov (Eds.)*
New Directions in Russian
International Studies
ISBN 3-89821-422-2

7 *Марк Григорьевич Меерович*
Как власть народ к труду приучала
Жилище в СССР – средство управления
людьми. 1917 – 1941 гг.
С предисловием Елены Осокиной
ISBN 3-89821-495-8

8 *David J. Galbreath*
Nation-Building and Minority Politics
in Post-Socialist States
Interests, Influence and Identities in Estonia
and Latvia
With a foreword by David J. Smith
ISBN 3-89821-467-2

9 *Алексей Юрьевич Безугольный*
Народы Кавказа в Вооруженных
силах СССР в годы Великой
Отечественной войны 1941-1945 гг.
С предисловием Николая Бугая
ISBN 3-89821-475-3

10 *Вячеслав Лихачев и Владимир
Прибыловский (ред.)*
Русское Национальное Единство,
1990-2000. В 2-х томах
ISBN 3-89821-523-7

11 *Николай Бугай (ред.)*
Народы стран Балтии в условиях
сталинизма (1940-е – 1950-е годы)
Документированная история
ISBN 3-89821-525-3

12 *Ingmar Bredies (Hrsg.)*
Zur Anatomie der Orange Revolution
in der Ukraine
Wechsel des Elitenregimes oder Triumph des
Parlamentarismus?
ISBN 3-89821-524-5

13 *Anastasia V. Mitrofanova*
The Politicization of Russian
Orthodoxy
Actors and Ideas
With a foreword by William C. Gay
ISBN 3-89821-481-8

14 *Nathan D. Larson*
    Alexander Solzhenitsyn and the
    Russo-Jewish Question
    ISBN 3-89821-483-4

15 *Guido Houben*
    Kulturpolitik und Ethnizität
    Staatliche Kunstförderung im Russland der
    neunziger Jahre
    Mit einem Vorwort von Gert Weisskirchen
    ISBN 3-89821-542-3

16 *Leonid Luks*
    Der russische „Sonderweg"?
    Aufsätze zur neuesten Geschichte Russlands
    im europäischen Kontext
    ISBN 3-89821-496-6

17 *Евгений Мороз*
    История «Мёртвой воды» – от
    страшной сказки к большой
    политике
    Политическое неоязычество в
    постсоветской России
    ISBN 3-89821-551-2

18 *Александр Верховский и Галина
    Кожевникова (ред.)*
    Этническая и религиозная
    интолерантность в российских СМИ
    Результаты мониторинга 2001-2004 гг.
    ISBN 3-89821-569-5

19 *Christian Ganzer*
    Sowjetisches Erbe und ukrainische
    Nation
    Das Museum der Geschichte des Zaporoger
    Kosakentums auf der Insel Chortycja
    Mit einem Vorwort von Frank Golczewski
    ISBN 3-89821-504-0

20 *Эльза-Баир Гучинова*
    Помнить нельзя забыть
    Антропология депортационной травмы
    калмыков
    С предисловием Кэролайн Хамфри
    ISBN 3-89821-506-7

21 *Юлия Лидерман*
    Мотивы «проверки» и «испытания»
    в постсоветской культуре
    Советское прошлое в российском
    кинематографе 1990-х годов
    С предисловием Евгения Марголита
    ISBN 3-89821-511-3

22 *Tanya Lokshina, Ray Thomas, Mary
    Mayer (Eds.)*
    The Imposition of a Fake Political
    Settlement in the Northern Caucasus
    The 2003 Chechen Presidential Election
    ISBN 3-89821-436-2

23 *Timothy McCajor Hall, Rosie Read
    (Eds.)*
    Changes in the Heart of Europe
    Recent Ethnographies of Czechs, Slovaks,
    Roma, and Sorbs
    With an afterword by Zdeněk Salzmann
    ISBN 3-89821-606-3

24 *Christian Autengruber*
    Die politischen Parteien in Bulgarien
    und Rumänien
    Eine vergleichende Analyse seit Beginn der
    90er Jahre
    Mit einem Vorwort von Dorothée de Nève
    ISBN 3-89821-476-1

25 *Annette Freyberg-Inan with Radu
    Cristescu*
    The Ghosts in Our Classrooms, or:
    John Dewey Meets Ceauşescu
    The Promise and the Failures of Civic
    Education in Romania
    ISBN 3-89821-416-8

26 *John B. Dunlop*
    The 2002 Dubrovka and 2004 Beslan
    Hostage Crises
    A Critique of Russian Counter-Terrorism
    With a foreword by Donald N. Jensen
    ISBN 3-89821-608-X

27 *Peter Koller*
    Das touristische Potenzial von
    Kam''janec'–Podil's'kyj
    Eine fremdenverkehrsgeographische
    Untersuchung der Zukunftsperspektiven und
    Maßnahmenplanung zur
    Destinationsentwicklung des „ukrainischen
    Rothenburg"
    Mit einem Vorwort von Kristiane Klemm
    ISBN 3-89821-640-3

28 *Françoise Daucé, Elisabeth Sieca-
    Kozlowski (Eds.)*
    Dedovshchina in the Post-Soviet
    Military
    Hazing of Russian Army Conscripts in a
    Comparative Perspective
    With a foreword by Dale Herspring
    ISBN 3-89821-616-0

29 Florian Strasser
    Zivilgesellschaftliche Einflüsse auf die
    Orange Revolution
    Die gewaltlose Massenbewegung und die
    ukrainische Wahlkrise 2004
    Mit einem Vorwort von Egbert Jahn
    ISBN 3-89821-648-9

30 Rebecca S. Katz
    The Georgian Regime Crisis of 2003-2004
    A Case Study in Post-Soviet Media
    Representation of Politics, Crime and
    Corruption
    ISBN 3-89821-413-3

31 Vladimir Kantor
    Willkür oder Freiheit
    Beiträge zur russischen Geschichtsphilosophie
    Ediert von Dagmar Herrmann sowie mit
    einem Vorwort versehen von Leonid Luks
    ISBN 3-89821-589-X

32 Laura A. Victoir
    The Russian Land Estate Today
    A Case Study of Cultural Politics in Post-Soviet Russia
    With a foreword by Priscilla Roosevelt
    ISBN 3-89821-426-5

33 Ivan Katchanovski
    Cleft Countries
    Regional Political Divisions and Cultures in
    Post-Soviet Ukraine and Moldova
    With a foreword by Francis Fukuyama
    ISBN 3-89821-558-X

34 Florian Mühlfried
    Postsowjetische Feiern
    Das Georgische Bankett im Wandel
    Mit einem Vorwort von Kevin Tuite
    ISBN 3-89821-601-2

35 Roger Griffin, Werner Loh, Andreas
    Umland (Eds.)
    Fascism Past and Present, West and East
    An International Debate on Concepts and
    Cases in the Comparative Study of the
    Extreme Right
    With an afterword by Walter Laqueur
    ISBN 3-89821-674-8

36 Sebastian Schlegel
    Der „Weiße Archipel"
    Sowjetische Atomstädte 1945-1991
    Mit einem Geleitwort von Thomas Bohn
    ISBN 3-89821-679-9

37 Vyacheslav Likhachev
    Political Anti-Semitism in Post-Soviet Russia
    Actors and Ideas in 1991-2003
    Edited and translated from Russian by Eugene Veklerov
    ISBN 3-89821-529-6

38 Josette Baer (Ed.)
    Preparing Liberty in Central Europe
    Political Texts from the Spring of Nations
    1848 to the Spring of Prague 1968
    With a foreword by Zdeněk V. David
    ISBN 3-89821-546-6

39 Михаил Лукьянов
    Российский консерватизм и
    реформа, 1907-1914
    С предисловием Марка Д. Стейнберга
    ISBN 3-89821-503-2

40 Nicola Melloni
    Market Without Economy
    The 1998 Russian Financial Crisis
    With a foreword by Eiji Furukawa
    ISBN 3-89821-407-9

41 Dmitrij Chmelnizki
    Die Architektur Stalins
    Bd. 1: Studien zu Ideologie und Stil
    Bd. 2: Bilddokumentation
    Mit einem Vorwort von Bruno Flierl
    ISBN 3-89821-515-6

42 Katja Yafimava
    Post-Soviet Russian-Belarussian Relationships
    The Role of Gas Transit Pipelines
    With a foreword by Jonathan P. Stern
    ISBN 3-89821-655-1

43 Boris Chavkin
    Verflechtungen der deutschen und
    russischen Zeitgeschichte
    Aufsätze und Archivfunde zu den
    Beziehungen Deutschlands und der
    Sowjetunion von 1917 bis 1991
    Ediert von Markus Edlinger sowie mit einem
    Vorwort versehen von Leonid Luks
    ISBN 3-89821-756-6

44 *Anastasija Grynenko in Zusammenarbeit mit Claudia Dathe*
Die Terminologie des Gerichtswesens der Ukraine und Deutschlands im Vergleich
Eine übersetzungswissenschaftliche Analyse juristischer Fachbegriffe im Deutschen, Ukrainischen und Russischen
Mit einem Vorwort von Ulrich Hartmann
ISBN 3-89821-691-8

45 *Anton Burkov*
The Impact of the European Convention on Human Rights on Russian Law
Legislation and Application in 1996-2006
With a foreword by Françoise Hampson
ISBN 978-3-89821-639-5

46 *Stina Torjesen, Indra Overland (Eds.)*
International Election Observers in Post-Soviet Azerbaijan
Geopolitical Pawns or Agents of Change?
ISBN 978-3-89821-743-9

47 *Taras Kuzio*
Ukraine – Crimea – Russia
Triangle of Conflict
ISBN 978-3-89821-761-3

48 *Claudia Šabić*
"Ich erinnere mich nicht, aber L'viv!"
Zur Funktion kultureller Faktoren für die Institutionalisierung und Entwicklung einer ukrainischen Region
Mit einem Vorwort von Melanie Tatur
ISBN 978-3-89821-752-1

49 *Marlies Bilz*
Tatarstan in der Transformation
Nationaler Diskurs und Politische Praxis 1988-1994
Mit einem Vorwort von Frank Golczewski
ISBN 978-3-89821-722-4

50 *Марлен Ларюэль (ред.)*
Современные интерпретации русского национализма
ISBN 978-3-89821-795-8

51 *Sonja Schüler*
Die ethnische Dimension der Armut
Roma im postsozialistischen Rumänien
Mit einem Vorwort von Anton Sterbling
ISBN 978-3-89821-776-7

52 *Галина Кожевникова*
Радикальный национализм в России и противодействие ему
Сборник докладов Центра «Сова» за 2004-2007 гг.
С предисловием Александра Верховского
ISBN 978-3-89821-721-7

53 *Галина Кожевникова и Владимир Прибыловский*
Российская власть в биографиях I
Высшие должностные лица РФ в 2004 г.
ISBN 978-3-89821-796-5

54 *Галина Кожевникова и Владимир Прибыловский*
Российская власть в биографиях II
Члены Правительства РФ в 2004 г.
ISBN 978-3-89821-797-2

55 *Галина Кожевникова и Владимир Прибыловский*
Российская власть в биографиях III
Руководители федеральных служб и агентств РФ в 2004 г.
ISBN 978-3-89821-798-9

56 *Ileana Petroniu*
Privatisierung in Transformationsökonomien
Determinanten der Restrukturierungs-Bereitschaft am Beispiel Polens, Rumäniens und der Ukraine
Mit einem Vorwort von Rainer W. Schäfer
ISBN 978-3-89821-790-3

57 *Christian Wipperfürth*
Russland und seine GUS-Nachbarn
Hintergründe, aktuelle Entwicklungen und Konflikte in einer ressourcenreichen Region
ISBN 978-3-89821-801-6

58 *Togzhan Kassenova*
From Antagonism to Partnership
The Uneasy Path of the U.S.-Russian Cooperative Threat Reduction
With a foreword by Christoph Bluth
ISBN 978-3-89821-707-1

59 *Alexander Höllwerth*
Das sakrale eurasische Imperium des Aleksandr Dugin
Eine Diskursanalyse zum postsowjetischen russischen Rechtsextremismus
Mit einem Vorwort von Dirk Uffelmann
ISBN 978-3-89821-813-9

60	Олег Рябов «Россия-Матушка» Национализм, гендер и война в России XX века С предисловием Елены Гощило ISBN 978-3-89821-487-2	68	Taras Kuzio (Ed.) Aspects of the Orange Revolution VI Post-Communist Democratic Revolutions in Comparative Perspective ISBN 978-3-89821-820-7
61	Ivan Maistrenko Borot'bism A Chapter in the History of the Ukrainian Revolution With a new introduction by Chris Ford Translated by George S. N. Luckyj with the assistance of Ivan L. Rudnytsky ISBN 978-3-89821-697-5	69	Tim Bohse Autoritarismus statt Selbstverwaltung Die Transformation der kommunalen Politik in der Stadt Kaliningrad 1990-2005 Mit einem Geleitwort von Stefan Troebst ISBN 978-3-89821-782-8
62	Maryna Romanets Anamorphosic Texts and Reconfigured Visions Improvised Traditions in Contemporary Ukrainian and Irish Literature ISBN 978-3-89821-576-3	70	David Rupp Die Rußländische Föderation und die russischsprachige Minderheit in Lettland Eine Fallstudie zur Anwaltspolitik Moskaus gegenüber den russophonen Minderheiten im „Nahen Ausland" von 1991 bis 2002 Mit einem Vorwort von Helmut Wagner ISBN 978-3-89821-778-1
63	Paul D'Anieri and Taras Kuzio (Eds.) Aspects of the Orange Revolution I Democratization and Elections in Post-Communist Ukraine ISBN 978-3-89821-698-2	71	Taras Kuzio Theoretical and Comparative Perspectives on Nationalism New Directions in Cross-Cultural and Post-Communist Studies With a foreword by Paul Robert Magocsi ISBN 978-3-89821-815-3
64	Bohdan Harasymiw in collaboration with Oleh S. Ilnytzkyj (Eds.) Aspects of the Orange Revolution II Information and Manipulation Strategies in the 2004 Ukrainian Presidential Elections ISBN 978-3-89821-699-9	72	Christine Teichmann Die Hochschultransformation im heutigen Osteuropa Kontinuität und Wandel bei der Entwicklung des postkommunistischen Universitätswesens Mit einem Vorwort von Oskar Anweiler ISBN 978-3-89821-842-9
65	Ingmar Bredies, Andreas Umland and Valentin Yakushik (Eds.) Aspects of the Orange Revolution III The Context and Dynamics of the 2004 Ukrainian Presidential Elections ISBN 978-3-89821-803-0	73	Julia Kusznir Der politische Einfluss von Wirtschaftseliten in russischen Regionen Eine Analyse am Beispiel der Erdöl- und Erdgasindustrie, 1992-2005 Mit einem Vorwort von Wolfgang Eichwede ISBN 978-3-89821-821-4
66	Ingmar Bredies, Andreas Umland and Valentin Yakushik (Eds.) Aspects of the Orange Revolution IV Foreign Assistance and Civic Action in the 2004 Ukrainian Presidential Elections ISBN 978-3-89821-808-5	74	Alena Vysotskaya Russland, Belarus und die EU-Osterweiterung Zur Minderheitenfrage und zum Problem der Freizügigkeit des Personenverkehrs Mit einem Vorwort von Katlijn Malfliet ISBN 978-3-89821-822-1
67	Ingmar Bredies, Andreas Umland and Valentin Yakushik (Eds.) Aspects of the Orange Revolution V Institutional Observation Reports on the 2004 Ukrainian Presidential Elections ISBN 978-3-89821-809-2		

75 Heiko Pleines (Hrsg.)
Corporate Governance in post-
sozialistischen Volkswirtschaften
ISBN 978-3-89821-766-8

76 Stefan Ihrig
Wer sind die Moldawier?
Rumänismus versus Moldowanismus in
Historiographie und Schulbüchern der
Republik Moldova, 1991-2006
Mit einem Vorwort von Holm Sundhaussen
ISBN 978-3-89821-466-7

77 Galina Kozhevnikova in collaboration
with Alexander Verkhovsky and
Eugene Veklerov
Ultra-Nationalism and Hate Crimes in
Contemporary Russia
The 2004-2006 Annual Reports of Moscow's
SOVA Center
With a foreword by Stephen D. Shenfield
ISBN 978-3-89821-868-9

78 Florian Küchler
The Role of the European Union in
Moldova's Transnistria Conflict
With a foreword by Christopher Hill
ISBN 978-3-89821-850-4

79 Bernd Rechel
The Long Way Back to Europe
Minority Protection in Bulgaria
With a foreword by Richard Crampton
ISBN 978-3-89821-863-4

80 Peter W. Rodgers
Nation, Region and History in Post-
Communist Transitions
Identity Politics in Ukraine, 1991-2006
With a foreword by Vera Tolz
ISBN 978-3-89821-903-7

81 Stephanie Solywoda
The Life and Work of
Semen L. Frank
A Study of Russian Religious Philosophy
With a foreword by Philip Walters
ISBN 978-3-89821-457-5

82 Vera Sokolova
Cultural Politics of Ethnicity
Discourses on Roma in Communist
Czechoslovakia
ISBN 978-3-89821-864-1

83 Natalya Shevchik Ketenci
Kazakhstani Enterprises in Transition
The Role of Historical Regional Development
in Kazakhstan's Post-Soviet Economic
Transformation
ISBN 978-3-89821-831-3

84 Martin Malek, Anna Schor-
Tschudnowskaja (Hrsg.)
Europa im Tschetschenienkrieg
Zwischen politischer Ohnmacht und
Gleichgültigkeit
Mit einem Vorwort von Lipchan Basajewa
ISBN 978-3-89821-676-0

85 Stefan Meister
Das postsowjetische Universitätswesen
zwischen nationalem und
internationalem Wandel
Die Entwicklung der regionalen Hochschule
in Russland als Gradmesser der
Systemtransformation
Mit einem Vorwort von Joan DeBardeleben
ISBN 978-3-89821-891-7

86 Konstantin Sheiko in collaboration
with Stephen Brown
Nationalist Imaginings of the
Russian Past
Anatolii Fomenko and the Rise of Alternative
History in Post-Communist Russia
With a foreword by Donald Ostrowski
ISBN 978-3-89821-915-0

87 Sabine Jenni
Wie stark ist das „Einige Russland"?
Zur Parteibindung der Eliten und zum
Wahlerfolg der Machtpartei
im Dezember 2007
Mit einem Vorwort von Klaus Armingeon
ISBN 978-3-89821-961-7

88 Thomas Borén
Meeting-Places of Transformation
Urban Identity, Spatial Representations and
Local Politics in Post-Soviet St Petersburg
ISBN 978-3-89821-739-2

89 Aygul Ashirova
Stalinismus und Stalin-Kult in
Zentralasien
Turkmenistan 1924-1953
Mit einem Vorwort von Leonid Luks
ISBN 978-3-89821-987-7

90 *Leonid Luks*
 Freiheit oder imperiale Größe?
 Essays zu einem russischen Dilemma
 ISBN 978-3-8382-0011-8

91 *Christopher Gilley*
 The 'Change of Signposts' in the Ukrainian Emigration
 A Contribution to the History of Sovietophilism in the 1920s
 With a foreword by Frank Golczewski
 ISBN 978-3-89821-965-5

92 *Philipp Casula, Jeronim Perovic (Eds.)*
 Identities and Politics During the Putin Presidency
 The Discursive Foundations of Russia's Stability
 With a foreword by Heiko Haumann
 ISBN 978-3-8382-0015-6

93 *Marcel Viëtor*
 Europa und die Frage nach seinen Grenzen im Osten
 Zur Konstruktion ‚europäischer Identität' in Geschichte und Gegenwart
 Mit einem Vorwort von Albrecht Lehmann
 ISBN 978-3-8382-0045-3

94 *Ben Hellman, Andrei Rogachevskii*
 Filming the Unfilmable
 Casper Wrede's 'One Day in the Life of Ivan Denisovich'
 Second, Revised and Expanded Edition
 ISBN 978-3-8382-0044-6

95 *Eva Fuchslocher*
 Vaterland, Sprache, Glaube
 Orthodoxie und Nationenbildung am Beispiel Georgiens
 Mit einem Vorwort von Christina von Braun
 ISBN 978-3-89821-884-9

96 *Vladimir Kantor*
 Das Westlertum und der Weg Russlands
 Zur Entwicklung der russischen Literatur und Philosophie
 Ediert von Dagmar Herrmann
 Mit einem Beitrag von Nikolaus Lobkowicz
 ISBN 978-3-8382-0102-3

97 *Kamran Musayev*
 Die postsowjetische Transformation im Baltikum und Südkaukasus
 Eine vergleichende Untersuchung der politischen Entwicklung Lettlands und Aserbaidschans 1985-2009
 Mit einem Vorwort von Leonid Luks
 Ediert von Sandro Henschel
 ISBN 978-3-8382-0103-0

98 *Tatiana Zhurzhenko*
 Borderlands into Bordered Lands
 Geopolitics of Identity in Post-Soviet Ukraine
 With a foreword by Dieter Segert
 ISBN 978-3-8382-0042-2

99 *Кирилл Галушко, Лидия Смола (ред.)*
 Пределы падения – варианты украинского будущего
 Аналитико-прогностические исследования
 ISBN 978-3-8382-0148-1

100 *Michael Minkenberg (ed.)*
 Historical Legacies and the Radical Right in Post-Cold War Central and Eastern Europe
 With an afterword by Sabrina P. Ramet
 ISBN 978-3-8382-0124-5

101 *David-Emil Wickström*
 Rocking St. Petersburg
 Transcultural Flows and Identity Politics in the St. Petersburg Popular Music Scene
 With a foreword by Yngvar B. Steinholt
 Second, Revised and Expanded Edition
 ISBN 978-3-8382-0100-9

102 *Eva Zabka*
 Eine neue „Zeit der Wirren"?
 Der spät- und postsowjetische Systemwandel 1985-2000 im Spiegel russischer gesellschaftspolitischer Diskurse
 Mit einem Vorwort von Margareta Mommsen
 ISBN 978-3-8382-0161-0

103 *Ulrike Ziemer*
 Ethnic Belonging, Gender and Cultural Practices
 Youth Identitites in Contemporary Russia
 With a foreword by Anoop Nayak
 ISBN 978-3-8382-0152-8

104 Ksenia Chepikova
,Einiges Russland' - eine zweite KPdSU?
Aspekte der Identitätskonstruktion einer postsowjetischen „Partei der Macht"
Mit einem Vorwort von Torsten Oppelland
ISBN 978-3-8382-0311-9

105 Леонид Люкс
Западничество или евразийство? Демократия или идеократия?
Сборник статей об исторических дилеммах России
С предисловием Владимира Кантора
ISBN 978-3-8382-0211-2

106 Anna Dost
Das russische Verfassungsrecht auf dem Weg zum Föderalismus und zurück
Zum Konflikt von Rechtsnormen und -wirklichkeit in der Russländischen Föderation von 1991 bis 2009
Mit einem Vorwort von Alexander Blankenagel
ISBN 978-3-8382-0292-1

107 Philipp Herzog
Sozialistische Völkerfreundschaft, nationaler Widerstand oder harmloser Zeitvertreib?
Zur politischen Funktion der Volkskunst im sowjetischen Estland
Mit einem Vorwort von Andreas Kappeler
ISBN 978-3-8382-0216-7

108 Marlène Laruelle (ed.)
Russian Nationalism, Foreign Policy, and Identity Debates in Putin's Russia
New Ideological Patterns after the Orange Revolution
ISBN 978-3-8382-0325-6

109 Michail Logvinov
Russlands Kampf gegen den internationalen Terrorismus
Eine kritische Bestandsaufnahme des Bekämpfungsansatzes
Mit einem Geleitwort von Hans-Henning Schröder
und einem Vorwort von Eckhard Jesse
ISBN 978-3-8382-0329-4

110 John B. Dunlop
The Moscow Bombings of September 1999
Examinations of Russian Terrorist Attacks at the Onset of Vladimir Putin's Rule
Second, Revised and Expanded Edition
ISBN 978-3-8382-0388-1

111 Андрей А. Ковалёв
Свидетельство из-за кулис российской политики I
Можно ли делать добро из зла?
(Воспоминания и размышления о последних советских и первых послесоветских годах)
With a foreword by Peter Reddaway
ISBN 978-3-8382-0302-7

112 Андрей А. Ковалёв
Свидетельство из-за кулис российской политики II
Угроза для себя и окружающих
(Наблюдения и предостережения относительно происходящего после 2000 г.)
ISBN 978-3-8382-0303-4

113 Bernd Kappenberg
Zeichen setzen für Europa
Der Gebrauch europäischer lateinischer Sonderzeichen in der deutschen Öffentlichkeit
Mit einem Vorwort von Peter Schlobinski
ISBN 978-3-89821-749-1

114 Ivo Mijnssen
The Quest for an Ideal Youth in Putin's Russia I
Back to Our Future! History, Modernity, and Patriotism according to Nashi, 2005-2013
With a foreword by Jeronim Perović
Second, Revised and Expanded Edition
ISBN 978-3-8382-0368-3

115 Jussi Lassila
The Quest for an Ideal Youth in Putin's Russia II
The Search for Distinctive Conformism in the Political Communication of Nashi, 2005-2009
With a foreword by Kirill Postoutenko
Second, Revised and Expanded Edition
ISBN 978-3-8382-0415-4

116 Valerio Trabandt
Neue Nachbarn, gute Nachbarschaft?
Die EU als internationaler Akteur am Beispiel ihrer Demokratieförderung in Belarus und der Ukraine 2004-2009
Mit einem Vorwort von Jutta Joachim
ISBN 978-3-8382-0437-6

117 *Fabian Pfeiffer*
Estlands Außen- und Sicherheitspolitik I
Der estnische Atlantizismus nach der
wiedererlangten Unabhängigkeit 1991-2004
Mit einem Vorwort von Helmut Hubel
ISBN 978-3-8382-0127-6

118 *Jana Podßuweit*
Estlands Außen- und Sicherheitspolitik II
Handlungsoptionen eines Kleinstaates im
Rahmen seiner EU-Mitgliedschaft (2004-2008)
Mit einem Vorwort von Helmut Hubel
ISBN 978-3-8382-0440-6

119 *Karin Pointner*
Estlands Außen- und Sicherheitspolitik III
Eine gedächtnispolitische Analyse estnischer
Entwicklungskooperation 2006-2010
Mit einem Vorwort von Karin Liebhart
ISBN 978-3-8382-0435-2

120 *Ruslana Vovk*
Die Offenheit der ukrainischen
Verfassung für das Völkerrecht und
die europäische Integration
Mit einem Vorwort von Alexander
Blankenagel
ISBN 978-3-8382-0481-9

121 *Mykhaylo Banakh*
Die Relevanz der Zivilgesellschaft
bei den postkommunistischen
Transformationsprozessen in mittel-
und osteuropäischen Ländern
Das Beispiel der spät- und postsowjetischen
Ukraine 1986-2009
Mit einem Vorwort von Gerhard Simon
ISBN 978-3-8382-0499-4

122 *Michael Moser*
Language Policy and the Discourse on
Languages in Ukraine under President
Viktor Yanukovych (25 February
2010–28 October 2012)
ISBN 978-3-8382-0497-0 (Paperback edition)
ISBN 978-3-8382-0507-6 (Hardcover edition)

123 *Nicole Krome*
Russischer Netzwerkkapitalismus
Restrukturierungsprozesse in der
Russischen Föderation am Beispiel des
Luftfahrtunternehmens "Aviastar"
Mit einem Vorwort von Petra Stykow
ISBN 978-3-8382-0534-2

124 *David R. Marples*
'Our Glorious Past'
Lukashenka's Belarus and
the Great Patriotic War
ISBN 978-3-8382-0574-8 (Paperback edition)
ISBN 978-3-8382-0675-2 (Hardcover edition)

125 *Ulf Walther*
Russlands "neuer Adel"
Die Macht des Geheimdienstes von
Gorbatschow bis Putin
Mit einem Vorwort von Hans-Georg Wieck
ISBN 978-3-8382-0584-7

126 *Simon Geissbühler (Hrsg.)*
Kiew – Revolution 3.0
Der Euromaidan 2013/14 und die
Zukunftsperspektiven der Ukraine
ISBN 978-3-8382-0581-6 (Paperback edition)
ISBN 978-3-8382-0681-3 (Hardcover edition)

127 *Andrey Makarychev*
Russia and the EU
in a Multipolar World
Discourses, Identities, Norms
With a foreword by Klaus Segbers
ISBN 978-3-8382-0629-5

128 *Roland Scharff*
Kasachstan als postsowjetischer
Wohlfahrtsstaat
Die Transformation des sozialen
Schutzsystems
Mit einem Vorwort von Joachim Ahrens
ISBN 978-3-8382-0622-6

129 *Katja Grupp*
Bild Lücke Deutschland
Kaliningrader Studierende sprechen über
Deutschland
Mit einem Vorwort von Martin Schulz
ISBN 978-3-8382-0552-6

130 *Konstantin Sheiko, Stephen Brown*
History as Therapy
Alternative History and Nationalist
Imaginings in Russia, 1991-2014
ISBN 978-3-8382-0665-3

131 Elisa Kriza
     Alexander Solzhenitsyn: Cold War
     Icon, Gulag Author, Russian
     Nationalist?
     A Study of the Western Reception of his
     Literary Writings, Historical Interpretations,
     and Political Ideas
     With a foreword by Andrei Rogatchevski
     ISBN 978-3-8382-0589-2 (Paperback edition)
     ISBN 978-3-8382-0690-5 (Hardcover edition)

132 Serghei Golunov
     The Elephant in the Room
     Corruption and Cheating in Russian
     Universities
     ISBN 978-3-8382-0570-0

133 Manja Hussner, Rainer Arnold (Hgg.)
     Verfassungsgerichtsbarkeit in
     Zentralasien I
     Sammlung von Verfassungstexten
     ISBN 978-3-8382-0595-3

134 Nikolay Mitrokhin
     Die "Russische Partei"
     Die Bewegung der russischen Nationalisten in
     der UdSSR 1953-1985
     Aus dem Russischen übertragen von einem
     Übersetzerteam unter der Leitung von Larisa Schippel
     ISBN 978-3-8382-0024-8

135 Manja Hussner, Rainer Arnold (Hgg.)
     Verfassungsgerichtsbarkeit in
     Zentralasien II
     Sammlung von Verfassungstexten
     ISBN 978-3-8382-0597-7

136 Manfred Zeller
     Das sowjetische Fieber
     Fußballfans im poststalinistischen
     Vielvölkerreich
     Mit einem Vorwort von Nikolaus Katzer
     ISBN 978-3-8382-0757-5

137 Kristin Schreiter
     Stellung und Entwicklungspotential
     zivilgesellschaftlicher Gruppen in
     Russland
     Menschenrechtsorganisationen im Vergleich
     ISBN 978-3-8382-0673-8

138 David R. Marples, Frederick V. Mills
     (Eds.)
     Ukraine's Euromaidan
     Analyses of a Civil Revolution
     ISBN 978-3-8382-0660-8

139 Bernd Kappenberg
     Setting Signs for Europe
     Why Diacritics Matter for
     European Integration
     With a foreword by Peter Schlobinski
     ISBN 978-3-8382-0663-9

140 René Lenz
     Internationalisierung, Kooperation
     und Transfer
     Externe bildungspolitische Akteure in der
     Russischen Föderation
     Mit einem Vorwort von Frank Ettrich
     ISBN 978-3-8382-0751-3

141 Juri Plusnin, Yana Zausaeva, Natalia
     Zhidkevich, Artemy Pozanenko
     Wandering Workers
     Mores, Behavior, Way of Life, and Political
     Status of Domestic Russian Labor Migrants
     Translated by Julia Kazantseva
     ISBN 978-3-8382-0653-0

142 Matthew Kott, David J. Smith (eds.)
     Latvia – A Work in Progress?
     100 Years of State- and Nation-building
     ISBN 978-3-8382-0648-6

143 Инна Чувычкина (ред.)
     Экспортные нефте- и газопроводы
     на постсоветском пространстве
     Анализ трубопроводной политики в свете
     теории международных отношений
     ISBN 978-3-8382-0822-0

144 Johann Zajaczkowski
     Russland – eine pragmatische
     Großmacht?
     Eine rollentheoretische Untersuchung
     russischer Außenpolitik am Beispiel der
     Zusammenarbeit mit den USA nach 9/11 und
     des Georgienkrieges von 2008
     Mit einem Vorwort von Siegfried Schieder
     ISBN 978-3-8382-0837-4

145 Boris Popivanov
     Changing Images of the Left in
     Bulgaria
     The Challenge of Post-Communism in the
     Early 21st Century
     ISBN 978-3-8382-0667-7

146 Lenka Krátká
     A History of the Czechoslovak Ocean
     Shipping Company 1948-1989
     How a Small, Landlocked Country Ran
     Maritime Business During the Cold War
     ISBN 978-3-8382-0666-0

ibidem-Verlag

Melchiorstr. 15

D-70439 Stuttgart

info@ibidem-verlag.de

www.ibidem-verlag.de
www.ibidem.eu
www.edition-noema.de
www.autorenbetreuung.de